mothering
teens

Understanding
the Adolescent Years

Edited by
Miriam Kaufman, M.D.

gynergy
books

10 9   8   7   6   5   4   3   2   1

Edited by: Wendy Thomas and Sibyl Frei

Printed and bound in Canada by: AGMV Marquis

gynergy books acknowledges the generous support of the Canada Council for the Arts.

Published by:
gynergy books
P.O. Box 2023
Charlottetown, PEI
Canada C1A 7N7

"Sexuality: The Desire to be Lovable and Loving" was adapted from *Facing Facts: Sexual Health for America's Adolescents* and is reprinted with the kind permission of SIECUS.

"What is Independence?: Teens with Physical Disability or Chronic Illness" is based on Miriam Kaufman's book, *Easy for You to Say: Q&As for Teens Living with Chronic Illness or Disability*, published by Key Porter Books and adapted with their kind permission.

Canadian Cataloguing in Publication Data

Main entry under title:

Mothering teens.

ISBN 0-921881-46-0

1. Parent and teenager. 2. Parenting. I. Kaufman, Miriam.

HQ796.M67 1997   649'.125   C97-950167-9

This book is for Jacob Benson Kaufman and Aviva Rose Benson Kaufman, who have taught me much about myself and about parenting, and whose teen years are just around the corner.

Acknowledgments

As always, my colleagues in the Division of Adolescent Medicine have been helpful in practical and emotional ways, including writing a couple of chapters. They are always available to provide information, give advice and commiserate when things aren't going well. In addition to her usual enthusiasm, Karen Leslie was also very helpful in providing references and statistics.

I appreciate the work of the contributors. Some of them had never written for publication before. Others graciously stepped in at the last minute to fill holes in the book. I thank them all for their interesting, professional-quality pieces.

Wendy Thomas is an editor's editor — wise, humorous, comfortable to work with, hard-working, tactful ... the list could go on. I hope I have the privilege of working with her again.

The books published by gynergy are an important contribution to feminist publishing. I appreciate the hard work, commitment and dedication shown by Sibyl Frei and Louise Fleming on this project.

My family has again put up with me staring at the computer in the middle of the night, coming home from work late, groaning and complaining when chapters were late, and generally acting more important than I am. I am ever grateful to all of them, most of all to my partner Roberta Benson.

Contents

Part Three: Parenting Different Kids

Introduction

When we, as parents, accompany our teens on their journey to adulthood, we are travelling with them through a country for which we have no map, or, at best, an outdated one. As progressive parents, most of us try to be flexible and to avoid parenting dogma. We endeavour to respect our children as individuals, encourage them to be involved in issues of justice and teach them that independence and assertiveness are important attributes.

Mothering Teens: Understanding The Adolescent Years is not a parenting book in the traditional sense, although some contributors share their parenting ideas. Its purpose is not to tell you how to parent, but to help you understand the process of adolescence. Parenting books almost all fall down in the end because every child is different: rigid rules can't be moulded to specific situations. This is one reason why cookie-cutter approaches to parenting, such as "tough love," don't work.

Many of us turn to books to help us understand our lives, and most of us have referred to parenting books, especially during our childrens' early years. There are excellent parenting books available, and wonderful books about individual issues in adolescence; however, I haven't found a book that provides a broad and inclusive context for parents. The twenty-one contributors to this book offer a guide to the cultural, political, developmental and social context of adolescence. Some material will apply only to girls or to boys, or to people of a particular race or culture, but all the essays contain insights and information that I hope you will find useful.

Is the process of adolescence a feminist issue? One of the basic tenets of feminism is that the personal is political. That is, the parts of our lives that have been considered inconsequential to history and politics are important, carry meaning that goes beyond the obvious, and therefore are intrinsically political. The politics of adolescence exist in the day-to-day lives of teens and their families. Conversely, the political is the personal. Such abstract notions as self-determination, reproductive choice and competency come alive during adolescence.

Adolescence is a concept that has been invented in recent history, and there are many cultures in which children move directly from childhood to adulthood, with puberty being the transitional event. Adolescence becomes a significant developmental stage when other changes are occurring in a culture. These include increased reliance on technology and a concomitant requirement for prolonged education, a movement of women into the "mainstream" work force and the resultant postponement of childbearing, and access to contraception and abortion, making the transformation from child to parent a more voluntary one.

Even puberty, encompassing the physical growth and development that occurs during adolescence, is not an absolute. Variations in puberty are a result not just of genetics, but also of nutrition: well-nourished children enter puberty earlier and grow taller than children who are undernourished. Thus, the politics of poverty have an impact on the age of onset of puberty and on physical growth. In many countries, poverty is linked to land management, with development money being funnelled to male-dominated bureaucracies. Rural women and other farmers are not usually involved in the planning and implementation of these programs. Poverty and lack of education have also been linked to the policies of the International Monetary Fund, an organization that has a large power base in the developing world. In some areas, girl children receive a smaller percentage of the family's resources than do the boys, resulting in a gender difference in pubertal development and adult health. In more developed countries gender-biased resource distribution is not as obvious, but still exists. Sports facilities are more available to young men than to young women, with more money flowing to organizations for sports for boys. As a result, girls get the message that they should be more sedentary. Schools may employ teaching methods that work more effectively with boys or girls, rarely finding ways to teach both appropriately. Parents may have very different gender-based expectations of their children.

The political nature of adolescence, the lives of adolescents in our culture and the personal development of parents throughout their children's adolescence are topics that we explored in the essays that follow, each one from a different perspective or focusing on a different issue. The whole question of gender in language was present as we worked on this book: we have decided to use "she" and "he" somewhat randomly to avoid an overall gender bias.

I have brought together a wide range of contributors for this collection. Almost all of the essays are published here for the first time, and the authors are from a mix of disciplines: academics, writers, health-care professionals, educators and activists. All are women. Many are mothers. Some are grandmothers. I have gleaned new information about adolescence from each one of them.

The book is divided into three sections. The first outlines some of the basic issues that underlie many teen experiences. I begin that section by examining adolescent growth and development. Questions of gender are explored in a conversation among a group of psychotherapists (Pier Bryden, Leora Pinhas, Michelle Marshall, Karin Jasper) and me. Merryl Bear and Kaca Henley, both of whom work in the field of body image and eating disorders, offer information about influences on body image and the effect on teens. The centrality of spiritual development to teens' identity is explored by Alison van Nie. Debra Haffner, of the Sexuality Information and Education Council of the United States, outlines the need for a practical, fresh approach to adolescent sexual health. To complete this section, Jacqueline Haessly discusses the many forms of violence teens face, and offers a hopeful, peaceful solution.

The second section looks at issues that many teens face in the world today. The culture teens are immersed in is unravelled by Kathleen McDonnell, author of the thoughtful and influential book, *Kid Culture*. Difficult questions about drug and alcohol abuse are examined by Cheryl Littleton, a nurse practitioner who works with teens with substance abuse problems. Carol Ricker-Wilson looks at the ways that teens are stimulated or stymied by the formal education system. Gail Winter elucidates Aboriginal culture in the context of raising a teenager on and off reserve. The effects of racism in school and in society, and effective tools Black families and communities have developed, are explored by journalist Pat Watson. Martha Fleming raises questions about class influences on teens. The challenges posed by family breakdown and divorce are explained by Rachel Geise. To close this section, Sheri Findlay offers insight and possibilities for grieving teens.

The third section deals specifically with special circumstances that may make a teen feel or seem different. Tara Cullis shares insights into her life with activist children. Margaret Schneider provides considerable information about homosexuality, and supports the efforts of teens and parents to come out. The difficulties, and the causes, of teen mothering are explored by internationally known researcher Judith Musick. I discuss the many issues faced by teens with chronic illness or disability. The final essay, by Bridget Lynch, offers a touching and empowering portrait of the life of her daughter, who has a development delay.

You have probably already thought about some of the issues we discuss in this book; others will be new to you. Some will be immediately relevant; others may acquire importance as time passes. You and your teen may bypass some of these issues altogether.

As our teens change in front of our eyes in erratic, radical and unpredictable ways, we can become much less secure about our abilities and be tempted to turn to approaches that tell us what to do, rather than ones that help us understand ourselves and our children. Instead, we can trust ourselves to figure them out, without anyone else's recipe, through an understanding of teens, their lives and their world. The process that occurs in discussions with friends, spouses, partners, professionals and strangers is as important as the information that we give and receive. I hope that the thoughtful material provided in this book will lead to some of those discussions. Much meaningful information about teens is generated and shared in an informal way between parents, in their neighbourhoods and workplaces, and I envision this book being passed across back fences, being discussed in line at the bank or being argued about at church potlucks. Through these conversations, we learn that we are not alone, even when our children are unique. We learn that we can work through situations and find solutions. We learn that we can apologize to our teens when we get it wrong the first time.

As a parent who reads, you are an important role model to your teen. As she sees you searching for information to help you as a parent, she may be more willing to seek information before acting. As he sees you finding comfort in books, so may he look for a broader network of fictional peers and models in his reading.

With teens, even more than with younger children, your actions speak louder than words. While most teens would find the idea horrifying, they are going to turn out like you in the end — smoking or not, drinking or not, going to demonstrations or not, caring or not, reading or not. Your teen will be examining your life for all of its hypocracies, large or small, real or imagined.

By reading about and discussing teens whenever you can, you will understand more about yourself and how your adolescence shaped who you are as a person and as a parent. You will better understand your children's friends, enemies, classmates and role models. You will see that their world and yours overlap, but are not the same. You will come to have a clearer picture of your own teen. And, with luck, you will smooth out a few of the bumps in the parts of her road that you share.

Miriam Kaufman
Summer 1997

part one

Basic
Issues

Change is the Essence: Adolescent Development

Miriam Kaufman

Change is the essence of childhood and adolescence, and keeping up with that change is the delightful, terrifying and bewildering task of parents. How many of us have thought when a parenting tactic fails, "But it worked yesterday!" How boring it would be to be a parent (or a paediatrician) if these challenges did not come up.

In this essay, I refer to early (age ten to fourteen), middle (fifteen and sixteen) and late adolescence (seventeen to twenty-one), but the reality is much fuzzier. Our teens move backward and forward through stages with kaleidoscopic frenzy. Each child is a unique human being, born, I believe, with a temperament that will persist into adulthood, and is then exposed to parents, friends and the world. The relative calmness of the years before adolescence lull us into believing that we understand our children, that there is hope that things will sail smoothly. But, even when they do, we are always second-guessing. As a colleague of mine at another centre once said, "When you're parenting a teen, every time you think you've got it right, you realize that you are an asshole!" A bit extreme, perhaps, but an understanding of adolescent development can help us second-guess what is going on.

Some of us may have forgotten that our own adolescence was a time of turbulence, with wild swings between elation and depression, even though we see our children experiencing these very same feelings. Despite the popular perception of adolescence as a period of temporary insanity, most adolescents are, in fact, mentally healthy. Although 10 to 20 percent of adolescents have, at any given time, psychiatric or significant behavioural problems, you'll be reassured to know that only a few have difficulties that persist. The vast majority of teens come through adolescence with no or only brief serious problems.

However, one of the hallmarks of adolescence is an increasing ability to experience emotions deeply, leading to a characteristically melodramatic approach to problems. As we come to understand adolescent development (the emotional and cognitive equivalent of growth), we not only understand our adolescent offspring, but also begin to appreciate the personal changes we, as parents, must make to be effective and to survive the experience of living with a teenager.

The bedrock of being an adolescent and living with an adolescent is development: the psychological and physical maturation that happens in the teen years. It may not seem like a maturing process while it is occurring, but at the end of adolescence it is clear that the young person has "grown up" to a significant degree. These changes do not proceed in a smooth, predictable fashion, and they seem to lack permanence, with a teen showing great maturity one day and utterly childish behaviour the next. This environment of constant change makes it difficult to pin down parenting strategies, as the "best" approach will vary from stage to stage, and sometimes daily.

Living with an adolescent can be frustrating, delightful, scary and thrilling. Understanding adolescent development may not alter any of these feelings, but it can help you see that you are living with someone who is undergoing huge changes over a relatively short period of time. Another important consideration is that we, as parents, also develop and mature, changing parenting styles to fit the situation, trying new strategies and, in the process, understanding ourselves better.

Paediatricians frequently speak of "growth and development," but although the end product of the two is the same (significant positive change), the processes are quite different. For a start, development is much more subtle. Also, whereas physical growth goes only in one direction, emotional development is like a tide, with increased maturity in any aspect of behaviour ebbing and flowing. In the long run, the move is toward positive change, but this is often not obvious on a day-to-day basis.

A model of adolescence that looks only at development would never explain the wide variety of teen behaviours and the potential richness of adolescents' lives. But the idea of adolescent development underlies many of the issues in this book, and an understanding of it helps us see how a teen may experience societal and political realities, such as gender, class and race, in a different manner than do children or adults.

Cognitive Changes

The majority of teens develop increased sophistication in their thought processes throughout adolescence. This growth underlies the ability to formulate personal ethics and perspectives that are different from those of parents and to assume new roles within the family and society.

In early adolescence, children are "concrete thinkers," usually unable to take a general concept and deduce from it a specific application, or, alternatively, to generalize from a specific idea or experience. At this stage, there may be only partial evolution of these thinking skills, even in teens of average intelligence, putting them on a par with a sizable minority of adults, who, despite some difficulty with abstract thinking, function well in society. The ability to think abstractly may develop earlier in areas least associated with the teens' life; thus, they develop thinking skills in an educational context long before these skills can be applied to personal and social thinking. Very bright early adolescents may seem more able to think in the abstract than they actually are, and, as parents, we see the result in a bright kid capable of complex arguments who does fairly "stupid" things.

Independence

Autonomy is one of the key goals of adolescence. It is intimately related to a sense of "mastery" over one's environment, an ability to accomplish some basic day-to-day tasks, an acceptance of growing up, and a feeling of personal security.

Autonomy needs appear in the second year of life, when parents see their previously charming baby change almost overnight into a toddler who has temper tantrums, throws food on the floor, and yells "no" at least once every five minutes. The successful parent of a toddler is one who realizes that this behaviour is normal and reflects neither evil intent nor a decrease in love felt toward the parent. These are not bad things to keep in mind when dealing with an adolescent.

All along, you have been encouraging your child to acquire the skills and knowledge needed for the healthy development of autonomy in adolescence. Learning to dress themselves, pick out their own clothes, tie shoes, dial the phone (don't we wish they had never learned this one!), walk to school alone, take responsibility for school work, learn to cook and do laundry, take public transit alone, all lead children to a feeling of control over their environment. As each of these tasks is learned, self-esteem increases.

In early adolescence, autonomy issues are expressed as a decrease of interest in participating in family activities and as mood swings. These rapid changes in mood are real, but are exaggerated by the teen's need to be separate from parents. The parent may see the teen as isolated and unhappy, although at school and with friends the teenager may not give this impression at all. As the teen gets a bit older, this isolation and moodiness may escalate into major arguments that revolve around the issue of who is in control. As parents adjust to teens taking charge of their own lives and teens (or young adults) become more confident of their ability to be effectively autonomous, things tend to calm down, with an increase in respect on both sides. Both teens and parents often become more accepting of the other's views at this stage.

For many parents who grew up in the '60s and '70s, one of the hardest jobs in raising younger children is learning to set limits. Brought up in the days of "children are just littler people," and being involved then (and, for many of us, still) with issues of social justice, we may find the idea of setting limits and making decisions for someone else unfair. By the time we figure out the importance of setting boundaries and expectations (without rigidity) in parenting, our children have turned into teenagers, and it can be hard for us to let go of some of the newly discovered skills of limit-setting. Certainly, it continues to be important to have clearly established limits and boundaries in the teen years, but these restrictions must be constantly monitored and updated, as young people become more capable of taking care of themselves. With teens who are argumentative or not talkative, it can be hard to loosen rules and trust them to take more responsibility. But they must be allowed to take chances and to make some mistakes. More and more, parents need to learn to negotiate with their children, to come to mutual agreement about rules and the consequences of breaking them. This is important role-modelling, with teens learning to negotiate and to see themselves as having the central role in their own life decisions.

Negotiation often takes place over choices about high school. Parents decide where their children will go to kindergarten, and have a great deal of input about middle school. At the high-school level, when educational options are available, most teens decide where they will go to school and what kind of program they will take. Parental input is important, but the final decision is made by the adolescent. This can be difficult for parents, especially if they feel that their children are making this critical decision based on such apparently frivolous determinants as where their friends are going or where the best social life will be. Teens who are forced to go to a high school not of their choosing often find a way to get back at their parents, usually by doing poorly academically or getting into trouble.

In mid- to late adolescence, autonomy may be explored and expressed in risk-taking. Frequently, these activities involve risk to family relationships, rather than risk to self. Such things as wild hairstyles or hair colours, wearing clothes unacceptable to parents, or breaking minor family rules can be ways to express independence without the damage that can come from major risk-taking, such as drinking and driving, having unprotected sex or dropping out of school.

Early teens often practise autonomy through fantasy. They will imagine themselves more grown up, and able to navigate complex situations that are beyond their current experience. Girls (and boys, occasionally) record these fantasies as fact in journals. This is one good reason for parents to avoid the temptation to read their teen's diary.

Parents may be less willing to let girls become autonomous, as they have (very real) concerns about safety. The issue is important, but we have to help teens learn to be safe and to protect themselves while not cloistering them. Early teens can learn martial arts, strategies for riding safely on public transit, and when it is imperative to be impolite. Recently a young woman wrote a column for a large, urban daily newspaper about being sexually assaulted on a crowded subway train. She quietly, politely and repeatedly begged her molester to stop touching her. He didn't stop, and it didn't seem to occur to her, even in retrospect, that she could have screamed at him or demanded help from other passengers.

Autonomy certainly does not mean cutting our children loose. They need to know that they can come to us for help and that we will listen without overreacting. It can be helpful to have a weekly or monthly time set up to get together. Choose a time that doesn't interfere with their schedule, and don't use the get-together as an opportunity to carp. Meeting away from home can remove the conversation from the site of battles or power conflicts. In early adolescence, the meeting should not be at a place where their friends will see them, as young teens are often embarrassed by being seen in public with parents. You don't have to talk about heavy issues, but when teens have something they'd like to talk about, such meetings provide a forum for the discussion.

Acceptance of the Physical Changes of Puberty

Over a short period of time, between ages ten and seventeen, girls and boys double their body weight (with boys gaining more, proportionately). Breasts start to grow, often either "too early" or "too late." Boys noticing their own breast development (a normal occurrence) may entertain worries that their bodies are switching gender. Pubic and underarm hair sprouts, acne flourishes, voices change and periods start. Teens may feel that they are waking up to a different body every day. Parents discover that the most innocent remarks about their teens' bodily changes can be greeted by tears or rage.

Worries about the speed or timing of puberty are almost universal, with each teen thinking that he or she is out of the ordinary. Teens may be teased by classmates if they are in the early group of developers or if they aren't showing obvious signs of puberty when most others are. In early adolescence, there is a huge preoccupation with one's body and comparisons with those of friends and classmates. Size (whether of breasts or penis) takes on great significance.

Eating disorders, discussed elsewhere in this book, are an extreme response to difficulty in accepting body changes, but many teens try to manipulate how they look in a less damaging way, with dieting or power eating, exercise, make-up, sanitary pads stuffed into bras, and other manoeuvres.

In early adolescence, teens watch their bodies closely and can seem preoccupied with each pubic hair or pimple. Often children who have seemed quite comfortable with how they look will become much more uncertain about themselves. As adolescence continues, they usually accept these changes; their experiments are no longer aimed at covering up or enhancing the signs of puberty, but are more an effort to fit into a norm of what is attractive. If one of the tasks of adolescence is to accept completely how we look and to develop a healthy body image, then — as a result of social pressures and media messages — it takes some women their whole lives to finish adolescence.

Pubertal changes can precipitate anxiety, confusion and anger. Even when teens know what is likely to happen, they often feel that their bodies are out of control. Also, these changes are a physical metaphor for the many emotional changes of adolescence. It would be easier to ignore the other changes of this age if there were not these obvious daily reminders that life will never be the same. The opposite can also be true. Teens whose bodies are late in maturing may feel that their internal changes are not being noticed or taken seriously.

As these physical changes begin, parents will first notice an increase in their teens' need for privacy. Not only do teens want to keep their bodies covered up, they also feel embarrassed seeing their parents' bodies. This need for privacy must be respected. Physical affection cannot be lavished as freely as with a younger child, and teens will often restrict when and where hugging and kissing occur and how much they will tolerate.

As adolescence progresses, teens increasingly accept their adult body shape. This happens with greater ease as the rate of bodily change slows. Although many people enter adulthood still feeling too fat, too thin, too short or too tall, most have accepted their pubic hair, voice changes, breasts, and so on. The acceptance of pubertal development is, again, a metaphor for the acceptance of an adult role.

Parents' outlook must also change. Day-to-day involvement with our children's physical lives decreases radically in adolescence. At a peak in infancy, when parents are aware of every bowel movement, hunger pang or sign of distress, parents' "ownership" of their children's bodies steadily decreases as childhood progresses, and is almost totally obliterated in mid-adolescence. Parents are aware of their daughters' first period and often of their sons' first wet dream, but, after this, parents have to let go, not only affording teens essential privacy, but preparing them to assume responsibility for their own health care and body maintenance.

Peers

Peer pressure is often identified as a negative part of adolescence and is blamed for cigarette smoking, drug and alcohol use and other risk-taking behaviours. I sometimes wonder who these mysterious "peers" are, as they never seem to be the children of my friends or colleagues, or my patients or their siblings. They are always the "other." During many age spans, a group mentality develops, and in groups people may do things that they would not do alone. But a move toward peers (and away from the family) is an important part of adolescence.

In the move toward an independent adulthood, teens' friendships are an important bridge from dependence on parents to reliance on self. Friends are sounding boards, people with less stake in a particular outcome than family. They can listen more dispassionately, give opinions that would not be heard if they came from parents and participate in the shared experience of growing up.

In early adolescence, this shift in alliance takes the form of a best friend, often of the same sex. This is one of the most intense relationships that exists. Teens will talk to their friends for hours, inventing shared fantasies. Girls will discuss the minute details of life. A teenager's mood frequently seems linked to this relationship. Parents often worry about close friendships that seem overly entangled and that take up time that could be spent studying or getting to know a larger group of friends. It is also at this age that teens first experience crushes, sometimes shared with the best friend.

Parents may feel jealous of this relationship, as the diminishing closeness with their teen is matched with the increasing closeness of the friend. However, any attempt to discourage the friendship just leads to further entrenchment. Many parents are able to maintain a fairly friendly relationship with their teens. These are often the parents who understand that you can be friendly without being friends. Parents who insist on being friends with their children block important aspects of growing up and burden their children with the friendship, often with the result that teens feel they are responsible for their parents' happiness.

In mid- to late adolescence, friendships broaden to include not only a larger number, but often a wider variety of people. Mid-teens will often have more than one group of friends. Peer activity is more group-focused, and identity with the group is expressed through clothing and hairstyles. Parents may feel they are losing touch with their teen's social life, but those who have welcomed their teen's friends into their home feel this less acutely. A receptive parent will often become an adviser/confessor to some of the kids who hang around the house and can hope that his or her own child has formed a similar relationship with a friend's parent.

In late adolescence, the peer group becomes less important. As longer-term romantic and sexual relationships form, friendships are often forged with other couples.

Identity

It is clear to most parents that children have a fairly set personality and identity long before adolescence. The task of the teen years is to become aware of what this identity is. Discovering it is often a matter of teens trying out different modes of being, and experiencing whether they feel more or less themselves with the "tried on" persona or behaviour.

Especially at the outset, the search for identity is a process of extremes. Teens often start with behaviours or beliefs that are the opposite of their parents'. Adopting what seem to be outlandish religious beliefs (or disbeliefs), clothing, hairstyles, friends and political convictions is a part of this process of self-definition.

Many of these behaviours or professed beliefs may be personally distasteful or incomprehensible to parents. Hardest of all is when parents see actions or categorical statements as judgments on their own deeply held beliefs. Combined with a phenomenal ability to perceive parental indecision and unsureness, and to label them hypocrisy, teens' behaviours are seen as an overt criticism of the parents' way of life. Parents who can maintain a sense of humour (not to be confused with making fun of a teen) usually weather this change more easily than those who take these statements at face value.

As our delightful, enquiring, independent ten- or eleven-year-old seems to turn into a monster overnight, we sometimes wonder if a parenting philosophy that encourages autonomy was the correct model to follow. We may feel like bad parents, with poor parenting skills that produced a child who won't behave the way we expect. Autonomy does mean that our teens will make decisions that we wish they hadn't made. Teens are not really autonomous if we give them only options that we want them to take. If we can stop judging our parenting by the palatability of our teens' choices, we can relax a bit and see what transpires.

It's fascinating to observe the emergence of a conscience as the teen's identity develops. At the beginning, the adolescent's idea of ethics is very concrete, with everything categorized neatly into neat "right" or "wrong." Moral ambivalence is not a concept associated with early adolescence. At first, these ideas exist in a vacuum, but gradually they evolve into a personal value system that teens see as applicable to their own lives. By late adolescence, teens should have developed a real conscience, with a clear idea that there are many fuzzy areas, but with a confidence that a moral decision can be made when the need arises, despite the inherent ambiguity in many situations.

Parents can have an impact on identity-formation through activities that enhance self-esteem (starting in earlier childhood). Their understanding of identity-formation as a long-term effort can provide some perspective to a teen who may be mired in the process.

Vocational aspirations tie in with identity-formation. In early adolescence, the teen often moves from standard "what I want to be when I grow up" ideas to grandiose plans, such as becoming a basketball star, a rock musician or ruler of the world. In middle adolescence, vocational aspirations tend to be more reachable, but often still have more to do with "What would I really like?" as opposed to "What would really suit my personality?" It is only in the last years of high school and the following two to three years that most young people have a practical vocational goal and a plan to move toward it.

Development of sexual identity is part of the overall process of identity-formation. Children have sexual feelings and express these as sexual behaviour from an early age, but the consciousness of oneself as a sexual being begins in early adolescence. Sexual dreams and fantasies and an undefined urge to be physically close to someone else often start the process of sexual self-awareness. Masturbation is a normal part of early sexuality, but can provoke feelings of guilt. Crushes often develop in early to mid-adolescence, and do not always correlate with eventual sexual orientation.

Sexual identity in early adolescence is often fairly amorphous, as teens discover who they are attracted to. They often don't identify themselves as heterosexual or homosexual. By middle adolescence, most heterosexual teens will identify as such, but many teens who will ultimately be gay or bisexual will not express a clear identity. In part, this delay occurs because they know that their orientation will not be accepted by their parents, teachers or friends. In part, it results because the process of identifying as something other than the mainstream, different from what is assumed, is longer and more difficult, especially at a developmental stage, when one wants to conform and identify with a peer group. Many teens acknowledge attractions to members of the same sex years before labelling themselves gay or lesbian. Gay and lesbian teens may develop dating skills much later than their heterosexual peers. There are several reasons for this: first, they often lack clear role models for how to date; second, the risk of asking someone out and being rejected is much higher; and, third, approaching someone who is not gay can result in ostracism, or even physical violence. Young lesbians may become monogamously involved with the first person they go out with and have a longer relationship than young heterosexuals. On the other hand, young gay men may experience a series of very short-term, or even anonymous, sexual contacts that involve little intimacy or romance.

Sexual decision making involves putting together this process of sexual identity-formation with cognitive development, the search for autonomy, and acceptance of physical pubertal changes and body image. Sexual decision making often requires impulse control and negotiation with others.

Many teens see sex as something they don't make decisions about, but rather as something that "just happens." Letting it happen is, of course, a decision in and of itself. Seeing sexual behaviour as spontaneous allows the teen a sense of diminished responsibility. Why should this be important to a young person? For one thing, embarking on extending one's sexuality to others, moving it beyond the personal realm of fantasy and feelings, is a huge step. To acknowledge making a decision about such a big thing can be hard, and it is easier to pretend it "just happened."

Conflicting messages that young people get about sex are another factor. Soap operas and movies assume that everyone normal has sex with other people, but religious and other beliefs can lead teens to see sex, and their own inherent sexuality, as bad, dirty, or even evil. Teens who chose to have sex may apply these negative judgments to themselves. Thus, it becomes much easier to see sex as part of a situation, rather than a conscious decision. Sex is then not linked directly to identity. Spontaneous sex as the ideal thus goes beyond an individual feeling and is incorporated into the cultural definition of romanticism.

The parental conflict here is to help our children and adolescents see sexuality as an essential part of everyone's selfhood, and sex as a normal, joyful part of some relationships, without feeling that we are encouraging our children to have sex at an early age. Early sex without the maturity that comes through the developmental process carries many risks, both emotional and physical. A concrete thinker (often the younger adolescent) is less likely to understand fully the link between what seems to be an isolated act and the theoretical risk of sexually transmitted disease or pregnancy. Teens who are struggling with identity and autonomy issues may end up in situations of emotional and physical abuse out of an overwhelming need for acceptance or a desire to define themselves as someone grown-up enough to have sex. In late adolescence, sex becomes less of an oppositional act, less of a thing to do because everyone does it, and sexuality becomes integrated with the other aspects of identity.

Each of these strands of development moves along at its own pace, sometimes seeming to be independent, sometime dormant, sometimes synergistic with one or more other strand. In the end (and there is no real way to define when that end has been reached), they come together into a self-acknowledged adult whole. When this happens, we, as parents, can settle into adult relationships with our offspring that are significantly different in tone and content from our earlier interactions.

What is the Role of Gender?

Pier Bryden, Leora Pinhas, Michelle Marshall, Karin Jasper and Miriam Kaufman

This essay summarizes a free-ranging discussion about gender and adolescence that involved five women, four of whom meet regularly. Specific questions were used to prompt the discussion.

What is the difference between sex and gender?

Leora: We often confuse sex and gender, and we collapse the two categories instead of being specific. Sex is biological, that is, what we appear to be. In most people, genetic sex, biological sex and reproductive functions all match up. Gender has more to do with behaviours that have become associated with masculinity and femininity, and with how people perceive their role — as male or female. It also has to do with how people define themselves, in that most people who are biologically one sex also self-identify as that sex, although not all the time.

Michelle: So, you're saying that sex is biologically based on anatomy, whereas gender is mainly socialized. When we use "feminine" and "masculine" today, we're using them in a conventional manner to describe how our society ascribes certain qualities to males and females. It doesn't necessarily mean we agree with that attribution; nor that any young person we're talking about today necessarily agrees with that attribution.

Miriam: In the context of adolescence then, we can talk about how those stereotypes affect young people, examine how those stereotypes might be changing. We can also look at how these issues affect parents. Do we treat our male and female teenagers differently? Do we react to their behaviour differently? Often "gender" is used as a codeword for "female." Women's studies get called "gender studies," for example. What this means is that men feel they don't need to examine these issues because they are excusively women's concerns; it lets men off the hook. I'd like to include men and boys as much as possible in this discussion, and not as some kind of enemy to girls, but as people who are affected by our ideas about gender.

What are the pressures on teens that are based on gender?

Leora: Little girls have been rewarded for dressing up and pirouetting, for showing off their bodies, whereas boys have tended to be rewarded for creating things, such as with Meccano sets. Girls soon find there's a line — that it's okay to show off to a point, but if you keep doing it you're being exhibitionistic and taking the limelight away from other little girls, and of course that's not very nice. There are huge pressures on young people who don't do these things, who don't behave in the correct way.

Growing up, for a girl, means primarily growing up into a sexual being, whereas growing up to be a man has traditionally had much more to it: a sexual component, of course, but also strength and height and increased efficacy in the external, rather than the domestic, world.

Puberty becomes a time that defines girls as sexual objects. Boys are permitted to take more pleasure in their bodies without that pleasure having sexual connotations.

Miriam: None the less, boys are objects, too. Girls talk about boys' bodies, rate them, look at them. Girls often don't take an active role in approaching boys, but I'm not sure that means boys aren't objects.

Leora: Even so, boys are more subjects than objects. The boys do the hugging, while the girls get hugged. The boys do the asking, while the girls wait by the phone. Already there's a difference between active and passive.

Karin: What about academic-performance differences in adolescents? There is a claim in recent articles that boys are actually doing worse than girls.

Pier: Maybe the school system is expecting more team learning. Girls are brought up to be good at forming relationships and communicating. When talking with adolescent boys, I have to be much more explicit about communication — what can be talked about, how to do it. When boys are given the opportunity, their interest in forming relationships is surprisingly high. It is important for adolescent boys to have alternative roles, to be able to see themselves in ways apart from gender stereotypes and to have the opportunity to view the girls that they go to school with, and their sisters and their mothers, in different ways.

Michelle: Boys are every bit as interested in their relationships ultimately as girls are, but they have been socialized away from that interest. We encourage them, from a young age, to be interested in things and activities. They don't learn the skills, the language needed to succeed in building relationships.

Karin: But boys are not penalized for wanting to test their limitations, and therefore have more freedom to explore what those limits are. For instance, within a popular group of kids in their early teens, the girls and boys seem to be a lot more willing to relate to one another sexually than those in a less popular group. There's a lot more sexual stuff, touching and jostling of one another, flirtatiousness and so on. Some kids just aren't ready to do that, and so are actually fine about not being in the popular group, but what if a girl were strongly attracted to that, and wanted to experiment, but was really nervous about it? She might feel left out, not being in this group, but not able to step in. Or say she was ready to step in, wanted to try it out, and her parents wouldn't give her the freedom that they might readily give to a boy, that would allow him to do the kind of experimenting he feels ready to. A possible consequence of these limits, of her parents preventing her from checking these things out, might be that she feels the need to do some other kinds of things in order to be recognized as a sexual being, an attractive young woman, like becoming thin.

Leora: Risk-taking is part of testing limits. Competitiveness around drinking is partly a contest around who can do the risk-taking thing better than the next guy. In the '50s, it would be playing chicken on the highway with cars. I'm not sure what sort of activities are popular now: rollerblading, skateboarding, snowboarding? It's interesting that risk-taking should still be associated more often with boys, and that teenage girls take different kinds of risks, usually involving relationships or sex. A girl might become involved in risky behaviour because the boy she's with does it.

Pier: For boys, drinking has traditionally been a test of masculinity. I remember that, at my college, everyone would place bottles in front of the male freshmen and see who could drink whom under the table. The more you were able to drink, the more of a man you were. Girls who got drunk met with a different reception. It was seen as stupid and promiscuous, in that if you drank a lot, you might end up in bed with someone, get raped, and you would be seen as asking for it.

Leora: It still seems to be the girl who's responsible for what happens sexually; there aren't consequences for the guy in the same way there are for the girl. Once she becomes a sexual being, her life changes. She has to deal with the fact that she gets looked at in different ways. She's responsible for how she gets looked at, and who's interested in her and what they do about their interest in her. That responsibility still isn't shared, and it should be. Even the language reflects this — it's a girl who is "promiscuous," not a boy, unless he's gay, then the term might be used.

Karin: Being the one who's responsible for what happens in sex means you're the one who has the most to lose. The girl's partner doesn't have to worry about being labelled a "slut" or about getting pregnant. Being a sexual object rather than a subject in this situation means the girl has almost all the responsibility and almost none of the power.

Pier: In some cultures, if you're a girl it isn't even okay to be friends with boys, let alone to experiment sexually.

Miriam: I see a lot of teens who tell me that the rules are very different at home for brothers and sisters. The boys get to go out with friends and don't have curfews. There is implicit approval of boys' sexual experimentation (although not with other boys). They often don't have to clean up or cook at home, or take care of younger siblings.

Karin: The teenage girl sees the inequities but can't convince her parents to change. In addition, she may be the one who is always expected to negotiate, to communicate; her brother doesn't have to do that. It's a woman's job.

Pier: Class comes into this too. A young person might be physically attractive but not be eligible for the "in group" because he or she is not of the same social class as that group. If you can't pay to do the things that the popular group does, then you're not going to be able to run with them. Obviously, race and sexual orientation may also be relevant, in addition to financial status, as part of class.

Michelle: The impact of class is partly gender-specific. An adolescent boy I know explains his difficulty meeting girls in terms of not having enough money to take them out. We have had conversations about why he assumes that it is necessary for him to pay for the date. I wonder if an adolescent girl would feel the same way. Would she feel that it was okay to have a richer boy take her out on dates and pay for it? I wonder if other ways in which class affects popularity for adolescents isn't also gender-related in quite a traditional sense, in that girls can "date up" more easily.

Leora: It would be an interesting thing to explore. A girl may be more able to "date up," but class affects whether you're in a popular group to start with, because fashion plays such a key role in popularity: wearing the right shoes and the right brand of shirt, having a cell phone or pager.

Karin: Girls still experience success as wrapped up with a more attractive physical appearance.

Michelle: This is where fashion takes on a big role. This also seems to affect young women disproportionately.

Leora: Popular girls will tell you that the most important issue for them is how you look. They will say quite clearly that popularity, for a girl, rests only on physical appearance, whereas, for a boy, a wide range of roles exists. You could be the jock, funny guy, smart guy, maybe good-looking guy, and still be considered popular. I've had long discussions with girls who are dating the most popular guy in class, a guy who is kind of pudgy and not conventionally attractive but dresses cool and is the funniest boy in class. He's got charisma, and yet, in terms of a girl's popularity, charisma is not enough. Even for the popular girls, for whom appearance is the most important thing, this can cause a great deal of stress. They're getting so much approval and attention because of their appearance, but status accorded on that basis feels transient and superficial because they know that their appearance could change. What happens if you start breaking out? What happens if you gain three pounds? They are not valued for who they are as people.

Pier: Very popular girls are often very restricted as to what behaviours are okay — whom they can even talk to, whom they can be seen talking to. And relationships are more central to self-esteem for girls than they are for boys. For boys, right from day one, achievement is made more central to self-esteem. So, for them to say "I can do this, I can do that, I can feel good about myself, even though I'm short, because I'm terrific at soccer" is more effective in building perception of self-worth. In fact, maybe "My shortness is an advantage in itself" would be an outcome for a boy with achievements. But, for girls, being good at something doesn't necessarily increase their status in terms of their relationship to their peer group. So I think self-esteem issues are more complicated for girls in that way as well.

Michelle: Appearance even becomes a factor in substance use. Tobacco is the drug of choice for young females. They're the only group among whom cigarette smoking has increased in the last five years. If you talk to them about quitting, they say they don't want to because they're afraid of gaining weight.

Leora: So, for girls, smoking and thinness are mechanisms of social acceptability, whereas we don't know if drug-taking behaviour in adolescent boys serves the same function. Substance and alcohol use and abuse are more common in adolescent boys.

Miriam: I think many boys define themselves socially by their drug taking. They are part of a crowd that drinks, or smokes up, or doesn't. My brother talks about learning how to smoke a cigarette "like a man" when he was a teen. If you did it wrong, you were ridiculed, but, if you did it right, you were a *de facto* member of the "macho guys."

Pier: People have talked about substance abuse as a relational issue in that it's a way of joining the popular group, but clearly, for a subgroup of boys, it separates them from their peers to a point where they're isolating themselves from everyone in order to do the drugs.

Karin: Dieting does the same for girls. At first it helps them feel like they fit in, but, if it becomes an eating disorder, they become isolated. What is initially an attempt to achieve social acceptability then removes them from their peer group.

Pier: In terms of the long-standing gender stereotypes, I think there's this idea that things are changing, and girls are now encouraged to go on to university and into the workforce. But there is a piling-on of roles, rather than an understanding that the early stereotypes have to change in order to accommodate these other expectations. The girls that I talk to discuss all the old concerns about appearance, weight, sexual desirability, popularity and sexual risks, but then also feel the need to perform in these other areas.

It can seem to adolescent girls that the only way to reject the traditional constraints of the female stereotype is to throw oneself into professional life. It becomes either this or that, but neither option is entirely satisfying. Given that most adult women have not yet sorted this issue out, how can teens learn to balance these conflicting demands? They see their mothers trying to juggle all of that, and I can understand why they see the solution as one or the other. A number of adolescent girls I've spoken to say: "I'll never have children." I find that really interesting, because I would imagine that that's different from what girls in a previous generation said. I see it, in many ways, as a rejection of tradition.

Miriam: I hear boys talking about wanting to be a different kind of father from the one they've had. They are assuming that they can do all the job/career stuff and still be a committed, involved parent. Yet it's still the rare boy who pictures himself doing the laundry and changing diapers.

It is very important to boys to fit in, to meld with the stereotype of what men are supposed to be. Boys who can't play that role are left out. But many of the boys who do play the role don't feel that they fit it, and worry about being found out. Many teens of both sexes don't fit in for lots of reasons: disability, class, personal style, whatever. In my experience, more girls are thinking about these issues in terms of power and gender, whereas many boys see them as personal issues and don't undertake the same level of analysis.

Leora: Girls are exposed to lots of admonitions: control yourself, control your body, control your desires and appetites. Adults seem more accepting of boys' needs to project themselves into the world.

Miriam: While it is the standard that boys will take more risks, be rowdier, all that stuff, they don't have as much permission to be gentle or nurturing. So there are limits on both sides.

Michelle: There are lots of examples where boys' behaviour is viewed differently. Staying out late and truancy are two of these. In extreme versions, they are considered acting-out behaviours for boys, but there is a much lower tolerance threshold for these behaviours in girls. For a lot of boys, that kind of behaviour gets encouraged as long as they aren't caught doing it — like, don't get a girl pregnant, don't get caught skipping class. It's the idea that you could get to do these things and get away with them. For girls, it's not okay to do them at all.

Miriam: Sometimes, when a teen gets pregnant, the parents of the boy tell him to deny that it's his. They say it will "ruin" his life, and so they think he shouldn't have to deal with the consequences of his behaviour.

Michelle: And there really are long-term consequences for girls who get pregnant. Girls who are sexually active at an early age tend generally to be the girls who continue pregnancies, so they never get the education, they can't support themselves.

Miriam: Often both the teen father and the teen mother are very impulsive; that's why they couldn't pause to use proper protection. Then they have a difficult kid who is impulsive himself. Everyone assumes bad behaviour in a child is the result of bad parenting but some of it is genetic. Also, of course, it is difficult to be a good, impulsive parent.

Leora: In many cases, by the time a girl becomes an adolescent, her mother is a certain age in a culture that has few models of mature women having a full sexual life. It may become complicated for young women to achieve sexual maturity because of the ambivalent responses of their fathers and mothers, for whom sexuality in adulthood may be associated with guilt. Boys and their parents take more pleasure in the boy's maturation and development: he's getting taller, he's filling out, he's becoming a man.

The whole issue of parents not touching a child's body when expressing affection has usually emerged earlier with sons than with daughters. At puberty, for most boys, the appropriateness of such displays of affection has already shifted. Although, as always, the importance of this issue will also depend on culture.

Pier: Another limit on self-expression is the change in the relationship between fathers and daughters that occurs at puberty. The physical affection and camaraderie that are important to both may be removed as a result of the father's discomfort with his daughter's emerging sexuality. Although this is rarely made explicit, comments such as, "You are too big to sit on my knee" sink in, such that most girls will learn to feel apologetic about their sexuality, realizing that this is something that has alienated their fathers from them.

How do gender-related pressures manifest?

Leora: For young women, the world can be a frightening place. They are less likely, given that they are constantly reminded of their vulnerability, to feel safe. Adolescents need to experiment with feelings of omnipotence and grandiosity. Girls are less likely to feel secure in their bodies or to express their omnipotence in the ways that boys do. Perhaps the one way that they can express their grandiosity is by protecting themselves from the world, which is where you see the emergence of depression and eating disorders. Some writers on the emergence of eating disorders in adolescent girls have pointed out that the expression of grandiosity for girls is often channelled toward their physical appearance.

Pier: A size-four girl with an eating disorder might go shopping with her mother, who has never been that small, and the store assistant says to the girl: "Oh, what a wonderful body! These clothes look great on you." The mother is ambivalent and in some ways jealous of her daughter's body. She has to deal with the realization that her daughter sees her as less valuable and less feminine because she cannot fit into these size-four clothes. The family shopping expeditions they have together represent a yearning for a commercial vision of a youthful, thin female sexuality that both mothers and daughters share in this society and that serves to devalue the mother in the relationship.

Miriam: And then that extends to other women — teachers, coaches, employers …

Leora: Right now there are things happening in high school that I think are unacceptable. In some schools, they've abandoned the school play in favour of the school fashion show, so, instead of talent or hard work, or finding out if you could do set design or whatever and still be part of the group, what matters is how you look. In some of these fashion shows, girls are modelling lingerie. That really outrages me. Of course these girls are going to be very conscious of their bodies if they're going to be walking on the stage in front of their peers in these little skimpy outfits.

Michelle: I gather the adolescent boys are not wearing underwear.

Leora: They do, but they wear boxers. It's not more revealing than what they would be wearing on a hot day in the summer. It's not a look that is solely sexual, as lingerie is.

Pier: You know you're going to meet the view that says, "This is the chance for these girls to explore their sexuality and to display it in a healthy way." How are you going to answer to that one?

Leora: I would say, that might be true if that was acceptable for girls of all shapes and sizes, but it becomes very clear that it's a sought-after position and it relates strictly to your body weight.

Michelle: I'm not sure that allowing yourself to be represented as a sexual object is the best way to explore your sexuality anyway, quite apart from body size.

Leora: When parents discover that their daughter has been experimenting with sex or drugs, the consequences are likely to be something in the realm of her not being allowed to talk or spend time with her friends from school. She may be forbidden to do sports or other activities that help her feel empowered or effective. The girl will feel trapped and ambivalent about her behaviour, and may run away or make a suicide attempt in response.

Pier: At the extreme end of the spectrum, we can look at psychiatric illnesses. Some are found much more often in one sex than the other. Girls experience eating disorders at a rate that's at least ten times that of boys. They also are diagnosed with unipolar depression three to five times more often. Girls attempt suicide anywhere from three to nine times more often, but three times as many boys than girls actually kill themselves. As a generalization, girls attempt suicide; boys commit suicide.

Karin: I think it's very hard for a young woman to actually express anger at what she feels around her, and she may have a hard time labelling her feelings. If she does end up hurting herself, she doesn't get a lot of support or understanding from the people around her. A lot of self-harming behaviours, like head-banging, suicide attempts, self-cutting and so on, may be related to post-traumatic stress such as sexual abuse. Sexual abuse has been established as probably four times as common among adolescent girls than boys.

Pier: One of the things that I find interesting is the way that gender differences and illness are discussed within the mental-health profession. Girls are considered to have the internalizing disorders. I sometimes have the impression that, when girls are discussed in terms of higher instances of depression and eating disorders and "unsuccessful" suicide attempts, they're seen as "whiny"; less effective in expressing their distress when boys go out there and complete the act. We all stand up and take notice then, and I sometimes have the impression that boys' distress is in some way taken more seriously because it's so much harder for them to articulate. There is a tendency to see girls' psychiatric symptoms as a call for attention. "Oh, I need attention, so I'm engaging in this suicidal behaviour," and that's spoiled-brat acting-out, and not that serious. The perception is not that the girl actually needs attention; it's that she wants it and she's manipulating to get it. A teen said to me, "I can't get anyone to listen to me unless I pull out my hair or bang my head on the wall. Why do I have to do all those things before you'll pay attention to the fact that I'm in pain?" We blame these girls for learning behaviours that the system has forced on them.

Miriam: So girls, then, are diagnosable. Boys who are having problems dealing with feelings are not. It's a double-edged sword. Boys aren't as misunderstood by the mental-health system because they enter the system less often. On the other hand, they often express their issues by hurting others, and then get into the justice system, where there is often no effort to help them, just to punish them for their actions.

What are the options?

Miriam: In *Reviving Ophelia*, Mary Pipher talks about the "false self" that girls create in early adolescence.[1] This persona matches their idea of who they need to be to fit in as an adolescent. Of course, this can block them from experiencing their real emotions. This "false self" may do things that are untrue to the nature of the "real" person. This idea is complicated by the reality that all teens, male and female, try on all kinds of different personae in a quest to identify who they really are.

The difference for boys and girls is that boys have a wider range of acceptable roles. Many boys also feel uncomfortable with these "Who am I?" issues, but I think that they start this process at a later age than girls, and go through it more quickly. As parents, inconsistency drives us nuts, but inconsistency is the hallmark of this process. It is unhealthy to be consistent, because it means that the teen is stuck in one persona and can't try on a variety of different modes of being. We might want our kids to be strong, healthy, non-destructive, feminist, all that stuff, but they won't be all the time. We also have to be aware of where we, ourselves, are coming from.

Pier: As a feminist therapist, I have to address my own attitudes before addressing them with a patient. Feminism, for most of us, has been a developmental, cultural and emotional experience. I have had to learn that I can't give feminism to a patient, that she may or may not learn or experience it on her own.

It's hard for me to come to terms with the fact that I can't talk girls out of their beliefs about their bodies, popularity and relationships any more than I could have talked myself out of them when I was fifteen. I have to work to understand that the opinion of their peers is far more important than my opinion. I've had to learn to work with their concerns, rather than against them. It's an unreasonable expectation that they should ignore their peers' opinion, and that they shouldn't worry about their weight or appearance. I know that it doesn't really relate to their value as a person. But it does relate to their value in their peer group, and that's of prime importance.

Leora: It is very tricky. I work with girls who come from very strict, traditional backgrounds who have their life pretty well planned out for them. As a feminist I find it hard to observe this, but the practical person in me recognizes that, often, for these girls who come from a particular community, that's all they know. All their friends are part of their parents' community, and to leave that community would be to leave every person they've ever known. There is no way that a seventeen- or eighteen-year-old kid can do that. So, the path that I've taken is: "How can you do the things you want to do and still remain a part of your community, in a way that that's manageable for you?" It's a compromise, clearly, but these girls aren't going to leave those communities where they have a sense of collectivity, warmth and positive support. So, the question for me is: "How do you do the stuff that fulfils you while at the same time maintaining the good part of your community?"

Karin: The experience of exclusion in high school or junior high school is so powerful that, even with supportive parents, it's very near intolerable. If it's an ongoing thing and there aren't ways of trying to resolve it, that may be the best that you can do — be very supportive around how to tolerate that. One day my twelve-year-old was brushing her hair, really brushing it hard, and saying how ugly and awful it was and how she was just going to have to do something different with it. Later that day, she said her friends from the previous year were "giving her the freeze-out." She didn't understand why, it didn't make any sense to her, and she tried all kinds of things, but they continued to talk over her and around her, or walk away when she came toward them. There was clearly pain in what she was saying. We talked more about this experience of being left out and how it felt. She told me about how, at school, the "in group" get to feel that they are "cool" by identifying others who are "uncool" — for instance, a boy had said to her that the way she wore her hair made her look like a baby. Her experience around this whole thing was of being excluded and feeling ugly. She said, and I'll never forget it, "Well, you think when you're left out that, if you could change something about yourself, then the others would like you and let you in."

We talked about her experience, and my own experiences, of exclusion. Then I asked her if her feeling of being ugly got bigger each time she was excluded, and she recognized immediately that that was how she felt. I said: "Well, when you're feeling like that, it doesn't matter what you do with your hair. It isn't going to look good enough, because your feeling of ugliness is coming from a different place — it doesn't really have anything to do with your hair." So she was thinking about that for a bit and we talked about other things — you know, the kind of conversation you have with a person this age is not happening in a linear fashion, but in bits and pieces — and we were walking down the street and the sun was shining . A woman passing us stopped and put her hand on my daughter's shoulder. I was freaking out, thinking: "What's this woman doing?", but then she said, "Oh my, your hair is gorgeous." It was a totally spontaneous comment, this "ugly" hair is the same hair that attracts a comment from a stranger on the street, and my daughter and I both laughed. My daughter said, "How much did you pay that woman to say that?" and we laughed some more. Although she was laughing, she was really confused. She knew that there was something about her own experience with her hair that was off because this wouldn't have happened otherwise, but she really didn't experience her own appearance as attractive, because of the underlying experience of exclusion. Now, we don't have a big appearance focus in our household, and what eventually happened was that these kids in her school decided that they had screwed things up, and wanted to have a more inclusive group in their class, and for the rest of the year she was part of a close group of friends who had previously excluded her. I don't recall her complaining about her hair for the rest of the term.

Leora: The popular group is not necessarily the best group. When I was fourteen, we moved to a new city, so I was automatically the outsider. At the same time, there was a girl who decided she wanted to be popular — she did a huge amount of sucking up and fawning to try to be accepted. The more popular girls physically and verbally abused her. She would make one friend in the popular group who would be a kind of ally, but who wouldn't really protect her. Even the popular boys would harass her, recognizing her position. After a year and a half, she was finally allowed to become part of the popular group. It was a life-changing experience for me, because I was certain that nothing was worse than what she had gone through, and I felt happy being less popular. We can help our kids recognize that the popular group often tends to be the cruellest, and maybe it's a better decision not to participate.

Pier: My parents were extremely appearance-conscious. How you looked was the passport to success, to living happily. When I talked to them later, they said, "How could we not want you to have access to happiness, success, approval when we had either suffered ourselves because we felt that we didn't have that opportunity or watched other people suffering from it? How could we not encourage you to make the best of your appearance?" I wish my parents had offered me alternatives to all that.

Karin: If a teen feels she must take risks to fit into the popular group, it is hard for parents to know what to do. Their support must be within a framework of safety, so they might say: "If you're going out, you must call us at such-and-such time. We need to know where you're going and with whom" — a structure of safety, with some rules, but some space to try these things out. A parent is one of the forces mediating how the child experiences cultural pressures.

Leora: It's inevitable that adolescents will experiment with all those things that are so powerful within the peer group. The hope is, if they have other role models who hold their attention, eventually they start to emulate them. We can encourage them to develop a group among the girls who play basketball, the girls who work on the yearbook — there are other options if they are able to tolerate the idea that they won't be in the popular group.

It can be a relief to be left out of the popular group. As much as you want to be popular and dating and all that, in some ways it can be scary. We can help our kids see that it's not all or nothing — if you're not in the popular group, you can still have friends. It's really hard to be in a popular group if you have an alternative set of values, and you really can't do it both ways, but you may be able to find a peer group that's similar to you.

Karin: We're talking about both the actuality of exclusion and the fear of exclusion, of losing that place. We can talk about what that experience is like and how to tolerate that experience. Maybe parents need to be looking at creating other opportunities for their kids to be connected with teens in other places, or even in the same school. Does it have to be this particular popular group? Are there other groups in the school where you can find people who have things in common with you? If not, why is this particular group so important?

Michelle: I think that there are real opportunities for being on the margin of the popular group, and I think that's something to teach children, that there's a real freedom in not being conventionally beautiful or not worrying about being conventionally beautiful.

Karin: There are more expectations piled up on top of the old expectations for girls. It is fairly common now to have a camp or workshops for girls with titles like "Be the Best That You Can Be." So it's not as though you can "be the best that you can be" at something-or-other; it's that you're supposed to "be the best that you can be" at everything, which means the best that you can be in physical education, in academics, as well in terms of your physical appearance. In other words, you should be perfect. So, to choose a marginal group instead of a popular group is not to be the best that you can be; it's to settle for something less than the best.

Pier: This "best that you can be" thing is a hard subject to negotiate with adolescents. With adolescents, you want to preserve a sense of infinite potential and grandiosity and omnipotence, but adults often have to come to terms with the loss of many of those beliefs about themselves and the world. I find it very hard to acknowledge that there are limitations to what young women can achieve, especially the parts that are gender-role related. They may or may not want to strive to overcome these things, so I don't want to push them too hard, but I also don't want to curtail their sense of being able to be the best, because, in the past, that lack of encouragement is something girls have experienced too often. I'm confused with regard to what's realistic for them, and am worried that I may do harm if I cannot help them balance, in their own minds, a realistic sense of limitation versus infinite potential.

Miriam: It's hard, too, because, as feminist parents, or parents who have learned a bit about life and gender, we may have ideas that are in direct conflict with the current thinking. Our kids may already feel marginalized because their family isn't totally "mainstream" — maybe we're vegetarians, or activists, or gay or lesbian, or just vocal about gender stuff. So they may feel they need to prove that they're normal, by doing very gender-stereotyped things. Our daughters might get into appearance-related stuff that we find offensive; our boys might not express their emotions, and inform us that boys don't cry. If we criticize this, they may see it as a criticism of who they are as people, but if we don't talk about it, are we selling out? Maybe we went through it ourselves, and we want to spare our kids the pain. But we can't leapfrog them past the adolescent years.

Michelle: Maybe we have to help our daughters in the beginning, show them that appearance is not important and that achievement should be valued for what it gives them, rather than how their peer group sees it. It isn't valuable for any other reason than their own experience of enjoying a new achievement. Otherwise it becomes another trap.

Pier: It's difficult. What are you going to say to your daughter? Are you going to say: "Hang in there until university, don't wear lipstick, don't diet," when at the same time you're seeing your daughter rejected, perhaps, or not feeling a part of life at school?

Michelle: We help them by being role models of self-acceptance. We should be conscious of not putting ourselves down or complaining about how we look. We can express our admiration for a wide variety of people, and not express our judgments as comments about appearance.

Leora: In any of these areas we're talking about, we would want to provide a young person with a little more choice. Even if we are appearance-conscious, we can be willing to challenge our personal values, challenge the cultural values around appearance. We can offer some support to our kids when they feel that they don't fit in.

Karin: Parents have to determine what limits are appropriate at this age, in this culture, and figure out how they can establish some safety, while giving their kids more room. This can be hard for parents who have given their kids a lot of freedom and now feel that things are out of control. The initial response is to just clamp down and say no, or to start being more rigid, rather than cooperatively to figure out issues around safety.

Leora: We tend to forget how much our kids' friends watch us. Every family is different, and they see these differences and wonder if that is how they want to be. If they come from a more restrictive family, it might be scary to see a more democratic family, but it will also open up possibilities. It works in the other direction too. Our kids may see more restrictive families as having clearer expectations. They might think it's an advantage not to have to think everything through, or process it to death.

Michelle: We can also look for things that will make our children and teens more resilient. Feminism can do this, as it can help them draw on a different construction of the woman's role or the male's role. It's an opportunity for adolescents to have another option available, especially if it's not forced down their throats. Adolescence can seem like a very humourless stage of life, but the teen with a sense of humour can often deal with stress more easily.

Miriam: I think it's also hard for us to have a sense a humour about teens — especially when we are thinking of them as sexual beings. There can be a lot of internal conflict. We want them to be sexually healthy, on the one hand, but, on the other, it would be a lot easier if they didn't get sexually involved, and we didn't have to worry about pregnancy, AIDS, all that. But, even more, we have our own confused feelings about sex. We don't want our kids to have those feelings, but we aren't totally comfortable with them not having them. We may also be surprised when we realize that we have a double standard about sex, that we are more comfortable with a boy having sex than with a girl having it.

Pier: We've talked mainly about girls — in part because we are all women, and in part because we work mainly with girls. There are many issues for boys, issues around masculinity and what it means, and how many boys actually feel comfortable with how they fit into male roles, and their own innate maleness.

Miriam: The big question is: What is the real role, biologically, of gender? If we could take out our culture's assumptions about masculinity and femininity, if we could remove the profit motive as a big part of why the media encourages young people to hate how they look and who they are, if we could expel our own hang-ups about gender, what would be left? Would there be a distinct difference between all men and all women? I think there would there be a continuum, with many women clustered at one end, and many men clustered at the other, but lots of both scattered in between.

We won't see that in our lifetimes, but if we can help our teens question the conventional wisdom about gender, question whether their behaviour is culturally programmed and maybe not always in their best interests, then we will help them weather the gender-related difficulties of adolescence, and, in the long run, change the world, even if only a little.

Notes

1. Mary Pipher, *Reviving Ophelia: Saving the Selves of Adolescent Girls* (New York: Ballantine, 1994).

Healthy Attitudes and Healthy Images

Merryl Bear and Kaca Henley

Our bodies are the most visible, concrete representations of our existence and our identities. How we view our bodies and appearance has immense psychological and social significance. We know how much that perception can affect our personal growth, self-image and sense of worth; there is no clear-cut border separating body and mind and feelings. Because our bodies carry so much emotional meaning and because they are so eloquent, developing and maintaining a good body image is central to healthy self-esteem. While it is possible to have a poor sense of self-worth along with a good body image, it is impossible to have good self-esteem and a poor body image.

How attractive we feel affects our attitudes, posture, facial expression — in short, our body language. And body language speaks volumes. In fact, 93 percent of what we communicate is not in the words we speak. Only 7 percent of our communication is conveyed by what we say. A surprising 55 percent is by body language, and the remaining 38 percent is by tone of voice.[1] Thus, the way we perceive ourselves will colour the way other people respond to us and will start a feedback loop: People are drawn to us when we are confident, which confirms our sense of our attractiveness. This in turn raises our confidence, which further attracts people to us.

From childhood, we are surrounded by contradictory messages about food, body size, appearance and exercise. These messages teach us to view our appetites and our bodies warily. This is especially true for adolescents, who are learning to deal cognitively, emotionally and physically with newly complex relationships.

Body image is an issue for both adolescent girls and boys. This essay discusses points common to both, as well as issues specific to one sex or the other, and what we, as parents, can do to moderate negative family, community and media influences. Because girls and women are particularly vulnerable to negative messages and can find it difficult to accept their bodies, and harder still to appreciate or even love them, our focus here is primarily on how body image is constructed and experienced by girls.

How Body Image Develops

Body image is generally defined as *the feelings, beliefs and attitudes that one has about one's body.*

Body image, like self-esteem, is not a constant; how we feel about ourselves can change from moment to moment, at the slightest provocation. There are days when we look at ourselves and are pleased with what we see. Those are the days we just fly through, with a good feeling about ourselves and a smile on our lips. On the other hand, we can have what some people call "bad hair days," the days when even our hair won't do what we think it should and we feel that we look "awful." This affects our willingness to be seen, and even to do things which, under other circumstances, we would do easily and comfortably.

Body image thus develops as an ever-changing sense of our comfort in, and our caring for, our bodies. It grows from the natural, spontaneous delight and exploration we have as infants. As we mature, it is influenced by the way people around us view and behave toward their own and others' bodies (including ours).

Children pick up popular and often contradictory notions about how their bodies should look, what should go into their bodies, what should and what can be done with their bodies, and how they should feel about their bodies. Examples of these notions include:

- what is healthy (e.g., meat and potatoes, or vegetarianism; mild or vigorous exercise);
- notions about waste (e.g. "Clean up your plate, think of the hungry children in …" or "Eat until you're full, then stop");
- beliefs regarding sex roles within the family (e.g., stereotypes of

women cooking and serving, men eating; small portions for women, large ones for men); and

- appropriate activity levels for girls and boys (e.g., boys run, girls walk; the feminine is passive, the masculine is active).

When linked to self-esteem, unrealistic standards of appearance can feed, or even create, insecurities about self-worth. In turn, the body becomes the focus of these insecurities. This happens in a variety of ways. The Western cultural phenomenon which associates the ideal body with success, popularity and high self-esteem is perpetuated by the entertainment, fashion and advertising industries. They imply that the slender, boyish body is the only acceptable "choice" for women, and, for boys, the sole "choice" is a lean body with well-defined muscles. And, above all, they imply that this "choice" is simply a matter of willpower, of exerting the requisite effort and, in many cases, emulating a given media star or buying a given product, to achieve that ideal.

These and similar messages come from a broad range of pervasive socializing influences, from religious, medical and educational institutions (and their practitioners) to the mass media and, of course, family and friends. Many of us who grew up with these messages take them for granted and never consider challenging them. We often live by them without being aware of their negative effects.

In addition to being affected by the complex and often contradictory aspects of the dominant culture in which we live, we have roots in other cultural contexts as well. Our religious, ethnic, class and racial heritages all affect the way we perceive the world and our bodies. For first-generation immigrants or their children, the new culture's stereotypes and messages can be a dramatic, or even incomprehensible, change from their own cultures. As a result of these ethnic and cultural differences, conflicts can arise between parents and teens. This may take the form of children wanting to conform to their peer group's standards while parents demand that they adhere to "the old country" ways. On the other hand, immigrant parents may encourage adaptation to the new culture's norms, especially in physical appearance, in the hopes that this will help the teen integrate, and even, in some instances, "pass" into the new culture. Some individuals may feel liberated from narrower sex roles and develop a solid sense of self-worth based on more than the limits of biology. Others may find the narrowness of the Western body ideal destroying their culture's broader, more inclusive notion of beauty.

Value conflicts are not, of course, limited to immigrant families. Families that have lived in a particular country or community for generations also struggle with the tensions between adolescent peer-group fashions and home values. Girls may want to wear clothes that expose their bodies the way their friends do, but their parents may perceive them as immodest. Boys may want to cut or grow or dye their hair, but parents may view that as making their son "effeminate," diminished as a male. Teens may pierce their bodies, or wear ragged clothes, or clothes perceived as deliberately bizarre. Many family tensions around such appearance-based issues come to bear just when teenagers are exploring the parameters of their independence from the family, trying to establish an identity, and when peer-group attitudes and behaviour are becoming the standard by which they generally measure their worth.

Against the backdrop of a society where "fitting in" can mean, for girls, being very slender; for boys, muscular and lean; and, for all, being tall, young, fair (Caucasian) and able-bodied, people who have other racial or ethnic backgrounds or other abilities or orientations are viewed as "different." Not only are teens in these groups obliged to live under the dominant white cultural norms and expectations, but also, at the same time, they may have to navigate the standards and expectations of their own culture or community. Conversely, their own culture's or community's values may support their resistance to conforming to a mainstream notion of success and happiness being predicated on slenderness or "good" looks.

Indeed, surveys of Black adolescent girls indicate that more central to their sense of beauty is the projection of a personal style, self-confidence and personality.[2] African-American women appear to evaluate their body size mainly in relation to that of other Black women and not to the Caucasian ideal. Given that their bodies are, on average, larger than those of their white contemporaries, this may permit many African-American women to develop a resistance to pressures to be thin. It also appears that Black women and adolescents are more likely than their white counterparts to give positive affirmation to one another on the basis of both self-presentation and achievements not tied to appearance. This helps to build a self-esteem which encompasses physical confidence, individuality and sensuality. Nonetheless, in a context in which racism is systemic, the better one "fits" the dominant (white) standard, the more likely one is to be widely accepted. It is thus important not to suggest that Black adolescents and women are immune to body-image issues, including food and weight preoccupation. As they move closer to acculturation, young Black women are increasingly exposed to the dominance of the white "beauty" ideal associated with acceptance and success. That is why we cannot assume that food and weight preoccupation, including eating disorders, are alien to Black adolescent women just because of their race, whether their cultural community accepts white norms or not. What is clear, however, is that we all have much to learn from the African-American idea of individual style and confidence as determining overall attractiveness.

Lesbians, gay men and individuals with chronic illness and disabilities are among those groups of teens who have additional issues which put them at increased risk of developing unhealthy attitudes toward their bodies. Within their own groups, a sense of one's individuality may be perceived as a badge of honour; in broader society, however, being "different" may be seen as a challenge to the dominant culture, and even as a personal failure. This may be compounded by pressures to conform to their communities' standards of appearance.

As they grow into their teens and as their physical, emotional and sexual experiences change, most children are inclined to separate themselves from their parents. Teenagers begin to turn to other sources of information and support, most notably their peers and the mass media. Their world revolves around their friends. They exchange ideas and impressions and experiences covering a range of issues, many of them related to physical appearance. Teenagers judge their acceptability on how they perceive their weight and appearance in comparison to their peers. This is a clear example of how other concerns are displaced onto body image. Peer support or rejection is a prime reference point for teens. They may become increasingly aware that girls and boys are perceived as having distinctly different roles and values, and are rewarded for different things. They will often accept as their own the constraints of other people's beliefs, such as the notion that adolescent women need to be more careful than boys and younger girls about how their bodies are perceived and used, and that they are more vulnerable to the intrusion of others.

Unhealthy Messages, Unhealthy Strategies

Young teens are coming to terms with bodies and appetites that are undergoing normal developmental changes; they are particularly susceptible to messages about what and how much (or how little) they should eat. The constant barrage of suggestions in the media can create an ambivalence about their natural hunger and their natural size, which is reflected in the attitudes of peers, parents and others.

Teens are still developing their ability to think abstractly, and the level of this development will affect their ability to articulate conflicts and solve problems. Since high self-esteem is generally equated with "looking good," they may have trouble separating external conflicts, successes and failures, and other concerns, from any body dissatisfaction or shame.

Complicating this picture is the fact that teens don't always understand the normal physical developments of puberty, and they can feel disappointed in themselves, mystified, or even betrayed, by their perfectly normal body changes at puberty. Many respond to weight gains, for example, with a sense of losing control of their bodies and resort to draconian efforts to regain that control, undertaking restrictive dieting and exercise routines. Part of the reason for this behaviour is that teens often cannot tolerate ambivalence. They see things in black and white, good and bad, making it easy to buy into the narrow range of "acceptable" body types touted by the Western mass media, as the way to fit in.

The natural physical changes of puberty and menopause are rarely acknowledged in Western society. On the leading edge of the trend to ignore these changes, the advertising and entertainment industries portray "normal" adult women as universally without any fat on their hips, thighs and breasts, creating the impression that the body weight and structure required for having children and for growing to healthy maturity is unnatural or undesirable.

Media images serve as the standard against which many, if not most, women (young and old) find themselves lacking, and it encourages them to believe that they don't "measure up." Adolescent women, exploring their newly burgeoning sexuality before they have had time to come to terms with it, may experience significant fear and uncertainty when they feel "different" from their mainstream peers. Taking control by regulating weight may be seen as a way of "fitting in."

Boys also need to be reassured about the changes their bodies undergo during puberty. The physical and cognitive developmental spurts they experience and see in their peers can create consternation. For boys who remain small or slight, measuring themselves against the traditional standard of the physically ideal man (tall, strong and muscular) may result in extreme confusion and shame, especially if they do not come to it with a strong sense of self-worth, and an understanding and appreciation of male developmental stages and the range of human bodies.

The power of these unrealistic norms, some dating back decades, is illustrated by the widespread response of boys to the 1950s "90-pound weakling" ads of Charles Atlas. On back pages of comic books across North America, Charles Atlas offered help (for "one thin dime") to boys and men who "got sand kicked in their faces" at the beach by bigger and stronger males. The image of the "90-pound weakling" has entered the language, and rumour has it that boys who find the ads in old comic books are still writing to the old address, sending a dime for Charles Atlas's booklet — and receiving it!

Today, teenage boys may feel even more confused. The physical range of successful men depicted in the media is narrowing, and masculinity is being redefined. Male sociocultural roles are in a state of flux, with the "'90s man" a supposed blend of sensitivity and traditional strength. The difficulty that arises is that there are almost no visible role models for young men to emulate; no visible men who successfully make their way in the world while simultaneously displaying traditionally feminine attributes of gentleness, compassion and caring, and who are not seen to be diminished in their masculinity. While young men may aspire to a fuller expression of their humanity, they don't want to be seen as feminine, which is a devalued attribute in this culture. To avoid being seen in this way, or as an outlet for their confusion and lowered sense of self, they, too, may do various things to take control of their bodies. While a smaller number of boys than girls develop eating disorders, an alarmingly high number of them use exercise and steroids to shape their physical appearance. For example, according to the Canadian Centre for Drug Free Sport, 47 percent of steroid users take these drugs specifically to change their physical appearance,[3] and Canada is not atypical in this regard.

Boys and men in the industrialized world are far from immune to the demand to live up to near impossible standards of appearance. Past generations had a protective factor in the broad range of physical attributes displayed by visible male role models. This is now being whittled away, however, as the media and advertising increasingly equate masculinity with a hard, lean male body — a body unlikely to be achieved by anything less than stringent exercise regimens, restrictive eating behaviour and a one-dimensional life, if not performance-enhancing chemicals. Even then, few men will be able to attain the "ideal" body, since the genetic range of human bodies is so broad.

Dieting and weight loss are often perceived by teens, and many adults, as ways of solving all problems and gaining control over numerous essentially non-related issues. In a landmark Arizona study of body image, one high-school girl commented, "If I went on a diet, I'd feel like it was a way of getting control … like a way to make myself thinner, and make my appearance and my social life better. So it would be like getting control over lots of different things, I guess."[4]

The fact that many teens do not eat regularly, or nutritiously, creates an inevitable physiological need to binge when the opportunity arises. Simply speaking, restricted eating (dieting) depletes the body. Our bodies cannot distinguish between a diet to lose weight and an actual famine, and respond by defending themselves. Our bodies become hungry and let us know that in no uncertain terms. Ignoring that hunger, and persisting with the diet, can lead to malnutrition, which in turn can lead to mood swings, fatigue and binge eating. When food deprivation or restriction leads to bingeing, it can create or fuel a sense of being out of control around food. This may increase the sense of shame, ambivalence and concern about food and weight, and, by extension, chip away at our sense of self-worth. It may also be the first behaviourial step toward developing an eating disorder.

Teenage girls are caught in a complex developmental dilemma. They are entering a world where women are no longer expected to be vulnerable, in need of protection, but rather to be confident, competent and independent. Yet, at the same time, they are expected to fulfil the traditionally feminine roles of nurturing and supporting others, and to look "feminine" too. At the very time that young women feel the greatest need to "fit in" and be seen as attractive (and hence worthy of acceptance), most of them are also dealing with the differences between their body shapes and the cultural "ideal." The general notion that only a slim body is attractive and a passport to acceptance is illustrated by another remark from the Arizona study: "I think that the reason that I would diet would be to gain self-confidence … but also that self-confidence I would want to use to like get a boyfriend. It seems like that's the only way that I'd be able to … be accepted."[5] Fifteen-year-old Kim[6] said, "If you're thin, a boy will forgive your other flaws."

At the same age, young men are more likely to be approaching the male cultural standard — getting taller, becoming more muscular. While some young men may lag behind their peers a bit, or try to hasten or alter their growth by obsessive body-building or through the use of steroids, their tendency to be less preoccupied with weight and food is grounded in society's inclination to accept a wider range of body types and attributes for successful males than for successful females.

The entertainment and fashion industries tout disturbed eating patterns as a tool for obtaining an ideal body image — they associate the fame, adulation and financial rewards heaped on celebrities with extremely restricted eating behaviour. In fact, they suggest that, by changing one's size and shape to the above-mentioned standard, "You, too, can have it all."

With manipulative repetition, these industries make abnormal eating attitudes and behaviours seem normal. In print, in movies and on television and radio, they model and encourage deprivation thinking (obsessing about dieting, food and weight issues). They consistently depict unnaturally small food portions as acceptable or normal, making ordinary hunger seem unacceptable, self-indulgent and out of control. Most media portrayals related to female body image are unrealistic or negative, and the high incidence of eating disorders among teenage girls reflects those influences.

Agism is another way the entertainment and fashion industries set unattainable standards. They use very young girls (or boys) to advertise practically everything, even clothing for adult women. Finalists in modelling agency contests often average fifteen years in age. Images of visibly older people are excluded except as consumers of incontinence products or, in the case of women, proponents of "anti-aging" products. Adolescents, and, for that matter, all of us, are left with few positive media images of growing older, especially for women.

Where there is an accepted climate of sexual harassment, insecurity about body image can be intensified. The sense of vulnerability and total exposure in high school gymnasiums and corridors is a case in point. It is often in these places that young women, people of colour, lesbians and gays, and other people of "difference," are (de)graded by others, often young men. To add to their insecurity, girls judge one another by their appearance as well, accepting or rejecting others and creating cliques in which restrictive eating and exercise behaviours are encouraged and socially rewarded. Where such behaviours are seen as permissible, even sanctioned, the experience of being an object is confirmed and intensified.

Young people's ability to truly live in and "stretch" their bodies can be further hampered by the mixed messages they receive about physical exercise. Exercise is known to enhance one's sense of both mental and physical competence, and thus can help raise self-esteem. But, more and more, exercise is used exclusively to control shape and weight rather than for fun, social engagement and health. Western youth are increasingly sedentary, which limits their experiences of, and trust in, their bodies. An increased number of youngsters are over their natural weight because of a sedentary lifestyle, putting them in a Catch-22 situation.

Being large is presented stereotypically as a deliberate choice — a bad, undisciplined and self-indulgent choice. And yet, the average North American woman is 5'3" tall and weighs 144 pounds.[7] That would correspond to about a size 14, which is outside the size range of many stores and boutiques. So the "ideal" is far from the "norm."

Before puberty, girls are generally freer to engage in unbounded physical activities and natural eating. Once puberty is reached, however, cultural messages about appropriate behaviour and appearance for girls tend to change and become more limiting. Thus, parents may tolerate, or even encourage, physical risk-taking and energetic activity in a pre-adolescent daughter; but, at puberty, they start to frown on such activities, labelling them "unfeminine," "undignified" or "unladylike."

As children become teens, they try even more intensely to live up to ideal body images: peers become increasingly influential, and teens become more invested in romantic attachments and fitting in with their peer group. Teens who are over the "normal" weight often internalize negative attitudes, such as: "Fat is bad; I'm fat, so I must be bad," which can lead to a variety of behaviours, including using food intake as a way of gaining a sense of control in a world that seems beyond their control.

A number of young girls will eat before a dinner date or ignore natural hunger signals and starve themselves. They do this in order not to appear too hungry, which is generally equated with being out of control or voracious. For girls, a full and natural appetite is often viewed as behaviour resulting from a consuming and uncontrolled character. As Kim said, "I'm really careful to eat only small servings of low-calorie foods when people are around, and then, when I'm alone and hungry, I sneak huge portions of leftovers from the fridge and binge on them. It makes me feel kind of ashamed and bad about myself."

The most pervasive message that women and men receive from media images is that, for women, success in all its forms depends on attaining and maintaining a slender body. The advertising and fashion industries tell us that women can choose the body they want (and that the only desirable choice is slender) and can attain it with willpower, discipline, and the "right" diet and exercise. They ignore scientific evidence that we each have our own inherited "set-point" (a certain weight to which we are genetically predisposed), in favour of the moral imperative not to be fat.

While there are many highly visible adult male role models of success who are tall, short, hairy, bald, thin and fat, women presented as successful are, with very few exceptions, slender and perfectly groomed, without a wrinkle, a blemish, or a hair out of place. The statistics for cosmetic surgery illustrate how successful the image makers have been.

The widely disseminated stereotype of "thin = good, fat = bad" becomes deeply ingrained well before puberty. A body-image survey quoted in *Psychology Today* describes the response of some pre-schoolers shown pictures of women of various shapes and sizes. They were asked which ones they would like to have as a teacher. The children invariably chose the slender ones, describing them as "nice, smart, fun" and rejected the fatter ones as "mean, lazy, ugly."[8]

Furthermore, inappropriate humour is one of many other ways that fashion and women's magazines contribute to women's insecurities. They create a climate in which anyone outside the "acceptable norm" is seen to be the butt of ridicule, an object of pity and even outright contempt. This can be illustrated by the jokes about, the devaluation of, or the flagrant dismissal of fat women. Even prodigious talent usually does not protect them: consider the ongoing excessive interest in and "pity" around Oprah Winfrey's weight-loss struggles; the implications that, as a fat woman, Roseanne Barr is acceptable only in a "lesser" role as a working-class woman on TV (with the double stigmatization of weight and social class); and the brutal "fat jokes" directed at Canadian singer Rita MacNeil.

Given the perception that one's body is never quite good enough, young women, regardless of their actual physical size or shape, may consistently feel themselves to be too fat. The Dairy Board of Canada published research results indicating that about 30 percent of normal-weight and 20 percent of underweight adolescent girls want to lose weight, with as many as 60 percent of underweight adolescent girls being satisfied with their weight.[9]

Body dissatisfaction is also in part the result of the fashion, cosmetics and advertising industries' portrayal of women's bodies as dismembered and disembodied; being shown parts, bits and pieces, we are led to objectify ourselves and see ourselves as a collection of body parts, some less problematic than others, rather than as whole, integrated beings, including body, mind and spirit.

Ask a woman about her body, and she will probably reply with a critique of specific bits and pieces of herself: "I hate my hips" or "My mouth is too broad" or "I can't stand my nose" or "My breasts are too big" or "… too small." Flipping through pages of advertising in women's magazines is like flipping through a parts catalogue of "shoulds," but when the disparate body parts offered up as desirable are put together, rarely does a physical being resembling a "real" woman emerge. This is particularly problematic when the media resorts to retouched, air-brushed, computer-modified or composite (youthful) images.

An example of the unreality that has influenced most North American girls as they were growing up is the Barbie doll, in all her (narrow) permutations. While many still talk of Barbie as "just a toy," the truth is that she is the ubiquitous messenger for the notion that success for women is related to looking a particular way, the Barbie way. But Barbie, if she were life-size, would possess the unlikely body proportions of a 40" chest, 18" waist and 32" hips, with feet on permanent tiptoe, that can fit only into high heels.

More confirmation of the internalization of this unreal image by girls comes from the Arizona study. It shows that white adolescent girls feel that the "perfect" girl would be 5'11" tall, just over 100 pounds, with long, flowing hair. Who is that, if not Barbie? (It should be noted that in that, same study, African-American girls proved far more accepting of a broad range of body types.)[10]

The media — in particular, women's magazines — show, on the one hand (or page!), articles that normalize and encourage the kind of starvation thinking mentioned earlier and, on the other, glorious, colourful images of luscious and "sinful" food for women to prepare, and presumably serve only to others. No wonder, then, that many women have problems staying in touch with their natural hunger and satiety patterns.

The "beauty" and advertising industries also demonstrate racism in the stereotypical portrayal of Black and Asian female models as "exotic" and sexually available. They further compound it by using models of colour whose body types and features are largely within the narrow Caucasian "acceptable norms" and, in that sense, atypical.

Finally, the open sexualization and objectification of female bodies creates a climate of ambivalence for a woman. Should she value and cultivate her other qualities, such as intellect, compassion and empathy, and her particular skills and abilities, or should she focus her life on being a sex object? In fact, the general perception of every woman's worth can be gravely undermined by the broadly held notion that, to be acceptable and worthy of love, a woman must look like a prepubescent boy. Mainstream media depict naked or almost-naked young girls in TV commercials and print advertisements and fashion photographs. Images that not too many years ago would have been seen as pornographic are retouched and airbrushed to near "perfection" and splayed out for the titillation, admiration and envy of viewers. Constant exposure to such depictions of vulnerability and potential exploitation can make it hard for young women to recognize the normality of their own bodies, or to feel safe in them. And if one cannot feel normal or safe in one's body, how can one reasonably be expected to appreciate, accept and nurture it? And, by extension, how can one allow it to carry one confidently about the business of being active and creative in the real world?

Parental Attitudes

Long before puberty, a variety of experiences affect how individuals live in their bodies and feel about them. In infancy and early childhood, parental attitudes are among the strongest of those influences. A parent's willingness to be physical, to touch and cuddle, and generally to be unconditionally accepting of the child's body and bodily functions can be crucial to the child's later acceptance and appreciation of her own body. These childhood influences continue to echo through her lifetime, along with continuing input from the surrounding world.

Adolescents often base their own developing sense of body on what parents expect of them. These expectations are coloured by our conscious or unconscious attitudes about our own appearance, and our own sexuality and sensuality. The messages we give our children, be they verbal or implied, can be a response to messages and incidents from our own childhood. Parents who examine their own attitudes and behaviours — and the signals these give to their children — may find that these signals are negative, or that they convey a fear or disgust with things sexual or physical, or indicate a tendency to measure people's acceptability (including their own) by size and shape.

Setting an example of healthy body attitudes and eating behaviour is crucial, and can be particularly difficult for mothers who have poor body image and disturbed eating patterns themselves. Research indicates that the dieting behaviour of mothers is likely to have a negative effect on post-pubertal daughters and to be copied by them.[11] This may be a response to increased parental concern about the child "fitting in" or/and an increased awareness of the social value of thinness for women. Fathers who have an emotional investment in their children's physical appearance, monitoring eating and exercise behaviour and rewarding weight loss, can also significantly lower the children's self-worth and body satisfaction.

Parents' preoccupation with their own weight and eating habits may even interfere with their general parenting skills and their attunement to the child. A mother or father who diets is more likely to be critical of the child's appearance and to apply pressure to lose weight. Some parents, especially mothers with daughters, will encourage their children to go on a diet with them. This gives the adolescent the idea that there is something wrong, not only with her developing body, but also with her mother's mature body. The message to the teenager is that she is not okay the way she is, that love is conditional on looking a particular way, and hence on her control of food and weight. It can also set up a state of unhealthy competition between parent and child.

Back to Kim, who limited food intake in family and public settings and binged in secret. She explains, "My mum tells me that I'm getting chubby and that I need to watch what I eat, but I think it's my dad's idea and not hers." This oblique communication has damaged Kim's sense of her own acceptability, and, what is more, it also hurt her relationship with both parents. "[Mum] says that it's because they love me and want me to be happy, but it makes me feel like I'm not good enough for my dad, and that mum ought to understand me and explain to dad instead of picking on me all the time. It feels like they won't love me if I'm not skinny." As a result of her own uncertainties and an adolescent's natural reticence around these matters, Kim was unable to address the issue with her mother because she felt the message did not originate from her; she was unable to address it with her father because he had not actually said it to her. Her distress led to her overt restraint and covert binges, creating a profound sense of shame and self-loathing focused on her body that will colour her entire adult life unless the issues are addressed.

Deliberately or not, many mothers' voices echo cultural beliefs, including those of male household members, about acceptable appearance, and related attitudes and behaviour around food. Even more than a mother's words, her attitude and the example she presents with her behaviour are a powerful influence, for the mother is the daughter's first reference point on womanliness, sexuality and sensuality. Research shows that, after puberty, daughters are more likely to be negatively influenced by mothers' pathological eating behaviours and attitudes.[12] This may be related to an increased fear of peer rejection, and an intensified vulnerability to notions about thinness as the bottom-line measure of social value. After all, the teenager's main life task is increasing her competence outside the family domain. When a daughter is unsure of her competence or her ability to manage as she moves in increasingly broader social circles, she may be even more influenced by her parents' expectations of her appearance.

Fathers and brothers, often unwittingly, can also wound girls by making comments or offering advice on appearance. Fathers may initiate such detrimental behaviours, which are then imitated by sons. Unchallenged, these attitudes can, from a very early age, have a negative impact on both the girl's and her brother's beliefs about body and behaviour patterns, and get passed on to the following generation as well.

Negative attitudes about body image may also come from peers and the media, and even from misreading some otherwise constructive messages. For example, one of the authors of this essay was told over and over as a child and adolescent, "Appearance doesn't matter; it's intelligence that counts." Certainly that is not a destructive message in itself, but it was repeated in a cultural climate that made it easy to misread. In her family's culture of origin, it was unacceptable for a woman to be vain or conceited, so her looks were never discussed at home. As a result, her mind distorted the message to "I'm ugly, but I'm smart." This had a powerful influence on her self-image for more than half her life. It was only many decades later that she could recognize what an attractive child and young woman she had been and get back on the road to self-acceptance.

Promoting Healthy Attitudes

As parents, we need to be aware of the strong desire of teens to "measure up" to body-image standards, and how easily they can find themselves lacking. We can consistently communicate our own appreciation of both sexes, and of the broadest range of body types for women and men. By our example, and by overcoming any discomfort we have with listening and talking about the fears, uncertainties and revulsions associated with a young person's physical changes, cycles and sexuality, we can help demystify them. We can remove some of the shame and disinformation that our daughters and sons will, without fail, pick up in locker rooms, on the street, in the media.

Comparisons with others on the basis of appearance and failing to live up to a self-imposed standard (inspired and reinforced by cultural ideals) makes many teens, especially young women, feel not only unattractive, but also "bad." This is where a parent or another trusted and supportive adult can help them accentuate the positive aspects of their bodies, rather than fretting about and trying to alter perceived flaws. They need to be encouraged to see themselves as whole physical beings rather than as a collection of flawed parts.

Parents' attitudes toward their teen daughters' burgeoning sexuality, especially their menses, will influence whether their daughters experience it — for decades to come — as a celebration of their femaleness, or with a sense of body-shame and dirtiness. Exposing young women to a genuine feeling of celebration, acceptance and/or matter-of-factness around menstrual functioning, will free them to develop a healthy self-concept and attitude toward their bodies and physical processes.

Boys' own comfort about their sexuality, and the changes brought on by puberty, as well as their attitudes toward their female peers, will also be strongly influenced by the attitudes and actions of their parents.

We must work hard to overcome our own as well as our daughters' reluctance to take a good, loving, compassionate look at our whole selves. We can take as our example the popular British actor and comic Dawn French, a large woman in a fat-unfriendly world. She has made a name for herself with a strong sense of self-acceptance based on all her attributes, including the beauty of her natural appearance. With that, her obvious self-esteem, her humour and her sense of her own competence, she commands respect and acceptance in a field of work that often values appearance over talent. French, and other women like her, wear their size and shape with comfort and pride. They demonstrate that women can develop and maintain an appreciation and acceptance of their normal, natural, real body as a whole, including their minds.

When mothers work through their own negative attitudes and practise self-acceptance and appreciation, both they and their children benefit. This applies to fathers too, as their expectation of the "ideal daughter or son" may also be projected onto their children. Judging by the authors' experience and many clinical anecdotes, the unconditional support that fathers provide for their children is significant in promoting healthy self-esteem, and, with it, a healthy body image.

During an eating disorder panel discussion not long ago, a mother in the audience described observing her three-year-old in a ballet class. The little girl, sturdy and healthy, had the rounded tummy of a child coming out of toddlerhood. The teacher instructed the child, "Tuck that tummy away!" The mother commented, "I took her out of that class then and there. I won't have anybody teaching her that part of her is bad, and needs 'tucking away,' especially when there's no place to put it!" This perceptive mother clearly recognized the harm that can come from critical remarks about her daughter's natural body.

If, later on, children who have had this kind of support about body image from parents or other caregivers are teased about body size or shape by peers or others, they may be more resilient, having grown up with supportive messages, reinforcing an appreciation of the inherent strengths and beauty of their own bodies. They could also be more able to deal with mixed messages about the social and economic value of bodies, especially women's bodies. The positive way they perceive their bodies could be reinforced by the knowledge that puberty is a natural phenomenon, to be appreciated as such, and that changes in their bodies before and during puberty are normal. They can get this assurance from the women and the men around them who model, demonstrate and openly discuss unconditional body acceptance at all stages of their development. In addition, knowing that their bodies are only a part of their overall identity will bring perspective to the relative importance of their other attributes and qualities.

Because media messages have such a profound effect on teens' self-image and self-esteem, burying our heads in the sand and ignoring degrading media images (in hopes that our children will do the same) can be harmful. We need to sit down with them and give them a safe and comfortable space in which to talk about these issues and decide for themselves how much of what they see in the press and on TV is an effort to manipulate consumers and audiences, usually for commercial profit in one form or another. It is also helpful for us, as parents, to call attention to agism in images, and to the absence of a diverse range of people in media images. We can encourage intergenerational activities in which children are provided with positive elderly role models.

We can also help by encouraging open discussion of the diet fads and the deprivation thinking popularized in the media. Teens may be very clever at disguising all their thoughts and feelings about restrictive eating. An impersonal approach can be helpful: talking about our own experiences with the deprivation/bingeing cycle, or perhaps referring broadly to a magazine article or a book. Learning that they are not alone with their feelings and behaviour around food, that they are normal and natural, can help youngsters restore their trust in their body and its signals.

Appropriately applied, humour can be a wonderful tool for instilling a sense of reality into this sphere; pointing out the comical aspects of some of the extremes in the media, fashion, and advertising will bring out the absurdity of the attitudes they foster. For example, poking fun at the number of women's magazines with weight-related articles featured on their cover can help us "lighten up" a "heavy" topic. We must, of course, be very careful that it not be hurtful or malicious humour, and that our sons and daughters do not feel they are being ridiculed along with the absurd social attitudes.

If teens are involved in restrictive eating behaviours, parents can help them look for the actual root of their discontent or emotional unease. Parents can also help them find other solutions to their difficulties, solutions that are more appropriate than food and weight preoccupation. Thus, for example, when a youngster recounts an incident where she has been the butt of a joke, it is important to help her put the incident in perspective. What might the tormentor have been feeling? Why did the person choose the body as a tool with which to hurt? Why is it hurtful? How could she have responded constructively? How can it be reframed to make the child feel better about herself and her body while attending to the real dynamic of the incident?

We can combat negative images, in part, by communicating other bases for self-esteem than physical appearance, and by encouraging activities that make one feel good about oneself, be it a team sport or involvement in an environmental protection group, or other activities that take advantage of a specific skill or interest. We can offer the example of incorporating movement and exercise into our daily lives and show our confidence in our children's ability to make good decisions about their own physical activities. An active mother who incorporates enjoyable, healthy and sustained physical activity in her life will be more credible when she offers her son or daughter options for physical activity. Better yet, if we can find an activity that our children will enjoy sharing with us, it serves a broader purpose than exercise. It will also strengthen family ties, and offer further opportunity to affirm our children. In addition, we can ensure that our children understand that height, weight and shape are inherited predispositions, and that healthy lifestyles will allow us to make the most of our bodies.

Being fatter than average can be difficult for both boys and girls to accept. As parents, we can foster children's self-esteem by genuinely hearing them, by not belittling their pain, and by working with them to develop strategies to deal with specific situations. We can help them develop self-acceptance by our own attitudes, and by providing them with accurate information about the genetic basis for body type and size, set-point and diversity. These children will also benefit by being encouraged to engage in activities (physical and/or mental challenges) which they enjoy and in which they excel. And they also need to know, from our words and our example, that caring for our bodies and dressing them comfortably and attractively is a factor in building and demonstrating body pride. In this context, it may be helpful to recognize and emulate many other cultures' strong encouragement of their youth to develop a solid sense of their own personal style of dress and appearance.

Children are frequently less preoccupied with food and weight if their parents have encouraged and supported in them an awareness of their specific attributes unrelated to appearance, such as their ability to make choices and accept consequences, a willingness to compromise, a sense of humour, or a natural curiosity and the motivation to satisfy that curiosity. Using physical appearance as the prime measure of acceptability and social competence creates a sense in the child that "not looking just right" means "not being all right."[13]

Conclusions

In adolescence, teens come increasingly under both the positive and the negative influences of their friends. While it is true that peer pressure is important, the example we as parents have set and continue to set for our children, the autonomy and the choices we have encouraged in them, will play a strong role in their ability to make wise decisions around issues of fads, diversity and critical thinking. We know that parental criticism of their attitudes and their friends is less effective than affirming young persons' inner wisdom and individuality. Often at this stage, the best thing we can offer is our example and our patience, as our sons and daughters test various points of view around issues of appearance, nutrition, shape and size.

There are some basic tools we can use as parents to ease our adolescent daughters and sons through the difficult territories of self-perception, body image and self-esteem. They hinge on our cultivating, as far as we are able, three things:

- a fundamental respect for both our children and ourselves;
- a non-judgmental acceptance of both ourselves and our children; and
- a basic consistency between what we say and what we do.

These attributes, along with the ability to admit it when we have departed from them, allow us to:

- model healthy values, behaviours and attitudes for our children by "walking the talk";

- demonstrate compassion, understanding and the conviction that they are competent, capable human beings;
- earn their trust and confidence in our knowledge and experience, without discounting theirs;
- listen to them and truly hear them, and respond credibly, without value judgments;
- give them information, including the possible consequences of various options, but allow them to make their own decisions and choices on the basis of that information;
- discuss difficult issues and encourage problem solving, with a breadth of options, including research and professional help;
- recognize their strengths and weaknesses, and, when appropriate, discuss them in an affirming, realistic and non-critical way; and
- confirm *their* right to make mistakes, which need not be perceived as failures, but as oppurtunities to learn.

Here are a few facts and suggestions that can inspire some interesting conversations on body-image issues between you and your teen:

- Your body is not a measure of your worth. Your value as a person is not defined by your weight, your size or the number of inches around your waist, any more than by, say, the shape of your toenails.
- You can replace negative thoughts with positive and respectful ones. Recognize your strengths and accomplishments, what you like about yourself, and respond to the critical voices in your mind.
- The notion that you can have any body you want is a fantasy. Enjoy and respect the body you have.
- If you respect your body and nurture it, you will find it settling at its healthiest weight, and you will feel attractive and energized.
- Do pleasurable things with your body: enjoy a bubble bath, a sauna, a massage, a stretch, a swim. Explore different ways that make you feel good in your body.

In order to have a good foundation for self-esteem and self-confidence, teens, like all of us, need to feel a sense of safety, competence, worthiness, and control within their bodies and person. We can help create resistance to poor body image, and hence to poor self-esteem, by modelling and nurturing respect of self and others, in the broadest of contexts.

Regardless of the context, our role as parents involves unconditional acceptance of our teens as young people, separate from us and our dreams for them, and as individuals inherently worthy of love and respect. This calls for:

- attentive listening;
- demonstrating a respect for their uniqueness as human beings; and
- setting an example of genuine self-acceptance and confidence as far more important than features such as size, weight and shape, and disability.

If we have a mutually trusting relationship with our children, if they know that we will be truthful and respectful with them, open discussion on these themes and honest self-assessment can be a liberating experience for both parent and youth.

While it is difficult to deal with the conflicts that arise in this context, parents are important mirrors in acknowledging and validating their children's strengths and attributes. This way, parents can help young people to fortify their self-esteem and body image during these trying times.

If parents will affirm the intrinsic value and beauty of all bodies, including their own, and help their children to see their bodies as an important part of their being while keeping physical appearance in perspective, the children will be better able to deal with negative attitudes to bodies, no matter where they arise.

If young people receive acceptance and affirmation from their parents, they are well on their way to a healthy image of themselves and their bodies. It is extremely liberating to realize that individuals come in a broad range of body sizes, shapes and weights which no one has the right to judge, which neither define them nor shape their characters, and which need not hamper the way they live their lives.

Notes

1. Albert Mehrabian, *Silent Messages*, as quoted in Peter Urs Bender, *Secrets of Power Presentations* (Toronto: Achievement Group, 1991), p. 99.

2. S. Parker, M. Nichter, N. Vuckovic, C. Sims and C. Ritenbaugh, "Body Image and Weight Concerns among African American and White Adolescent Females: Differences that make a difference," *Human Organisation* 54, 2 (1995) [referred to as the "Arizona study"].

3. Canadian Centre for Drug Free Sport (now the Canadian Centre for Ethics in Sport), *The National School Survey on Drugs and Sport* (Ottawa: Price Waterhouse, 1993).

4. S. Parker, M. Nichter, N. Vuckovic, C. Sims and C. Ritenbaugh.

5. Ibid.

6. Personal communication with the authors.

7. R. Sheinen, "Body Shame: Body Image in a Cultural Context," *National Eating Disorder Information Bulletin* 5, 5 (November 1990).

8. D. Garner, "The Psychology Today 1997 Body Image Survey Results," *Psychology Today* 30, 1 (January/February 1997).

9. Dairy Bureau of Canada, "Myths and Malnutrition: A growing problem" in *A Summary of Clinical Papers and Recent Studies* (Montreal: Dairy Bureau of Canada, May 1993).

10. S. Parker, M. Nichter, N. Vuckovic, C. Sims and C. Ritenbaugh.

11. J. Sanftner, J. Crawford, P. Crawford et al, "Maternal influences (or lack thereof) on daughters' eating attitudes and behaviours," *Eating Disorders* 4, 2, pp. 147-59; R. Streigel-Moore and A. Kearney-Cooke, "Exploring parent's attitudes and behaviours about their childrens' physical appearance," *International Journal of Eating Disorders* 15 (1994); and R. Katz, C. Mazer and I. Litt, "Anorexia nervosa by proxy," *Journal of Pediatrics* 107 (1985).

12. Ibid.

13. For further reading, see: Frances M. Berg, *Afraid to eat: Children and teens in weight crisis* (Healthy Weight Publishing Network, 1997); Kaz Cooke, *Real Gorgeous: The Truth about Body and Beauty* (New York: W.W. Norton, 1996); Teresa Pitman and Miriam Kaufman, *All Shapes and Sizes: Promoting Fitness and Self-esteem in Your Overweight Child* (Toronto: HarperCollins, 1994); and Evelyn Tribole and Elyse Resch, *Intuitive Eating* (New York: St. Martin's Press, 1995).

Spirituality:
A Lifelong Journey

Alison van Nie

*A belief in powerlessness is seductive, and so is belief in a
Higher Power. They both let one off the hook too easily.*
— Janette Turner Hospital, in *Oyster*[1]

The Nature of Spirituality

Spirituality is not some vague, esoteric state of mind attained by a
chosen few; nor is it exclusively the domain of any particular religious
ideology or tradition. The word "spirituality" means, simply, "concerned with the spirit"; that is, a person's animating principle or
intelligence, a person's soul or essence. It also refers to a person's mental
or moral nature, attitude, state of mind, vivacity, and the principle or
purpose that underlies our lives. Spirit is not something that we need to
find or to create; it is innate.

Spirituality is not tied necessarily to a particular religious ideology.
Indeed, it is much broader than religion and does not need to align
itself with any one religious outlook. Nonetheless, spirituality often is
closely associated with some form of religious ideology and tradition.
Religion and religious thought have to do with a particular system of
belief and form of worship that often include establishing a structure
in which to experience and express elements of the human spirit. Not
all religious practices are healthy and life-affirming; yet, there are

religious forms, encompassing traditions, ideologies and rituals, that are based on a sincere desire for the expression of the human spirit and that may be helpful in the development and manifestation of our spirituality. Thus, for some individuals, the outward expression of spirituality may occur in part through identification with a particular religious tradition. For others, religious traditions and beliefs are not required for the expression of one's spiritual nature. But no matter what means is chosen for their outward expression, our spirit and our spirituality are essential elements within each of us, and the discovery, acknowledgement and identification of our spiritual nature is a lifelong process.

Thomas Moore, in his book *Care of the Soul,*[2] offers some insights into the nature of spirituality and soul. He notes that one of the great losses in contemporary society seems to be the "loss of soul," and that this loss has a role in the creation of addictions, obsessions, violence, and loss of meaning and sacredness. A spiritual life of some kind is seen as absolutely necessary for psychological "health," although some forms of spirituality can be detrimental rather than healthy. Knowing how to differentiate between healthy and unhealthy spirituality is important. Healthy spirituality is centred in an acknowledgement of the individual within the context of family and community, and encourages the awareness and the expression of spirituality within a caring and supportive community in positive and life-affirming ways. This expression of spirituality includes the exploration of attitudes, ethics, intelligence, purpose in life, and the way in which one's life is lived. Unhealthy spirituality may isolate the individual; may place stringent demands in the form of time, monetary contributions, belief systems and lifestyle; may claim to provide the answers to all of life's concerns.

Caring for the soul seems to be essential for all human beings and includes a process of understanding and of listening to our inner spirit. This awareness and cultivation of our spirituality is not a remedy for unpleasantness or a relief from the concerns of everyday life, but is a means of mending the split that seems to have taken place between mind, body and spirit. It is a way of substituting for the myth of the pursuit of happiness and success as a means of engendering hope and faith, with a truth, based in a reality, that incorporates the power of faith and spiritual sustenance to engender hope in life.

Moore claims that the importance of the soul can be made clear by naming symptoms of the loss of soul, which he identifies as feelings of emptiness, meaninglessness, depression, a loss of values, disillusionment about relationships, a yearning for personal fulfilment and a hunger for spirituality. The soul is identified as being related to place and culture, as having an articulated world-view, as being composed of a set of values, as existing within an holistic frame of reference, as a myth of immortality and as an attitude toward death that transcends place and culture. Understood within this perspective, the acknowledgement of the presence and the meaning of one's spirituality may mean that one will not accept uncritically the values of the "world," nor assume a lifestyle determined primarily by media advertising, but will choose a life based on a search for wisdom and informed by spiritual values. Solutions to problems in life will reside within one's self primarily, and by acknowledging the inevitability of unanswerable questions and mysteries in life.

The need for symbolic and reflective experiences associated with spirituality may be partially fulfilled by participating in religious traditions that help the individual to recognize the sacred dimensions of life. Some religious traditions help to remind us of the importance and the necessity of spiritual life and the importance of bringing the sacred into daily life. These religious traditions are often repositories of stories or myths that help to explain things to us. Myths are sacred stories of spirituality that throughout time have been important as significant elements in understanding ourselves and our place in the world. Myths, or sacred stories, are offered to us as universal guides for the spirit.

As parents, we should be aware of our own sense of spirituality and its development as we help in the process of discovery that accompanies the development of a young person's sense of the spiritual. This may include telling stories, recounting myths and discussing their place within our understanding of life, recognizing and promoting the role of the sacred in life, celebrating community and understanding, and conveying the importance of finding our place in the world. We can teach our children about the *sacred* by telling them fairy tales and recounting family histories, being aware and careful consumers committed to the principles of reducing consumption, reusing and recycling our waste, paying attention to the environment and acting to ensure its preservation, talking about and showing concern for the wider world and its people. In all of these ways, we teach, discover and affirm our own spiritual nature, and in so doing affirm the spiritual nature of our children.

The Development of Spirituality

Spirituality does not reside exclusively within our psyche but is connected intimately with other areas of our being. The search for spirituality is not only ongoing and difficult, but also replete with opportunities for exciting and profound discoveries. The development of our spiritual sense begins early in our lives and is constant. It is connected to our sense of identity and to our development as individuals. As children, we are very much dependent on the roles provided for us by adults; they help to define who we are, how we should behave and how we should think about things. Children's sense of spirituality is developed along with their sense of self and is expressed often in a form of magic realism;[3] that is, a way of identifying ideas and perceptions that contain elements of "realism" combined with elements of "fantasy" and provide a means of understanding the world. Children tend to think of their essential being, and to express it, and their sense of the world outside themselves, with wonderment and fantasy. They may visualize God as an actual physical being with human characteristics and attributes who lives in the sky; as someone who has powers to grant wishes and to perform magical feats, similar to Santa Claus and the Easter Bunny. These are elements of spirituality that children embrace without reservation, and that we, as adults, often have lost. Parents can choose to disabuse children of ideas that contain elements of magic and fantasy and can substitute ones of their own, or they can allow the child to have these ideas in the knowledge that with age comes more sophisticated and mature thinking, while acknowledging and rejoicing in the sense of wonderment and the unknowable that will always be a part of spirituality, and which includes mysticism and miracles.

As children proceed into adolescence, they start to think about and to explore a personal identity, separate from that of parents and peers. Teenagers may also begin to combine earlier ideas about spirit and fantasy with other, more down-to-earth and mundane understandings. The influence of parents and peers remains important, but, in a sense, during this process of growth, it changes in intensity and meaning; often teenagers explore their own sense of being by reacting against their parents' beliefs. They may reject their parents' values while they search for their own individuality and meaning in their lives. This search also may be expressed within religious traditions and thought, for there is a strong connection between our spiritual nature and the expression of that nature in religious traditions.

The search for personal identity during the teenage years includes a struggle with spiritual issues, as well, a struggle traditionally full of conflict and tensions. For adolescents, part of this search involves challenging the assumptions they encounter and rejecting the ideas and values of parents, and even of peers. Adolescents, like most of us, often think that, in order to understand themselves as individuals, they need to be separate, to be unique, to declare their differences. How they go about that varies from person to person and may involve all sorts of explorations that take them to many places. This discovery of self seems to be necessary, but it can make those around them uneasy, and resistant to the process and to the outcome of the struggle. When we allow adolescents, as we allow ourselves, to complete their own exploration, we must be prepared for challenges to our own sense of being, and even to outcomes that may be difficult for us to accept.

Adolescence is a time for trying on identities, for rejecting accepted values, for breaking the rules, for experimenting with philosophies and ideologies and religious traditions. It is also a time for establishing and for maintaining a sense of self and a sense of community. These two elements or needs are deeply entwined, and so, although adolescent soul-searching is often accompanied by a rejection of one's family or by a distancing from family, and even from culture, it is also tied to an intense need to be connected to the community — beginning with the family and extending to those outside the family — and to be placed within that context of community life. Without this sense of community, of belonging, there is the danger of the adolescent becoming a person without a sense of commitment or loyalty, without a sense of responsibility that is outside the narrow bounds of the self. Too often if an adolescent's rejection of parental and adult values is met with family rejection and disapproval, the familial bonds are broken, and so are those with the wider community. It is necessary for parents to accept an adolescent child despite disapproving of certain attitudes and/or behaviours, and even while experiencing elements of personal rejection. For with feelings of rejection comes the potential for hurt, dismay, and even anger, and it is equally necessary not to direct these responses at the adolescent child in destructive ways, leading to relationships perhaps being harmed, or even destroyed. Patience, understanding and flexibility are essential, and a willingness to view personal attacks with detachment. Thus, it is important for adolescents to explore their identity, including a developing spirituality, while the family continues to accept them and to keep them within the circle of family, friends and community.

A resurgent interest in myths and the popularity of works of fiction such as *The Celestine Prophecy*[4] attest to a general fascination with, and indeed hunger for, spiritual sustenance. These popular writings tend to simplify the essence of spirituality and to imply that enlightenment can be found by following a few easy steps. In them, the "search" for spiritual enlightenment is emphasized, as if it were some abstract entity to be acquired, rather than spirituality being seen as arising from a recognition of the profound spirit inherent in each of us.

Spirituality involves a quest for answers to questions that by their very nature remain unanswerable and focuses on a search that is rooted in the process of asking questions rather than in finding answers. In a culture that often demands immediate and clear solutions, it is difficult to remember that some of the most profound questions have no easy or definitive answers. The development of spiritual awareness lies in the asking of the questions rather than in the ability to find the answers. Spiritual awareness provides a framework in which we can live with unanswerable questions rather than satisfying ourselves with simplistic insights. Simplistic insights tend to focus on feelings rather than thoughts, on a belief in the universality of particular spiritual needs rather than needs informed by individuality and culture, on predictions that come true in magical ways rather than a search for meaning, on the right to assume the beliefs of others rather than to search for meaning within one's own cultural and personal context. Adolescents can explore the spirituality and the insights of others without changing their own essential nature or cultural background. As parents, we can encourage young people to find their own spiritual identity in ways that accept the premise that one can explore ideas without denying the validity of one's own experience and culture. The current environment encourages us to think about and to develop our spiritual nature. We can do the same for our children, as parents who have an understanding of our own spiritual nature.

The Importance of Rituals

Rituals are often identified as actions that can speak to the soul, and thus have meaning for the spirit. In reality, rituals can take many forms and have many meanings. We all practise many sorts of rituals in our daily lives, but the rituals that speak to the soul are different in nature and purpose from other forms of rituals, such as brushing our teeth before bed or having tea at four-thirty each afternoon. Rituals that speak to the soul are different from ordinary rituals in that they maintain the holiness of the world and can ascribe meaning in life. Although many rituals that we associate with religious traditions, such as prayer, songs, sacraments of communion and baptism, and the way in which holy scriptures are read and listened to, seem healthy and acceptable, there are other rituals that are unhealthy and unacceptable. Some of these latter rituals include those that oppress or exploit individuals, exert inappropriate power and manipulate the hearts and minds of individuals. Rituals that involve degrading practices or that cause physical suffering and mental anguish, that dictate inappropriate initiation rites or questionable rites of passage, are harmful, and we need to be concerned about them. If our adolescent child is engaged within a setting that practises inappropriate rituals or which demands actions or ways of thinking with which we are uncomfortable, then we, as parents, need to prevent such involvement. We need to question the nature of rituals and to make sure that the rituals that we practise are healthy and life-giving. Spirituality, as expressed through rituals and traditions, can be powerful, but, because of its nature, has the potential for evil as well as for good.

Fundamentalism and Cults

Adolescents have a strong need for belonging and for certainty, a need to get a foothold on the chaos and to be able to reassure themselves there is purpose and meaning in life. Some adolescents are strongly attracted to the rigid ideas of fundamentalist thinking and the confining practices of cult religions. There is a similar attraction in both these settings for people looking for a level of certainty that is not a part of their own lives. By succumbing to the sway of charismatic figures, whether they are part of traditional forms of religious expression or of the more bizarre forms of cults that are beyond the bounds of general acceptance, adolescents can fulfil their need for the rejection of commonly held beliefs and practices, and the seemingly incompatible need for a sense of place and for the certain knowledge of what is right and how life should be lived. Fundamentalist ideas, including right-wing ideologies, perform the same function; they allow participants to give up all sense of deciding for themselves and claim to provide indisputable answers to all of life's questions. Such theologies, ideologies and cults are harmful and dangerous to the individual's well-being, and, for the parent dealing with the adolescent who has chosen these expressions of self, they require great care, and even resistance. It is frightening for a parent to realize the powerful nature of the desire or the tendency of someone to submit to some belief system that claims to have all the answers, and whose members are compelled to acquiesce to an ideology in order to be accepted into the community. Although we are surprised by such tendencies and involvements, we know that the spiritual self is capable of great love, of great loyalty, and sometimes of great blindness.

As a parent, it is appropriate to intervene when an adolescent has become involved in a cult that dictates not only beliefs, but lifestyle and daily practices. This is a difficult thing to do, especially when a child has been encouraged to explore his or her spirituality and its manifestation in various religions and religious practices. Sometimes we are forced to declare our own disapproval and dismay at the particular choices that our adolescents make, especially when those choices seem harmful and destructive. This may mean talking about the aspects of the involvement that we find unacceptable, setting restrictions on the child's involvement, and even prohibiting continued membership, when possible. There are resources that families can seek out to help with adolescent involvements in cults or membership in groups to which the parent objects, if parental influence is not enough to correct a situation that is unacceptable. At the same time, we need to consider the myriad of other religious traditions that have arisen as an expression of spirituality and are identified less easily as good or bad. How does a parent know when to encourage or to discourage involvement? The process of knowing when and how to intervene depends on your own orientation and affiliation within this realm, but it is important to remain open to new expressions of the spirit while being aware of the potential dangers inherent in this process of self-discovery.

Responding as a Parent

Being an authentic person is something that is required of us throughout our spiritual lives. In my experience, that means being as open and honest about who you are as you can possibly be while continuing to explore your own sense of self and your system of beliefs. Recognizing your own struggle for identity and how your thinking is affected in the search helps you to identify with the young person's search. Finding the truth within yourself is not an easy task. Nor is being consistent, especially when called to account by someone for whom one is a role model — and teenagers are notorious for challenging the parent's sense of self! The more rigid we see ourselves as being, the more difficult it will be to accept differences that appear in others, especially in our own children and other young adults. Being consistent and having integrity, though, are not same as being absolutely right all the time and never wavering when confronted with different ideas. Showing flexibility and listening to others' ideas and their expressions of their own spiritual natures is not a sign of weakness or insecurity; rather, it is a sign of self-confidence, wisdom and strength. This search for self-identification and the discovery of the nature of our spirituality is a common thread that unites rather than divides individuals, even parents and their adolescent children.

As a parent, you may choose to participate in a religious tradition that includes certain practices and experiences or you may choose not to participate at all. It is important to communicate to your child the reasons for either participation or non-participation. Include children in any participation you have as a parent, from an early age, and continue to encourage independent participation as the child matures, if this is an important aspect of your life. This is not necessarily an easy task. Articulating your beliefs can be difficult. We may be forced to reconsider our beliefs and practices when questioned about their nature and importance. Nevertheless, it is important to talk about any religious traditions, or lack of them, within the family. This provides children with a sense of being included in the discussion rather than having demands placed on them to conform to the practices and beliefs held by the parents. We all expect teenagers to reject the parents' religious practices and to stop attending services with the family. They are likely to turn away from any or all religious beliefs espoused in the home.

They may refuse to participate in opportunities for involvement, or even discussion. How do we deal with this rejection? Even when we expect rejection, we are surprised and often hurt by it. Our spiritual beliefs have acquired significance within our lives, and to be challenged on them can be threatening. These beliefs may involve religious practices, but also lifestyle and moral issues. Still, we may be able to recall that we as teenagers ourselves rejected our parents' values, and we can console ourselves with the knowledge that the rejection is not always as permanent or as significant as it seems at the time. As a parent, you might be prepared also to encourage your adolescent to explore other religious traditions, and this may involve an open-mindedness and an acceptance of practices and beliefs outside your own experience. Allowing, and even encouraging, choices in these areas may be easier for some parents than for others. As a parent, you may be tempted to try to bend the adolescent's will to yours, but winning cooperation[5] from children, rather than demanding cooperation or compliance, leads to a more fulfilling relationship. Winning someone's cooperation creates a more equitable division of responsibility, shows more respect for the individual and acknowledges that there are choices. This concept of winning cooperation can be understood as an approach to relationships with others that is centred on respect, acknowledgement of the other as a partner in the process, and an assumption that there is a way of arriving at some sort of consensus. Demanding cooperation, on the other hand, predicates a relationship in which power is the determining factor and where consensus is not required. Of course, the risk inherent in this commitment to winning cooperation is that you may not achieve cooperation. But the alternative — demanding compliance and cooperation — may lead to increased rebellion, resistance and distancing, and does not acknowledge that each of us needs to discover the nature of our spiritual life and practices. We need to allow our children to make choices for themselves, whether we approve of these choices or not. Naturally, we would choose to have our children accept the values, beliefs and traditions that we cherish, but we cannot force acceptance on anyone, no matter how sure we are about the value of these things for ourselves. That said, there are instances when we need to try to exert influence. We have the right and the responsibility to try to prevent our adolescents from participating in value and belief systems or behaviours that we know to be harmful. It is one thing to reject the parents' values and another to replace them with values that are dangerous and harmful. In those situations, we must continue to model our values and beliefs for our children. Our actions and words speak for themselves, and we must believe that our most positive and admirable attributes will be remembered, if not modelled, by our children. Sometimes the different life the adolescent chooses in the search for independence becomes a permanent change. We may not approve or agree, but we must accept that this is so. Giving up control in a parenting role may not be easy, but it is sometimes necessary.

The task of a parent is to allow the adolescent to explore her or his sense of spirituality without hindrance, although with watchfulness and interest, and to offer acceptance and guidance when required, and to know when intervention is needed.

If we are able to communicate our understanding of spirituality and our attachment to, or rejection of, certain religious traditions and practices, we will be able to support and to confirm the search for soul our adolescent children have embarked upon. We cannot control or determine the outcome of this process, but we can provide as much empathy and acceptance as possible while being aware of the dangers of attachments to particular ideologies and practices.

The inward and the outward progression toward spirituality is a lifelong journey that we can share with our children if we so choose. By sharing our own journey, we can participate in the journey of others and be enriched by their sense of spirituality and the profound nature of their souls.

Notes

1. Janette Turner Hospital, *Oyster* (Toronto: Alfred A. Knopf, 1996), p. 116.

2. Thomas Moore, *Care of the Soul* (New York: Harper Perennial, 1994).

3. "Magic realism" is defined in Jan Ousby (ed.), *The Cambridge Guide to Literature in English* (Cambridge, U.K.: Cambridge University Press, 1993), p. 561.

4. James Redfield, *The Celestine Prophecy* (New York: Warner Books, 1994).

5. "Winning cooperation" is explored by Rudolf Dreikurs in *Children: The Challenge* (New York: Hawthorn Books, 1964).

Sexuality: The Desire to be Lovable and Loving

Debra Haffner

Adolescent sexuality has changed dramatically during the past forty years.[1] In the 1950s, petting was the most common intimate teenage sexual experience, adolescents reached physical maturity later and married earlier, and teenage intercourse was uncommon except among the oldest (usually engaged or married) adolescents. Patterns of sexual behaviour differed widely among young men and young women, as well as among youth from different backgrounds.

Today's teenagers reach physical maturity earlier and marry later. There has been a steady increase in the percentage of young people having sexual intercourse, and in the percentage doing so at younger and younger ages. Almost all teenagers experiment with some type of sexual behaviour. Patterns of sexual activity are now fairly similar among young men and women, and among young people from different ethnic, socio-economic and religious groups.

There is public and professional consensus about what is sexually unhealthy for teenagers. Professionals, politicians and parents across the political spectrum share a deep concern about unplanned adolescent pregnancy; out-of-wedlock childbearing; sexually transmitted diseases (STDs), including AIDS; sexual abuse; date rape; and the potential negative emotional consequences of premature sexual behaviours.

However, there is little consensus about what is sexually healthy for teenagers. The public debate about adolescent sexuality has often focused on which sexual behaviours are appropriate for adolescents and has ignored the complex dimensions of sexuality.

Some groups support the "just say no" approach to adolescent sexuality. They believe that the only healthy adolescent sexuality is abstinence from all sexual behaviours until marriage, and that adults should work to eliminate teen sexual experimentation. Another approach could be described as "just say not now." This philosophy encourages young people to abstain until they are more mature but, given the high rates of teenage sexual involvement in intercourse, recommends that it is important to provide young people with access to contraception and condoms whether or not adults approve of their behaviour. This approach might also be labelled "if you can't say no, protect yourself!" Other adults adopt a "don't ask, don't tell" posture and simply pretend that adolescent sexuality and sexual behaviour do not exist.

It is important to recognize that sexuality is a natural and healthy part of life. Sexuality encompasses the sexual knowledge, beliefs, attitudes, values and behaviours of individuals. It deals with the anatomy, physiology and biochemistry of the sexual response system, as well as with roles, identity and personality. Sexuality encompasses thoughts, feelings, behaviours and relationships. All human beings are inherently sexual. Infants, children, adolescents and adults at different stages experience their sexuality in distinct ways. Sexuality evolves during childhood and adolescence, laying the foundation for adult sexual health and intimacy. Adolescent sexual health is defined by a broad range of knowledge, attitudes and behaviours, and cannot be defined solely on the basis of abstinence or preventive behaviours. In fact, "sexual behaviour" is not synonymous with heterosexual penile-vaginal intercourse. Although there are serious medical problems related to adolescent sexual behaviour and these diseases have a significant negative impact on adolescents, this essay focuses on sexual health, and not disease or pregnancy.

The available research on healthy adolescent sexuality is extremely limited. Most of the existing research has focused on adolescent women, particularly those who attend family-planning clinics, and on the medical problems associated with adolescent sexual behaviour.

Most studies have examined heterosexual intercourse and contraceptive practices. Few studies are available on adolescent romantic relationships, non-coital behaviours, and healthy adolescent sexual relationships. Much of the research reported in English comes from the United States and focuses on European-American and African-American adolescents, and information relating to education or income is often unavailable.

Adolescent sexuality is a highly charged emotional issue for many adults. All adults are former adolescents, and one's own personal biography often colours the understanding of this complex issue. Parents can put their own experiences and hopes for their children into the context of the experience of adolescents today. In addition, adolescents grow up in a variety of contexts and communities. It can be difficult to define adolescent sexual health in its broadest context while respecting the difficulty of extrapolating across our complex society. Young people who face special physical, mental, emotional, social, cultural and economic challenges confront a wide range of barriers to sexual health and require particular attention.

There is an urgent need for a new approach to adolescent sexual health. Parents have a responsibility to help adolescents understand and accept their evolving sexuality, and to assist them to make responsible sexual choices, now and in their future adult roles. Adults must focus on enabling young people to avoid unprotected and unwanted sexual behaviours. As parents, and teachers, we must help adolescents develop the values, attitudes, maturity and skills to become sexually healthy adults.

Stages of Adolescent Sexual Development

Becoming a sexually healthy adult is a key developmental task of adolescence. Achieving sexual health requires the integration of psychological, physical, societal, cultural, educational, economic and spiritual factors.

There is no such thing as an "average adolescent." Individual adolescents vary widely in the pace of their development, with a high degree of variation within each individual: for example, a physically mature fifteen-year-old might function emotionally as a twelve-year-old in dealing with his parents, and yet cognitively as a late adolescent in dealing with math problems.

Adolescent sexual development is not singular or stable; it is plural and dynamic. For most young people, adolescence does not entail an absolutely predictable, consistent set of developmental tasks; nor does it unfold in a singular, universal fashion. Adolescent sexuality emerges from cultural identities mediated by ethnicity, gender, sexual orientation, class, and physical and emotional capacity. This development is affected by parents, other family members and other adults, as well as school culture and the peer group.

Although girls tend to begin and move through adolescence somewhat earlier than boys, both proceed through similar stages of development, often divided into early, middle and late adolescence. In early adolescence, the teen experiences body changes more rapidly than at any time since infancy — secondary sexual characteristics begin to appear; growth accelerates; and physical changes require psychological and social adjustments on the part of the adolescent, family and other adults.

Experimenting with some sexual behaviours is common, but sexual intercourse of any kind is usually limited. Males may initiate intercourse during this stage but most often delay regular sexual activity until middle or late adolescence. Adolescent girls are much less likely to begin sexual intercourse at this age. Of those who do, many are in relationships with much older men.

Young adolescents seek to develop a sense of identity, connection, power and joy. For many adolescents from communities that do not support the development of personal identity in other ways, drugs and sexual experimentation may be a short cut to achieving these feelings. Early sexual involvement is one way that disadvantaged youth may meet developmental needs for power, identity, connection and pleasure.[2] Involvement in sexual behaviours may not be about sexual pleasure, but rather may reflect peer norms, boredom, conflicts with adults, low self-esteem and poor ability to control impulsiveness.[3]

Middle adolescence is the stage that most typifies the stereotype of "teenagers." The transitions in this stage are so dramatic that they seem to occur overnight. Secondary sexual characteristics become fully established, and, for girls, the growth rate decelerates.

Middle adolescents are sometimes described as feeling omniscient, omnipotent and invincible. These feelings provide young people with the support to develop greater autonomy, but may also put them at risk, as they may believe that their behaviour cannot lead to harm (such as pregnancy or STDs).

As adolescents continue the process of separation from the family, they cling more tightly to the peer group that they defined for themselves in early adolescence. This desire to be accepted by the peer group can influence sexual behaviours.

Sexuality and sexual expression are of major importance in the lives of many middle adolescents. As they move through rapid developmental changes, adolescents at this stage often focus on themselves and assume others will focus on them equally. Many middle adolescents choose to show off their new bodies with revealing clothes such as miniskirts and muscle shirts. Although parents may see this as sexually provocative, it may be more the adult's perception than the intent of the middle adolescent.

Middle adolescents often fall in love for the first time. Again, because they are self-centred, the love object may serve as a mirror and reflect characteristics that the teenager admires, rather than being loved for him- or herself. Sexual experimentation is common, and many adolescents first have intercourse in middle adolescence.

By late adolescence, most teens are explicitly moving toward adult roles and responsibilities. Some are beginning full-time jobs; others are beginning families. Many are preparing for these adult roles. The late adolescent completes the process of physical maturation. Many achieve the ability to understand abstract concepts, and they become more aware of their limitations and how their past will affect their future. They understand the consequences of their actions and behaviours, and they grapple with the complexities of identity, values and ethical principles. Within the family, they move to a more adult relationship with their parents. The peer group recedes in importance as a determinant of behaviour, and sexuality may become closely tied to commitment and planning for the future. Intimacy skills increase during late adolescence. By this time many teens are fairly sure of their sexual orientation.

Physical Maturation

Adolescents ask themselves: Am I normal? Am I competent? Am I lovable and loving?[4] Much of adolescent sexual behaviour can be attributed to the search for affirmative answers to these questions.

The onset of sexual maturation is significantly different for young men and young women. On average, young girls start puberty one to two years before boys. This discrepancy in maturation is one factor that may contribute to some young women seeking partners older than themselves. The difference in age places young women at considerable risk for sexual exploitation. The adolescent female completes the process of puberty in three to five years, whereas for males the process takes four to six years.

Young people today are reaching sexual maturity at much younger ages than they did in the past. Today, most girls experience menarche (first menstruation) at 12.4 years of age. Records from family bibles around the time of the American Revolution indicate an age of menarche of approximately 17 years. In 1860, the average age was somewhat more than 15 years in Europe and North America. During the past century, the age at menarche declined an average of three months per decade until 1960. Over the past three decades, the average age of menarche appears to have remained constant, with slight ethnic and urban-rural differences.[5]

Early pubertal development is associated with an increased likelihood for early experimentation with sexual behaviours, in particular, intercourse.[6]

Adjusting to the biological changes of puberty is a major task of early adolescence. Society does not adequately prepare or support young people during these changes. A significant minority of young women do not receive education about menstruation before menarche, and few adult men can recall receiving information of pubertal maturation prior to their first ejaculation or nocturnal emission. Many adolescents are embarrassed by or ashamed of normal pubertal events.

Sexual health for adolescents includes an ability to appreciate their bodies and to view pubertal changes as normal. Achievement of these goals is dependent on parents' and other trusted adults' preparing young people in advance of pubertal events, as well as supporting them during this important transition.

During adolescence, young people develop a range of intellectual characteristics that increase the probability that they will be able to become sexually healthy adults. Ideally, this includes developing the ability to reason abstractly, foresee consequences of actions and understand the social context of behaviours. Adolescents develop an increased ability to control impulsiveness, identify the future implications of their actions and obtain control of their future plans. All of these factors combine to increase decision-making abilities.

Developmental age and cognitive and emotional development may influence adolescent sexual decisions and contraceptive use. A teen's degree of cognitive maturity may place limits on his or her ability to plan for sexual relationships, clearly articulate personal values, negotiate with a partner, and obtain contraception and condoms. Further, the adolescent's ability to form empathetic relationships is dependent on "social cognition" because being able to see a situation from another person's perspective is one aspect of cognitive development.

Sexual self-concept, an individual's evaluation of his or her sexual feelings and actions, emerges during adolescence. Young people develop a stronger sense of gender identity. An understanding of personal sexual orientation also develops during adolescence as young people become more aware of their sexual attractions and love interests, and adult-like erotic feelings emerge.

During adolescence, young people solidify their gender identification by observing the gender roles of their parents and other adults. Gender identification includes understanding that one is male or female, and the roles, values, duties and responsibilities of being a man or a woman. Most young people have a firm sense of their maleness or femaleness prior to adolescence, but in adolescence clear identification with adult masculine and feminine models emerges. It is essential that teens have men and women in their environment who convey the attitudes of appropriate gender-role modes. By interacting with psychologically healthy adult men and women, adolescents learn who they are and how to behave in appropriate ways.

Gender-role stereotypes impede both young men and young women in attaining sexual health. Young women may learn that "it is better to be cute and popular than smart," that "girls have few sexual feelings," and that "girls who carry condoms are bad." Boys may learn that "real men are always ready for sex" and that "guys should never act like girls." One study found that teenage males who agree with traditional cultural messages about masculinity use condoms less consistently (if at all) than other young men and will say that, if they get a partner pregnant, they will feel like a "real man"; they are less likely to think men share the responsibility for preventing pregnancy.[7]

It is important to note that, although patterns of sexual involvement are increasingly similar in boys and girls, persistent gender stereotypes mean that young women still experience their sexual behaviours quite differently.[8] In a 1994 poll, young women reported that they were more likely to regret their sexual experience, more likely to label the relationship "love," less likely to report their sexual experiences as pleasurable, and more likely to bear the brunt of negative outcomes than were their male counterparts.[9]

Sexual orientation often emerges in adolescence. Uncertainty about sexual orientation diminishes with age; one large study showed that 26 percent of twelve-year-olds were "unsure" about their orientation compared with only 5 percent of eighteen-year-olds.[10] If teens express some confusion, parents can help them talk about their feelings and show love for who they are, regardless of sexual orientation. More information can be useful for both teens and parents in this situation, and going to counsellors who are accepting of gay and lesbian sexuality might be an option for teens. "Coming out," or confiding one's sexual orientation with family, friends and co-workers, generally does not occur until very late in adolescence or adulthood. Families can help by being as accepting and supportive of the teen as possible.

Characteristics of a Sexually Healthy Adolescent

The characteristics and behaviours of a sexually healthy teen can be defined in relationship to self, parents and other family members, peers, and romantic partners. Attributes of sexually healthy teens are also those of a sexually healthy adult. Sexual health is not defined by which sexual behaviours a teenager has or has not engaged in.

To appreciate their own bodies, it is important not only that young teens understand the pubertal changes they are undergoing, but also that they are able to view these changes as normal. This appreciation leads to the practice of health-promoting behaviours such as limiting alcohol, cigarette and drug use; undergoing regular check-ups; and abstention from dangerous dieting.

Sexually healthy teens take responsibility for their own behaviour. To do this they must identify their own values, deciding what is personally "right." To act on these values, they must understand the consequences of their actions. They must be able to distinguish personal desires and values from those of their peer group and from media messages that can create unrealistic expectations of sexuality. An awareness of how alcohol and other drugs can impair decision making and an ability to recognize and seek help for self-destructive behaviour are also part of taking responsibility.

Both an intellectual understanding of and a personal insight about sexuality issues are key to sexual health. Sexually healthy people enjoy their sexual feelings without a compulsion to act upon them. They make personal decisions about sexual behaviour based on knowledge and beliefs. They are clear about their own gender identity and understand the effect of gender-role stereotypes. Sexually healthy teens are on the path to understanding their sexual orientation and accept people with different orientation, experience and values. They seek further information about sexuality as needed.

Effective communication with family members both leads to and is rooted in an appropriate balance between family roles and responsibilities and a growing need for independence. Teens need to be able to negotiate with parents about rules and boundaries in a way that respects the rights of other family members. Teens who can ask their parents about values and can take the answers into consideration when making decisions (or at least try to understand the parental viewpoint) are more likely to be sexually healthy.

Sexually healthy teens communicate effectively with friends of both sexes and are able to form empathic relationships while avoiding exploitative relationships. They reject sexually harassing behaviours and respect others' rights to privacy. They understand pressures to be popular and accepted, and make decisions consistent with their own values.

Sexually healthy teens believe that boys and girls have equal rights and responsibilities for love and sexual relationships. They communicate sexual desires and wishes, including the wish not to engage in sexual behaviours, and accept the wishes of their partners. Sexually mature persons are able to distinguish love and sexual attraction and also try to understand and empathize with their partners. Sexually healthy teens talk with their partners about sexual behaviours before they occur, and communicate and negotiate sexual limits. These limits take into account an understanding of low- and high-risk behaviours. If they have heterosexual intercourse, they lower the risk of pregnancy by using effective contraception. They prevent STDs by practising safer sex. They know how to use and access the health care system, community agencies, religious institutions and schools to get advice, information and needed services.

Adolescent Sexual Behaviour in the '90s

Almost all North American teens engage in some type of sexual behaviour. Although the media tend to focus on sexual intercourse and its negative consequences, young people explore dating, relationships and intimacy from a much wider framework. An accurate picture of adolescent sexual behaviour will help us understand our teens within the context of our culture and will perhaps alleviate some anxiety regarding their behaviour.

Historically, young women and men did not reach physical maturity until their middle-teenage years. Marriage and other adult responsibilities followed puberty closely.

Today's teenagers are different from young people of generations ago. They reach puberty earlier, have intercourse earlier and marry later. Women and men who marry today do so three to four years later than young people did in the '50s.

The majority of teens move from kissing to other more intimate sexual behaviours during their teenage years. Some data suggest that the progression from kissing to non-coital behaviours to intercourse varies among different groups of adolescents. While many teenagers move through a progression of intimate behaviours, lower-income teens are less likely to follow this progression, moving more rapidly from kissing to sexual intercourse.[11]

Most teens who have intercourse do so responsibly. More than 80 percent of North Americans first have intercourse as teenagers.[12] In Canada, 40 percent of sixteen-year-olds and 53 percent of seventeen-year-olds attending high school have had intercourse.[13] Despite the large numbers of young people who experiment with a variety of sexual behaviours, intercourse is generally less widespread, and certainly less frequent, than many teens and adults believe. The majority of adolescents use contraceptives as consistently and effectively as most adults.

Teens have always engaged in sexual behaviours. However, in the past, at least for young women, intercourse was reserved for engaged or married couples. When an out-of-wedlock pregnancy occurred, "shotgun" marriages were frequently the answer, or girls were sent away to stay with a relative until the baby was born and adopted.

The birth rate for American adolescents actually peaked in 1957. The adolescent birth rate is now significantly lower than it was forty years ago. In Canada, rates of births to teenagers declined consistently between 1977 (at forty-four per thousand) and 1992 (at twenty-two per thousand), while the proportion of young women who admitted being sexually active during the junior high and high school years increased.[14]

Nevertheless, in the last two decades there has been a significant change in the numbers of young people who have had intercourse at a young age. At each stage of adolescence, higher proportions of teenage men and women have had sexual intercourse today than their counterparts had twenty years ago. At the same time, contraceptive use has also increased. The majority of teens who have heterosexual intercourse use contraception, two-thirds of adolescents use contraception the first time they have intercourse and more than three-quarters do so on an ongoing basis.[15] Almost 60 percent used a condom the last time they had intercourse.[16]

Most teens say they do not feel peer or partner pressure to have intercourse, and those who have intercourse do so with partners they love or date seriously.[17] Typically, teens who have sexual intercourse do so less than once a month.[18]

Although sexual involvement is pleasurable and safe for many adolescents, these behaviours can be quite risky and dangerous for a significant minority of young people. In particular, young adolescents who become involved in sexual behaviours prematurely face a host of risks.

Intercourse is developmentally disadvantageous for young adolescents as they do not have the cognitive or emotional maturity for involvement in intimate sexual behaviours, especially intercourse. There is no set chronological age of readiness for intercourse.

Teenage women have male sexual partners on average three years older than they are. This age difference is especially noticeable with teen mothers. A California study showed that the younger the mother, the greater the partner age gap. Among mothers aged eleven and twelve, the fathers were, on average, nearly ten years older.[19]

The earlier a teen begins having intercourse, the more partners she or he is likely to have, increasing the risk of sexually transmitted diseases and other consequences. Good communication between parents and their teens, along with a willingness to answer any questions about sex that their children ask, even if it is information parents may feel the child is "too young" to know, can help younger teens make healthy choices for themselves. Opportunities to provide information and guidance on how to avoid unwanted sexual activity and what "safer sex" really means can be created by parents.

Unfortunately, not all adolescent sexual behaviour is voluntary, and sexual assault is not uncommon among adolescents. Six percent of boys and 15 percent of girls are sexually assaulted prior to their sixteenth birthday.[20] Nearly three-quarters of young women who had intercourse before age fourteen report having had intercourse involuntarily.[21]

A disproportionate number of young women who become pregnant during adolescence are victims of childhood sexual abuse. In one study of teenagers who were pregnant or already parents, 70 percent of Whites, 42 percent of the African-Americans and 37 percent of Hispanics had been sexually abused as children.[22] In another study, 64 percent of parenting and pregnant teens reported that they had had at least one unwanted sexual experience.[23]

Gay, lesbian and bisexual teenagers face an additional form of abuse related to their sexuality. A study in New York City found that, of lesbian, gay and bisexual teenagers reporting an assault, almost half reported the assault was related to their sexual orientation, and, for almost two-thirds, the assault happened within their families.[24]

We should encourage adolescents to delay sexual behaviours until they are ready physically, cognitively and emotionally for mature sexual relationships and their consequences. This readiness can be supported through education about intimacy; sexual limit-setting; resisting social, media, peer and partner pressure; and pregnancy and STD prevention. Prevention of sexual violence also depends on such education, as well as on measures to increase self-esteem and assertiveness.

Society must also recognize that a majority of adolescents will become involved in sexual relationships during their teenage years. Adolescents should receive support and education for developing the skills to evaluate their readiness for mature sexual relationships. Responsible adolescent intimate relationships, like those of adults, should be based on shared personal values, and should be consensual, non-exploitative, honest, pleasurable, and protected against unintended pregnancies and sexually transmitted diseases, if any type of intercourse occurs.

The Adult Role in Promoting Adolescent Sexual Health

Many adults have difficulty acknowledging teenagers' emerging sexuality. Adults' denial and disapproval of teenage sexual behaviour may actually increase teenagers' risk of pregnancy and sexually transmitted diseases. The majority of adults disapprove of teenagers having intimate sexual relationships, and adolescents often perceive this disapproval. Many teenagers are willing to risk pregnancy and disease rather than damage their "reputation" with their parents, or experience the disapproval of adults with whom they must interact to obtain contraceptives and condoms.

Policy makers must remember that adolescents grow up in families and communities, and that these communities must be involved in promoting adolescent sexual health. All sectors of the community — parents, families, schools, community agencies, religious institutions, media, businesses, health care providers and government at all levels — have important roles to play.

Too much public-policy debate about adolescent sexuality has focused on whether adolescents should abstain from sexual behaviours, particularly intercourse, or whether contraception and condoms should be available to them. Some sexually healthy adolescents abstain from intercourse; some sexually healthy adolescents have intercourse. As noted above, there are circumstances where abstinence will be the healthiest choice for a young person. All adult sectors of society (parents, schools, religious institutions, community youth programs, media and government) should give adolescents consistent and age-appropriate messages about abstinence.

These messages should clearly communicate to teenagers that abstinence from sexual intercourse is the most effective method of preventing pregnancies and sexually transmitted diseases. Delaying first intercourse until late adolescence is likely to result in lower rates of pregnancy, STDs and childbearing.

Educational programs that are designed to provoke fear and shame in adolescents about sexuality in order to enforce abstinence from all sexual behaviours do not help teens become sexually healthy, and create guilt and fear in teens who have intimate sexual relationships.

Within this context, it is important to recognize that very young adolescents are not mature enough for a sexual relationship that includes intercourse, and that most young adolescents do not have intercourse. Teenagers who date should be encouraged to discuss sexual limits with their romantic partners, and to respect those limits.

Teens should be told that there are many ways to give and receive sexual pleasure and not have intercourse, and that they should talk to a trusted adult before having intercourse. Family belief systems, including religious beliefs that sexual intercourse should occur only in marriage, should be communicated to teens. Realistic discussions about any conflict between teens' activities and families' beliefs can be very important.

Older teens should know that many teens have had sexual intercourse and many have not, and that sexual intercourse is not a way to achieve adulthood. Parents can affirm that people in romantic relationships can express their sexual feelings without engaging in sexual intercourse, and that many adults experience periods of abstinence.

Instead of advocating abstinence as public policy, the primary goal of sexuality education should be the promotion of sexual health. Children and youth need age-appropriate comprehensive sexuality education. Schools are only one site for sexuality education. Community agencies, religious institutions and youth serving organizations should develop sexuality-education programs that are appropriate for their settings. In addition, education programs should be available for parents of children and adolescents to help them provide sexuality education within their homes.

Comprehensive sexuality education seeks to assist children in understanding a positive view of sexuality, to provide them with information and skills about taking care of their sexual health, and to help them acquire skills to make decisions now and in the future. A comprehensive sexuality-education program includes information as well as an opportunity to explore attitudes and acquire skills in such areas as human development, relationships, personal skills, sexual behaviour, sexual health, and society and culture.[25] In seeking a comprehensive sexuality-education program for your teen, look for one that:

- is experiential and skill-based;
- is taught by well-trained teachers and leaders;
- discusses controversial issues;
- provides multiple sessions through multiple mediums;
- is relevant to all teenagers, regardless of sexual orientation;
- is culturally specific and sensitive;
- is linguistically appropriate;
- discusses social influences and pressures;

- reinforces values and group norms against unprotected sexual behaviours;
- provides age — and experience — appropriate messages and lessons;
- teachs skill-building, including refusal skills;
- is integrated within comprehensive health education; and
- uses peer counselling and peer support when appropriate.

An essential component of adolescent sexual health is the quality of health care and information that they receive. Health providers and organizations should make affordable, sensitive and confidential sexual and reproductive health care services available to young people. This includes mental health counselling; support services for gay and lesbian youth; family planning; abortion; STD screening, diagnosis and treatment; and prenatal care.

School-based and school-linked programs, special adolescent health-care services, and private practitioners all have special roles to play in reaching adolescents. It is also important that there be formal linkages between health-care delivery and education programs.

In these programs, all staff must have both an interest and special training in working with adolescents. Programs should be offered during convenient times for teens and in locations that are physically accessible, as well as inviting. Confidentiality should be routine, although parental involvement should be encouraged when appropriate. Staff who speak more than one language, or the availability of translators unrelated to the teen, will help promote cultural sensitivity. Most successful programs use a multidisciplinary approach. Their goals can be best attained when youth are involved in designing and implementing the program.

Community youth-serving programs (such as girls' and boys' clubs, scouts, guides, sports organizations, public libraries, recreation departments, after-school programs, work sites, camps, juvenile-justice centres, job-training programs and religious organizations) can play a major role in ensuring adolescent sexual health by developing sexuality-education programs as well as a variety of opportunities to provide young people with education and employment.[26]

Community programs should work together to give young people a consistent set of messages regarding community values about such issues as sexual behaviours, responsibility and future planning. Programs should reinforce each other.

Mass media have become a major source of young people's information about sexuality. Parents can advocate for youth needs by encouraging the media to provide accurate information and model responsible behaviours. The communication of accurate information adds realism and helps adolescents gain insights into their own sexuality and make more responsible decisions about their behaviour.

As parents, individually or in groups, we can encourage writers, producers, programming executives, reporters and others to provide diverse and positive views of a range of body images and to eliminate stereotypes about sexuality and sexual behaviours — for example, eliminating the ideas that only beautiful people have sexual relationships or that all adolescents have intercourse.

When describing or portraying a sexual encounter, they should include steps that should be taken, such as using a condom to prevent unwanted pregnancy and sexually transmitted diseases. It should be recognized and demonstrated that the majority of sexual encounters are planned events, not spur-of-the-moment responses to the heat of passion. Teens can be shown to communicate about upcoming sexual encounters. If the sexual encounter includes unprotected intercourse, possible short- and long-term negative consequences should be addressed.

Although there is clearly a need for dramatic tension and conflict in some relationships, and for the accurate portrayal of stressful relationships when they exist, typical interactions between men and women or boys and girls should be portrayed as respectful and non-exploitative.

Existing barriers to contraceptive and condom advertising should be lifted.

We can ask that teenage idols be used to promote responsible adolescent behaviour and to model appropriate actions, highlighting youth success stories.

Public television and radio are especially well placed to provide ways for young people to obtain additional information about sexuality and related issues, such as by listing addresses and telephone numbers of public-health organizations and support groups.

Strategies for Parents

Parents are the primary sexuality educators of children. We educate both by what we say and by how we behave. It is important to begin deliberate education at the earliest childhood level; however, adolescence poses new challenges for many parents. In homes where there is open communication about contraception and sexuality, young people often behave more responsibly. At a minimum, such communication may help young people accept their own sexual feelings and actions.

With open communication, young people are more likely to turn to their parents in times of trouble; without it, they will not.[27]

Many parents have difficulty communicating with their children about sexuality. Parents must receive education about sexuality and how to provide this education and information to their children.

Individual adults, especially parents and other trusted adult family members, can play an important role in encouraging adolescent sexual health. Adults can assure that young people have access to accurate information and education about sexuality issues by direct communication and by providing books, pamphlets and videos. Adults need to foster responsible sexual decision-making skills and need to model healthy sexual attitudes and responsible behaviours in their own lives.

Parents and families can play a major role in ensuring adolescent sexual health, and often have to do so earlier than they might have thought necessary. Parents of a sexually healthy adolescent:
- value, respect, accept and trust their adolescent children;
- model sexually healthy attitudes in their own relationships;
- maintain a non-punitive stance toward sexuality;
- are knowledgeable about sexuality;
- discuss sexuality with their children;
- provide information on sexuality to their children;
- seek appropriate guidance and information as needed;
- try to understand their adolescent's point of view;
- help their adolescent gain understanding of values;
- set and maintain limits for dating and other activities outside of school;
- stay actively involved in the young person's life;
- ask questions about friends and romantic partners;
- provide a supportive and safe environment for their children;
- offer to assist adolescents in accessing health care services; and
- help them plan for their future.

Notes

1. This essay was adapted from *Facing Facts: Sexual Health for America's Adolescents*, edited by Debra Haffner (New York: SIECUS, 1995).

2. R. Selverstone, "Adolescent Sexuality: Developing Self Esteem and Mastering Developmental Tasks," *SIECUS Report* 18, 1 (1989), pp. 1-5.

3. M. Durban, R. DiClemente and D. Siegel, "Factors Associated with Multiple Sex Partners among Junior High School Students," *Journal of Adolescent Health* 14, 3 (1993), pp. 202-7.

4. P. Scales, *A Portrait of Young Adolescents in the 1990's: Implications for Healthy Growth and Development* (Chapel Hill, NC: Center for Early Adolescence, University of North Carolina at Chapel Hill, 1991).

5. L.S. Neinstein, *Adolescent Health Care: A Practical Guide* (Baltimore, MD: Williams & Wilkins, 1996).

6. C. Chilman, "Family Life Education: Promoting Healthy Adolescent Sexuality," *Family Relations* 39, 2 (1990), pp. 123-31.

7. J. Pleck, F. Sonenstein and L. Ku, "Masculinity Idealogy: Its Impact on Adolescent Males' Heterosexual Relationships," *Journal of Social Issues* 49, 3 (1993), pp. 11-30.

8. S. Thompson, "Putting a Big Thing into a Little Hole: Teenage Girls' Accounts of Sexual Initiation," *Journal of Sex Research* 27, 3 (1990), pp. 341-61.

9. Roper Starch Worldwide, *Teens Talk about Sex: Adolescent Sexuality in the 90's* (New York: Sexuality Information and Education Council of the United States, 1994).

10. G. Remafedi et al. "Demography of Sexual Orientation in Adolescents," *Pediatrics* 89, 4 (1992), pp. 714-21.

11. J. Brooks-Gunn and F.F. Furstenburg, "Coming of Age in the Era of AIDS: Puberty, Sexuality, and Contraception," *The Millbank Quarterly* 68 (1990), Suppl. 1.

12. The Alan Guttmacher Institute, *Sex and America's Teenagers* (New York: The Alan Guttmacher Institute, 1994).

13. Alan King, *Canada Youth and AIDS study* (Kingston, ON: Social Program Evaluation Group, Queens University, 1988).

14. S. Wong and H. McKilligan, "Trends in Births to Teenagers in Ontario 1971-1992," in *Public Health and Epidemiology Report* (Toronto: Government of Ontario, 1994), pp. 167-9.

15. The Alan Guttmacher Institute.

16. Centers for Disease Control and Prevention, *Pregnancy, Sexually Transmitted Diseases, and Related Risk Behaviors among US Adolescents* (Atlanta, GA: CDC, 1994).

17. Roper Starch Worldwide.

18. The Alan Guttmacher Institute; and F. Sonenstein, J. Pleck and L. Ku, "Sexual Activity, Condom Use, and AIDS Awareness among Adolescent Males," *Family Planning Perspectives* 21, 4 (1989), pp. 152-8.

19. California Vital Statistics Section, *California Resident Live Births, 1990, by Age of Father, by Age of Mother* (Sacramento, CA: California Vital Statistics Section, Department of Health Services, 1992).

20. D. Polit, W. Cozette and D. Thomas, "Child Sexual Abuse and Premarital Intercourse among High Risk Adolescents," *Journal of Adolescent Health Care* 11 (1990), pp. 231-4.

21. The Alan Guttmacher Institute; and Child Welfare League of America, *A Survey of 17 Florence Crittendon Agencies Serving Minor Mothers* (Washington, DC: CWLA, 1994).

22. D. Boyer and D. Fine, "Sexual Abuse as a Factor in Adolescent Pregnancy and Child Maltreatment," *Family Planning Perspectives* 24, 1 (1992), pp. 4-11.

23. Child Welfare League of America.

24. J. Hunter, "Violence against Lesbian and Gay Male Youths," *Journal of Interpersonal Violence* 5 (1990), pp. 295-300.

25. National Guidelines Task Force, *Guidelines for Comprehensive Sexuality Education: Kindergarten — 12th Grade* (New York: Sexuality Information and Education Council of the United States, 1991).

26. Carnegie Corporation of New York, *A Matter of Time: Risk and Opportunity in the Out-Of-School Hours* (New York: Carnegie Corporation of New York, 1992).

27. R. Blum, M. Resnick and T. Stark, "The Impact of a Parental Notification Law on Adolescent Abortion Decision Making," *American Journal of Public Health* 77, 5 (1987), pp. 619-20.

From Violence to Peace: Families Confront Challenges and Embrace Possibilities

Jacqueline Haessly

Families today face significant challenges, often of global proportions. Among the most threatening of these challenges are the escalating levels of violence which occur in our society. Conflicts abound. At times, disputes within and between families, neighbourhoods and governments turn violent. In the midst of these challenges, parents and teens ask: How can we prepare ourselves for our future? In what ways can we work together to reduce violence and shape a peaceful future for our family and others, and for future generations? How do we ensure our physical, emotional, spiritual and moral development in this complex and, at times, violent society? How do we develop the awareness and skills necessary to respond creatively as a just people in our society? What attitudes and values will assist us to live humanly with all others who share life with us on this small planet we each call home? These are the challenges we as families face as we move forward with hope into the twenty-first century.

This essay examines the issue of violence as it affects families, and addresses the responses to it that can generate peace within the family, in the community and throughout the world. Part One presents an overview of violence and manifestations of violence which threaten teens and their families. Part Two identifies values, attitudes, knowledge and skills families need both to respond to violence and to live in peace. Throughout this essay, the relationship between parents and teens is addressed in ways that foster respect between them and generate opportunities for shared responsibility in reducing violence, resolving conflicts non-violently, and working together to create a just peace within the family and beyond.

Part One: Violence as a Threat to Families

Violence! The very word stirs fear in the hearts of parents everywhere. Will our son be hassled on the school bus or on the playground? Will our daughter be the next victim of a mugging for a team jacket? a rape? a gunshot wound? Or will one of our loved ones be the next victim of a mass killing in a fast-food restaurant or a terrorist attack such as those that occurred in Beirut, Munich or Oklahoma City? Might it be our teen who taunts another, or wields the knife or gun, causing emotional or physical harm to others? In the midst of such threats to the safety and well-being of our young, families ask, can we make the world safe for our children, and our children safe for the world? These questions plague parents, with good reason.

Reports of domestic violence, drug violence, gun violence, gang violence, racial and ethnic violence, military violence, rape of women and children, as well as senseless killings in a schoolyard fill the daily news. Mass murders, terrorist attacks and random bombings increase, while conventional, chemical or nuclear warfare threaten the existence of whole populations.

By the mid-1970s, the increase of domestic and community violence in the United States was compared to an unchecked medical epidemic, leading to the establishment of a violence prevention project by the Centers for Disease Control in Atlanta, Georgia, in 1983. In 1994, Gene Stephens, criminal justice editor for *The Futurist*, reported that violence is a growing phenomenon worldwide, and that youth violence, which has the highest incidence in the United States, is increasing at an alarming rate throughout the world.[1] Violence poses a particular threat to family and community well-being. In too many communities, not only do teens view acts of real violence and terrorism on the news, but many witness violence in their own lives. Moreover, in some communities, teens are both victims and perpetrators of violence, especially gun violence. Conferences have been held throughout the United States, in Canada, and elsewhere to examine this threat to society.

Understanding Violence

To grasp how deeply violence affects families, it is important to understand the breadth of the term. For most of us, our awareness of violence is limited to physical acts: battering of children or partners in a home; rape, robbery, muggings or gang violence on the street; or bombings and other forms of terrorist activity that threaten the safety of us all. Violence, however, is much more than this. Violence consists of any intentional behaviour that causes physical, as well as emotional, mental or psychological harm to another, and includes any act — physical, emotional, verbal or psychological — which threatens or forces a person or a community to act in ways that right reason, law or moral suasion could not.[2]

Violence, some believe, is becoming a defining characteristic of life in the world today. Peace scholar John Galtung makes the point that the two theorists who most strongly purport that aggression is natural to human life, Konrad Lorenz of Germany and E. Wilson of the United States, come from countries with a history of being among the most aggressive in the world.[3] Others, such as Kenneth Boulding and Ashley Montagu, suggest that human violence is a learned behaviour.[4] While high levels of violence are observed in some societies, it is evident that not all people, nor all cultures, engage in acts of aggression and violence in conflict situations.

Violence takes many forms. It can be overt, manifested in physical, emotional, and verbal attacks, or covert, manifested in psychological abuse or in systemic, structural or institutional oppression, exploitation, manipulation and/or coercion of others. Physical violence involves actual threats to the person or life of another. Emotional and verbal violence threaten a person's sense of self-worth. Psychological violence occurs when one or more people in positions of authority intimidate others without use of actual force, generating a sense of disease in victims, who learn to distrust their own senses. Systemic violence, also known as "structural" or "institutional" violence, occurs when basic human and civil rights and freedoms are denied anyone on the basis of law, policy or community practice. Parents who share a concern about violence and safety for the members of their family need be as concerned about eliminating verbal, emotional, psychological and systemic violence as they are about eliminating acts of physical violence in their home, in their children's classrooms and on the streets of their own communities.

Manifestations of Violence

Violence, which has multiple expressions, is manifested in the diverse places where we live our lives, including the family, school and community at the local, national and international levels. Expressions of violence which transcend place include cultural violence; corporate violence; military violence; and systemic, institutional or structural violence. Below, we examine each of these manifestations in turn to grasp its impact on teens and their families.

Family Violence

Family or domestic violence takes place both within the privacy of the home and in public places such as shopping centres, parks, religious congregations, community centres and wherever else family members gather. It is almost a truism that all parents love their children. Yet, in too many communities around the globe, as each day draws to a close, reports of new instances of child abuse fill the evening news. Within such an environment, children's longing for love, or even their basic survival needs such as safety and security, often go unmet. Where a sense of personal security and self-worth is lacking, it is difficult indeed to identify and meet either one's own or another's needs.

Family violence can be both emotional and physical. Perhaps no threat to teens is as potentially harmful to their emotional well-being as the threat of abandonment. Marriage and other forms of committed relationships are, by their very nature, the act of bonding people together into a family. Marriage is also an act that connects the generations. When abandonment occurs — physical, emotional, or both — this connection between young people and others in their family is severed. Literature on the dysfunctional family is replete with stories linking emotional and physical abandonment, childhood trauma, and adult life scars which often take years to heal.

Emotionally violent homes foster an atmosphere where competitiveness, rivalry, bitterness, revenge, and even hate, thrive. In emotionally abusive families, disagreements are seen as threats to the authority or emotional stability of one or more people — usually, but not always, a parent — and are promptly censored. In such families, there is no open dialogue about differences in interest, needs, opinions or skills, or about complex issues such as dating, sexual orientation or religious practices. Young people have no safe way to make their needs known, or to express ordinary disagreements or ordinary anger. In such households, in fact, anger is often denied. But the rage that rumbles just beneath the surface occasionally erupts with a force violent enough to send children scampering under beds, and teens and adults fleeing from the house to places of safety or hiding.

Occasionally, in such families, emotional abuse erupts into physical violence, leading to spousal, partner, child and/or elder battery serious enough to send one or more persons to hospital for treatment of severe physical or emotional wounds. Rape and incest are other manifestations of physical and emotional violence occurring in far too many homes. Suicides and attempted suicides are common, and a legacy of fear, distrust, suspicion, revenge and hate keeps people who have not yet learned to love each other well apart.

School Violence

Schools are places where teens spend six or more hours five days each week engaged in activities meant to ensure their intellectual, physical, mental and emotional growth. Increasingly, violence in schools diminishes the opportunity for learning and, at times, threatens safety or life. A poll conducted by Louis Harris and Associates describes the effect violence has upon the behaviour of teachers and students in some school districts: Academic performance has decreased, teachers show less enthusiasm for teaching, and students who are unwilling to risk exposure to violence at school drop out or change schools frequently.[5] Educators in the United States report that the Federal Gun-Free Schools Act of 1994, which requires a minimum one-year expulsion of any student found to have carried a firearm onto school grounds, has resulted in an increase in the number of students suspended or expelled. Educators and counsellors who work with these young people consider them at risk because too often expelled youth neither continue their education, nor receive counselling or other support services while away from school. Without such services, professionals believe, students will fall behind in their studies and, more important, if they return to school, will still lack skills needed to face and resolve conflicts peacefully.[6] Because expelled students often escalate their violent behaviours, they are also more at risk of becoming involved with criminal justice or welfare systems later in life. Thus, there are long-term social consequences to families and communities when the causes of anger and the resulting violent behaviour go unaddressed.

Community Violence

Violence in our villages and cities causes widespread fear for personal safety. Shootings — for clothing or shoes, to settle a playground dispute or to obtain drugs — are rampant. Violence by strangers results in the rape and murders of young girls innocently riding their bikes, the death of teens struck by stray bullets while playing basketball or the random killing of young people at a restaurant or college. Each of these forms of community violence involves both perpetrators and victims of violence, and either could be our children!

Escalating incidents of youth violence have a profound impact on the emotional and psychic health of a society. Daniel Goleman, author of *Emotional Intelligence*, references several hundred studies linking poor emotional intelligence of individuals and society with exposure to and participation in acts of violence.[7] The Louis Harris poll cited above indicates that fear of violence exists more heavily in low-income, inner-city neighbourhoods where "almost half of all young have changed their behaviour as a result of crime or the threat of crime."[8] Young people and their families avoid favourite parks and playgrounds, bypass particular shops and malls and alter travel routes in efforts to assure their safety. The threat of violence has led some to carry weapons or take other precautions to protect themselves and their loved ones. Such behaviour deters healthy interaction with others in the community and the world.

Cultural Violence

Cultural violence takes many forms. Perhaps this question can be posed: Is there a form of community and cultural violence that is peculiar to adolescents? While families in our own community may never witness incidents of gun- and gang-related violence so prevalent in the daily experience of some communities, or the acts of terrorism and warfare prevalent in others, there is a culture of violence that permeates the behaviours of many adolescents. Name-calling, labelling, taunts, shunning and other forms of verbal and emotional abuse destroy the sense of self-worth of those abused, and can escalate into physically violent confrontations. Swarming is another common adolescent behaviour designed to intimidate others, often teens from groups different from themselves, or small-business owners and their clientele.

Movies, television, commercials and billboards glamorize the pleasures of alcohol and drugs. Peer pressure is strong among young people who hear these messages and act on them. At the same time, young people often lack even basic knowledge about how these affect their physical, emotional, and mental well-being and functioning. Impaired by drugs or alcohol, some teens risk engaging in activities that can turn violent.

A culture which glamorizes and objectifies sex and promotes it as "the" way for young people to feel good about themselves and relate with others leads to a variety of complications. Many risk infection with AIDS and other sexually transmitted diseases (STDs). If pregnancy results, some mothers toss unwanted babies into trash bins, where most are left to die. Rape, especially date rape, is a growing phenomenon among the young, made more vicious with the rising use of Rohypnol, which renders young women powerless to defend themselves and permits young men who meet no resistance from acknowledging the violence of their act. Pornography and the growing sex industry glamorize sex while exploiting our young in our own communities and worldwide.

Competitive play offers a chance to test and improve skills; too often, however, competitive games and sports simply glorify individual and group acts of aggression and violence. A culture based on competitiveness values superiority over collegiality and cooperation. Add to this the violence that young people worldwide are exposed to through war toys, and certain video games, movies and television programs that glorify violence. Through these and other forms of entertainment, young people learn that violence generates excitement as well as posing as a culturally acceptable way to react to personal and social problems.

Language adds to the confusion about what is violence and what is not. Sports metaphors include "enemy," "kill them," and "bury them," while media coverage of wars, especially of the Gulf War, is replete with sports imagery. To add to the confusion of language usage, military terms creep into ordinary conversations and professional literature. For example, in *Emotional Intelligence*, the term "trigger" is used as many as four or five times per page when non-military terms such as "evoke," "stimulate" and "generate" would communicate an idea just as effectively.[9]

Social forces unleashed through rapid political and economic change lead to a clash of values which, at times, turns emotionally and verbally, if not actually physically, violent. A culture which limits roles for women and men generates widespread debate and conflict about the "proper" role of women and men in a society's child-rearing and homemaking practices, in places of work, as well as in government and other policy-setting institutions. A commitment to a social value based on individualism; a cultural value based on racism, sexism, classism, materialism and consumerism; or a corporate value based on competitiveness promotes a culture counter to the values of caretaking and cooperation essential to healthy family and community life.

Lastly, a cultural value which fails to honour a respect for the life ethic across the continuum of human life becomes imbedded in conflict which often turns violent on such controversial issues as abortion, imprisonment, capital punishment, government regulation and euthanasia. Each of these issues has an impact on someone's family. Dangers surrounding these controversies include an undervaluing of life; a search for easy solutions to complex social, economic and legal problems occurring in any society; and a mentality that places a propensity for violence in the "other," who must be locked away or killed. Violence, then, erupts at abortion clinics, government compounds, federal buildings, and prisons, resulting in too many deaths and an untold pain that scars a community and the psyche of its people. Most troubling, many of us see these controversies in terms of either/or. When our pleading, our demands, our lobbying and our protests are fuelled by the urgency of our beliefs, the fury of our chants and the violence of our actions, we fail to teach our young to respect the precious life of each one of us who is already here.

Corporate Violence

Corporate policies and practices which exploit managers, workers, communities and resources add to the levels of violence in a society. Corporate violence is a particularly virulent form, blending as it does aspects of both cultural and systemic violence, and is made more so because, on the surface, it appears so bloodless. Corporate greed compels owners of some companies to place a higher value on profit than on worker or community well-being and safety. Products shoddily produced break or threaten lives. Banking and insurance companies use a practice called "redlining" (singling out specific populations or sections of a community to deny loans, mortgages, fire insurance and so on). Whole communities face economic devastation when companies relocate to take advantage of lower labour costs or less restrictive environmental or safety regulations in other parts of the world, while the new host country faces threats to its environment and to worker safety.

Military Violence

War and threats of war impede individual growth and family unity; cause community disruption and political disenfranchisement; and lead to widespread loss of property, limb and life. Many of the problems of violence in the modern world come from a commitment to militarism to solve problems. In the past, mobilization for war was temporary. Today, military preparedness is a constant, with continuing stockpiles of conventional, chemical and nuclear weapons, and personnel trained to use them.

Military solutions to life's cultural, racial, political and economic problems threaten our young, and do so in three ways. First of all, it is our sons and daughters — some too young for secondary school — who are the ones called to fight for our countries and our causes and, at times, to die.[10] Second, it is our young who live with fear for their future, and even their lives. One young man who once spent three days in our home as part of the Children of War Tour sponsored by the Religious Task Force, a collaborative international effort of the Fellowship of Reconciliation and the Mobilization for Survival, expressed amazement that "American children play Ping-Pong in their basements." In Lebanon, his home, "basements are places you go to get away from the bombs." Third, because military violence alters a nation's budgetary priorities, moneys that should be used to support families, build schools and recreation centres, hire teachers and youth workers, and otherwise provide for family and community well-being, are no longer available.

Systemic Violence

Most of us recognize incidents of physical violence in a community; however, few of us recognize that decayed homes, garbage-strewn streets, clusters of unemployed who slouch on porches and at street corners are other manifestations of community violence, a violence caused by social, political and economic decisions made by government and corporate leaders as well as by ordinary citizens within a community which fails to care for the needs of all its members. Sadly, members of our families can be both victims of any of these forms of violence, as well as perpetrate such violence by personal, professional and political decisions we make each day of our lives.

Systemic or institutional violence and injustice occur when basic human and civil rights and freedoms are denied others based upon public law or policy, or corporate or community practice. Systemic violence, which affects groups of people rather than just individuals, is based on practices which discriminate against others because of differences in gender, race, age, religion, national and ethnic origin, marital status, sexual orientation, ability level, as well as political persuasion, economic class and/or lifestyle choices.

If there are places you don't want your teen visiting or "hanging out," places you and your family want to avoid because of a reputation for crime and violence, look for systemic violence as a root cause. Systemic violence is evident in unjust social, political and economic policies and practices that limit access by members of any specific group to adequate food, shelter, education, employment, recreation, health care, wealth and other basic human rights. Social violence limits people's access to full participation in the life of a society. Political violence restricts people's access to education or the right to participate in decisions which affect their lives. Economic violence denies people access to adequate reimbursement for meaningful work or, through "redlining," access to the goods, resources and services in a society. Environmental violence threatens the welfare of families whose health is at risk due to polluted streams and landfills; whose food source is destroyed due to unproductive land use; whose family life is disrupted as members flee from chemical and nuclear accidents, acts of aggression or war; or whose very existence is at risk due to depletion of the rain forest and the ozone layer. Corporate violence, addressed above, can thrive only within a framework of institutional and systemic violence. Systemic violence raises the question of who makes and enforces the social, political or economic decisions that affect family and community life.

Increasingly, teens are growing up in communities that limit their options for development and full participation in their society. Many live without family support in homeless shelters in the urban centres of our world or in refugee camps in disaster or war-torn areas of the world, visual reminders of the crisis systemic violence causes teens and their families today. The United Nations 1994 International Year of the Family was inaugurated specifically to address concerns about the negative impact this violence has upon communities, its families and our young people. "The inability to raise children in a way that sustains society in the long run has become a social crisis of global proportions," according to Urie Bronfenbrenner, professor of Family Studies at Cornell University, who adds, "secure families determine the degree of society's security. Families must survive if society is to survive."[11]

Part Two: Peacemaking as a Family Response to Violence

How, then, do teens and their families counter this epidemic of violence so that they not only survive, but thrive? Can families both protect teens from violence and ensure, to the best of their ability, that teens will never intentionally violate another? Can families respond to the threats of violence in their lives in a way that will provide security for teens and lead to the survival of society? Part Two suggest ways to protect teens from violence, educate teens for peace and empower teens for global citizenship.

Protecting Teens from Violence

Peacemaking is a lifelong process which is fostered, first of all, in a positive and nurturing home environment. Teens need to know that their family will nurture, educate, protect and support them. Gene

Stephens suggests that we can help young people become responsible citizens if we treat them "with the respect they deserve. Children need and deserve tender loving care and attention. When they feel wanted and gain attention and approval for socially desirable activities, they are unlikely to become serious lawbreakers as adolescents or adults."[12] Within the safety and comfort of the home, parents can promote healthy, loving relationships and empower both sons and daughters to be people of strong character who know how to act with integrity, and treat themselves and others with gentleness and respect.

Knowing that violence is a reality of life, families can encourage activities that reduce exposure to violence. Making our home inviting for teens and their friends to "hang out" in; engaging in family or community gardening, sports, or a hobby shared with a group; volunteering in the community — all provide opportunity for worthwhile, safe activities. Parents and teens can also develop guidelines for self-protection. These might include using a buddy system when out with friends; going out in groups rather than alone or with just one romantic interest; trusting instincts when there is a possibility that activities might turn unsafe; avoiding rides with those who have been drinking or using drugs; and calling home to report whereabouts when delayed or for help to get out of a potentially dangerous situation. Parents who want teens to call home need to express willingness to arrange transportation after any event — no matter how late — if their ride falls through or the situation feels unsafe.

Open and honest family communication is important if we want our young to confide in us. This is especially true when it is our son or daughter who is the victim of violence. Parents and other caregivers can provide a safe space where children can express their pain, their fear, their outrage. We can listen respectfully, without judgment. We can assure them that most adults in their world will care for them and not cause them harm. They need to know that people can disagree and still resolve both simple and serious conflicts without resorting to violence or acts of terrorism. Even when they have been violated, they don't need to stay in a victim role. When we encourage them to seek help when violated, we empower them to see themselves as survivors, not victims, of violence.

Perhaps the most difficult task parents face is knowing how to respond to violence when it is their teen who taunts others, rapes, or is guilty of wielding the knife or gun, ready to cause harm to another, or their teen is charged with assault or murder. With youth violence rising throughout the world, we know that, for too many families, it is their own teens who perpetrate such evil deeds. When it is our teens who violate others, we can offer support by letting them know that we continue to love them while despising their deed. We can advocate to ensure that services be provided to meet their legal, physical, emotional and intellectual needs, and we can encourage them to assume financial, legal and moral responsibility for their actions. We can write and visit them in prison to let them know we care. It is essential, too, that we, as parents, seek support for ourselves in such times of trial. Some religious congregations provide a prison ministry program for both inmates of prison and their families to aid in this process.

Educating Teens for Non-violence and Peace

Teens not only need our protection, but also education which provides them with attitudes, values, knowledge and skill for living with others peacefully in the world. Educating our young for peace and non-violence consists of three distinct yet intertwined components.

Creating a Peaceful Environment

Within the safety and security of the home, families can create an environment where the values and skills of peacemaking are practised. (1) Affirming our own and others wants, needs, interests and ideas provides a counter to the put-downs, name-calling, labelling and other forms of verbal abuse common in schoolyards, classrooms, on playgrounds, and even in our homes and places of work. (2) Communicating effectively depends upon a willingness to share honestly, listen respectfully, and offer positive, caring, and clarifying comments to each other. (3) Respecting differences empowers people within the family to recognize and respect differences outside the family. (4) Nurturing encourages both our sons and our daughters to care for each other and maintain the home; tend to the physical needs of the young and the infirm; engage in gentle, not hurtful touch; and provide emotional support to others in times of sadness and times of joy. (5) Valuing cooperation in work and play counters the very competitive society in which many of us live, where a need to win, to be first, or to be best permeates work, study and play. (6) Celebrating in simple ways with laughter, song, music, dance and play enables young and old to express their joy in and commitment to each other in ways that contribute to the building-up, not the tearing-down, of the earth and its people.

When each member of the family feels affirmed and treasured; where differences are acknowledged, accepted, respected, treasured, and even celebrated; and when everyone has learned to play and work with others cooperatively so that all win, then we can begin to examine conflict in a new and different way. We can begin to see conflict, not as a struggle to prove one of us right — the winner — and the other, wrong — the loser. We can begin to view conflict as a given of human life, presenting us with challenges to be met and problems to be resolved for the mutual benefit of all.

Resolving Conflict Peacefully

Conflict, simply defined, is the existence of two or more needs interfering with each other. Conflict can occur within an individual who is faced with opposing choices or needs as well as between two or more persons or social groups whose interests or needs interfere with each other. Conflict, by itself, is neither right nor wrong. In fact, the existence of conflict can be good, for it challenges everyone in the family to examine choices and options, and to clarify values and goals. Conflict is a given of human life, presenting us with challenges to be met and problems to be resolved in caring ways that respect the legitimate needs of everyone involved.

A number of common conflict themes occur within families. These include sharing (of games, toys, sports equipment, clothing, space, time, self); personal responsibility (for grooming, homework, social life, house tasks — including who does what and when to ensure that the needs of the home and the family are met); leisure-time activities (TV, video games, dating, use of the car, sexual activities,"hanging around" — including use of alcohol and drugs); money: (family needs, jobs, allowances — including how much and how used); communication: (really sharing with another our own wants, needs and feelings, and listening to and understanding what another wants, needs and feels); availability (to each other).

While conflict itself may be neither right nor wrong, what families do with conflict certainly can be. Conflict within a family can be trying at best. However, it isn't always the "what" of conflict that creates stress in the family circle. Often it is the atmosphere in which conflict is viewed.

Thus, families need effective tools and skills for the creative and peaceful resolution of conflict. The following skills help families resolve conflicts creatively and non-violently. (1) Understanding perceptual differences encourages children to validate both their own and others' experiences, opinions and feelings without fear of being judged right or wrong. (2) Strengthening the imagination expands awareness of possible uses of common items or solutions to any problem. (3) Providing the opportunity to make choices enables teens to affect decisions in their lives, teaches them that every choice involves consequences, and empowers them to accept responsibility for their actions, reduce conflict, and grow into wise decision makers. (4) Brainstorming a list of three or more alternatives to simple and complex problems develops skill in critical thinking and expands the possibility that solutions to problems can be found. (5) Participating in family meetings provide teens an opportunity to develop both conflict resolution and leadership skill. All members of the family can suggest items for the agenda. Teens can assist even very young children in leading a family meeting by providing gentle and loving encouragement.

Faced with a culture permeated with violence, parents and other caregivers can engage with teens in open and honest dialogue about the pain and brokenness in our families and in our world. An environment conducive to affirmation and effective communication makes this task easier. As they learn to acknowledge, accept and treasure differences; to cooperate in work and play; and to resolve conflict peacefully, both parents and teens become better prepared to communicate about more complex issues they face. They can share concerns about use of drugs, alcohol and firearms, pressures and dangers associated with gangs, as well as fears they might have related to threats of sexual or physical violence. As they gain in skill, they will be strengthened in voicing objections when others are harassed in school or when they hear offensive jokes or comments. In all these ways teens and parents are learning to name forms of violence in their lives, and identify non-violent ways to respond to that violence.

Building Family Support Networks

Teens and parents need contact with others who share values and attempt to make peacemaking an important part of their lives. Families who gather together with other families to play, to work and to share parenting concerns in networks of support benefit everyone involved. Our daughters and our sons will feel more secure when they know there are other families like themselves who are learning to express positive, caring statements in the midst of the put-downs so prevalent in our society; others learning to respect and celebrate diversity when people whose race, religion, sexual orientation, age or other differences are ridiculed; others like themselves enjoying the challenge of cooperative as well as competitive play and work.

Communities that provide opportunity for safe, fun activities for teens are saying that the interests and needs of young people are valued. It isn't enough to teach teens and pre-teens to "Just say no!" to drugs, alcohol, sex, vandalism or crime. Parents, caregivers and business and community leaders who work together with teens to provide safe places and positive, socially acceptable alternatives — movies, concerts, athletics, and other forms of participatory and spectator entertainment, as well as volunteer activities they can do with groups of friends — show they care for young people in their community. Some homes and businesses post window signs encouraging young people to seek shelter when danger lurks.

Community leaders who want to end violence can offer support in other ways. Communities can survive the uncivil wars that erupt on the controversial issues of our times if parents and community leaders model ways to engage, not attack, others in efforts to raise issues in public forums. Youth violence can be reduced or stopped through mentoring programs such as those offered in the United States by One Hundred Black Men and the National Compadres Network, which work to reduce the incidence of substance abuse, domestic violence, teen pregnancy and gang violence that plague communities. The international Parenting for Peace and Justice Network and their Families Against Violence Project does the same with teens and families.[13] Aware of their children's fear of verbal, sexual or physical harassment, and gang-related violence, terrorism, or warfare, some parents have sought support from school administrators, teachers and religious leaders to establish education programs which address these concerns. Such programs provide an opportunity to examine values, develop skills, and engage in a methodology for educating about self-respect, non-violence, peace, justice and global citizenship.

Family and community education for peace programs are directly related to the promotion and establishment of a healthy, secure society. Participants in such programs build self-esteem and acquire both an understanding of the theory of non-violence and an awareness that there are alternatives to dysfunctional violent behaviours. Role-playing helps teens prepare for the possibility of violence and helps them develop skill to respond non-violently if threatened. Moreover, by participating in these programs, teens and their families discover that non-violence is more than a technique to reduce danger to oneself or others. It is more than a strategy to effect changes one desires in others. It is, most of all, a commitment to a way of life which respects oneself, others and one's world.

Empowering Our Young for Global Citizenship

The journey from violence to peacemaking is a lengthy one. Playing and working together, respecting the rich diversity among us, seeking effective ways to resolve the conflicts that occur in our daily lives all enable us to grow in peacemaking ways within the safety and security of our own families. But the challenge of peacemaking urges us to expand our concerns beyond the doors of our home and neighbour-hood and into the broader society, where the conflicts and crisis that confront us are often of global proportions. Given that global interde-pendence is a fact, how do we help our families live as peacemakers who recognize that we share a common bond, a common land, common resources, and a common heritage with all of humanity?

Addressing Systemic Violence

In order to do justice to the multitude of issues which have an impact on families today, and which are caused as much by systemic as by personal acts of violence, families need knowledge of and sensitivity to the multiple expressions of violence and injustice addressed in Part One of this essay.

Teens who have developed critical thinking skills and who have learned to share and cooperate with others can begin to make a significant impact on these important justice issues. Teens and parents can talk about how each of these issues affects our own family, and reflect on two intricately related questions. What effect do these issues have on other people, other families different from ourselves in colour, culture or country, yet — like ourselves — an important part of the human family? And second, what impact does our family have on these issues? That is, what impact does our family's daily lifestyle choices have on the critical issues before us? Do our personal, professional and political choices contribute to or heal the suffering of others?

Building the Peaceful Community

Henryk Sokalski reminds us that the family, as the most basic level of human communion, must be strong if a sense of community is to be extended in the greater society.[14] Strong families value service to each other and to the broader community. Strong families also value an ability to image peace, knowing that it is from our images that we can build a peace-filled world. Lastly, strong families are grounded with a sense of hope for their future.

Service empowers teens and their families to act as citizens of a civic and a global society. Through acts of care, families witness their connection to each other and experience the importance of service to a broader community. Marjorie Tuitt of Church Women United suggests service can take one or more of five forms: direct service, advocacy, empowerment, solidarity and stewardship.[15]

Some parents and teens, along with younger children of all ages, enjoy performing direct service to others by gathering canned goods for the hungry; collecting toys, clothing or books for others; visiting the sick, lonely or elderly; offering support in times of disaster; and simply sitting with others in quiet prayer. Direct service helps with people's immediate needs and, at times, even helps keep people alive. However, it does not usually address the underlying causes of need. Therefore, families who are serious about living justly also consider other forms of service equally important for community and global peacemaking.

Several of these areas of service address issues of policy and practice which undergird systemic violence. Families advocate for others by speaking out for those in need. They talk about issues that matter to them; work together to address those issues; write letters to leaders in the community or workplace, to editors of local newspapers, and to legislators and the leader of their country in an effort to change laws or policies that keep people hungry, homeless and otherwise in need; and participate in boycotts, protest marches, and other forms of public witness to raise awareness to important issues. Families empower others when they provide knowledge and tools and teach those in need the skills to use them, thus empowering them to act in their own behalf. Families act in solidarity with others when they stand alongside those who suffer discrimination, accepting the risk, pain and suffering directed toward another individual or group.

Through acts of care for the earth, families also serve as stewards, caring for the resources of our earth which have been entrusted to us for safekeeping. Concern for the environment and equitable distribution of both human and natural resources affect all members of our family. Stewards consider how resources are used and what changes, if any, might be necessary in order to live in kinship with all others in this fragile ecosystem.

Building peaceful communities also involves our ability to image a world at peace. It has been said that we create only what we can first image. What, then, is our image of a peace-filled world? Does it include a world which values equality, mutuality, diversity, and justice for all? Are our images of a world at peace as vivid and concrete as our images of a world at war? Do we share our images of peace with others in our family, with our classmates, neighbours, co-workers and those at our place of worship? Dare we risk working to bring such a world into being? And, if so, what are the risks that we, in our family, are willing to take? These are important questions for each person in the family to address. Our own future and the future of our children depend upon the willingness of all of us to rechannel our creative energies, and reallocate time, talent and treasure to the visioning and teaching of new ways to live together cooperatively and caringly with peoples of diverse cultures, lifestyles, races, religions, philosophical and/or political persuasions to build a non-violent, just and peaceful world.

Perhaps the greatest gift parents can share with our young is a sense of hope in their future. They need to see us witness the hope that lives within us. In a world of brokenness and violence, our young must experience signs of this hope in their daily lives if they are to have a healthy sense of themselves and value their efforts for building a peaceful world. They need to see that our hope flows from spiritual values that connect us both to a spirit-force who goes by many names and to each other. Our hope, which is grounded in a belief that we are each participants in the building of a safe and peace-filled world, springs from our awareness of the joint efforts of many people who are working to bring healing and wholeness to all who share life with us on planet earth.

Conclusion

The children we parent and educate today will be the leaders and decision makers of tomorrow. It is within the family that we can prepare them for their future in a holistic manner. Let us gift them with our love, that they may know the experience of love and learn to pass it on. Let us gift them with those values and skills which will enable them to make a difference for good in their families, their communities and their world. This is the gift, the legacy, we leave to our children and our children's children, a promise and a vision of how to live humanly with others as together we prepare for life in the twenty-first century. Let us empower our young to welcome the future and all the challenges it presents. Let us start today to teach them well the ways of peace.

Notes

1. Gene Stephens, "The Global Crime Wave and What We Can Do about It," *The Futurist*, July/August 1994.

2. This definition of violence is taken from undated lecture notes from a Theology of Non-violence course taught by Professor Daniel Di Domizio, Ph.D., at Marquette University in the fall of 1971. Much of the material that follows is developed from courses team-taught by Dr. Di Domizio and this author during the past twenty-five years.

3. John Galtung, "The Next Twenty-five Years," in *Peace Research: Achievements and Challenges*, Peter Wallensteen (ed.) (Boulder, CO: Westview Press, 1988).

4. Ian Harris and Jacqueline Haessly, "Violence and Alternatives to Violence: An Educational Perspective," unpublished paper (accepted for publication in the January 1998 special peace issue of *Holistic Education Review*).

5. Louis Harris and Associates, *The Metropolitan Life Survey of the American Teacher: Violence in America's Public Schools* (New York: Metropolitan Life Insurance, 1995), p. 10.

6. E-mail from Dr. Ian Harris, Professor of Peace Education, University of Wisconsin-Milwaukee, May 1997.

7. Daniel Goleman, *Emotional Intelligence* (New York: Bantam Books, 1996).

8. Louis Harris and Associates.

9. Daniel Goleman.

10. Yael Azmon, "War, Mothers, and a Girl with Braids: Involvement of Mothers Peace Groups in the National Discourse in Israel," in *Families as Educators for Global Citizenship*, Judith Myers-Walls and Peter Somali (eds.) (U.K.: in press). Yael Azmon describes the "Girl with Braids" to reveal the dilemma of using children for war-making poses to opposing military leaders fighting in Israel.

11. Urie Bronfenbrenner, "Who Cares for the Children?" in *The International Year of the Family* (Geneva: United Nations Department of Public Information, Non-Governmental Organizations Section, DPI/NGO/SB/91/17), p. 5.

12. Gene Stephens.

13. To learn more about the Families Against Violence network, contact Parenting for Peace and Justice at: 4144 Lindell Blvd., St. Louis, MO, USA 63108; phone (314) 533-4445.

14. Henryk Sokalski, "International Year of the Family," statement at a seminar on Family Life Education for Peace, University for Peace, Escazu, Costa Rica, January 16, 1992.

15. These five forms of service were developed by Marjorie Tuitt, Daniel Di Domizio and this author for the "Quest for Peace" workshop, part of a series of workshops we offered for the Wisconsin and National Church Women United in the late 1970s and early 1980s.

Select Bibliography

A. Children's experiences of war and peace

Filipovic, Zlata. *Zlata's Diary: A Child's Life in Sarajevo*. New York: Penguin, 1994.

Frank, Anne. *The Diary of a Young Girl*. Garden City, NY: Doubleday, 1952.

Hoose, Phillip. *It's Our World, Too! Stories of Young People Who Are Making a Difference*. Boston: Little, Brown and Company, 1993.

Kome, Penny and Patrick Crean (eds.). *Peace, A Dream Unfolding*. San Francisco: Sierra Club Books, 1986.

Lystad, Mary. *A Child's World*. Rockville, MD: National Institute for Mental Health, 1974.

Nagasaki Prefecture Hibakusha Teachers Association. *In The Sky Over Nagasaki: An A-Bomb Reader for Children*. Wilmington, OH: Peace Resource Center, 1977.

Rosenblatt, Roger. *Children of War*. Garden City, NY: Doubleday, 1983.

Volavková, Hana, ed. *I Never Saw Another Butterfly: Children's Drawings and*

Poems From Terezin Concentration Camp, 1942-1944. New York: McGraw-Hill, 1962.

Vornberger, William (ed.). *Fire From the Sky: Salvadoran Children's Drawings.* New York: Writer's and Reader's Publishing Cooperative, 1986.

B. Family education for non-violence and peace

Altergott, Karen (ed.). *One World, Many Families.* Minneapolis: National Council on Family Relations, 1993.

Curran, Delores. *Traits of a Healthy Family.* Minneapolis: Winston Press, 1983.

Edelman, Marian Wright. *The Measure of Our Success: A Letter to My Children and Yours.* Boston: Beacon Press, 1992.

Haessly, Jacqueline. *Learning to Live Together.* San Jose: Resource Publications, 1989.

Judson, Stephanie. *Manual on Children and Non-violence.* Philadelphia: New Society Press, 1984.

McGinnis, James, and Kathleen McGinnis. *Parenting for Peace and Justice.* New York: Orbis Press, 1981.

Montessori, Maria. *Education and Peace.* Chicago: Regnery, 1949.

Muller, Robert. *Most of All They Taught Me Happiness.* New York: Image Books, 1985.

Orlick, Terry. *The Cooperative Sports and Games Books.* New York: Pantheon Books, 1976.

Taylor, Dena (ed.). *Feminist Parenting.* Freedom, CA: The Crossing Press, 1994.

True, Michael. *Homemade Social Justice: Teaching Peace and Justice in the Home.* Chicago: Fides Claretian, 1982.

C: Establishing a peace education program

Haessly, Jacqueline. "Peace Studies." In *Ready Reference: Ethics*, John K. Roth (consulting ed.). Pasedena, CA: Salem Press, 1994. pp. 647-9.

Haessly, Jacqueline. *What Shall We Teach Our Children: Peace Education in the Schools.* Milwaukee: Peace Talk Publications, 1985.

O'Reilley, Mary Rose. *The Peaceable Classroom.* Portsmith, NH: Boynton Cook Publishers, 1993.

Prothrow-Stith, D. *Violence Prevention: A Community Health Curriculum for Adolescents.* Newton, MA: Education Development Center, 1987.

Prutzman, Priscilla and Lee Stern. *A Friendly Classroom for a Small Planet.* Philadelphia: New Society Publishers, 1987.

Reardon, Betty. *Comprehensive Peace Education: Educating for Global Responsibility.* New York: Teachers College Press, 1988.

Teens in the World

Doin' It for Themselves: Teen Rites and Teen Culture

Kathleen McDonnell

Some years ago I encountered a woman whose daughter was just entering her teenage years. The woman was very upset about the changes she was witnessing in her daughter's personality. "She's not the person I knew," the mother complained. "She's turned into someone else." "How is she different?" I asked. The woman was very specific: Her teenage daughter had become angry, demanding and unpleasant, where once she had been unfailingly compliant and good-natured. The mother made it clear to me — and I don't doubt she made it just as clear to her daughter — that she wanted nothing to do with this "other person." The sooner she reverted back to her former self, the better.

At the time I didn't think of myself as someone who knew the first thing about kids or how to raise them. Still, something about this woman's attitude really bothered me. She seemed awfully ready to reject this "other person" outright. How, I wondered, did she know it wasn't just a side of her daughter's personality she hadn't seen before? But I didn't have kids. What did I know? I kept my thoughts to myself.

Now I'm the mother of a teenager and I'm experiencing the "other person" phenomenon first-hand with my own daughter. I must admit I understand now exactly what the woman was talking about. But, after all these years, her words still stick in my craw. Because I think they sum up, in a kind of verbal shorthand, the prevailing attitude toward adolescence, one that, to some degree, we adults all buy into. It's like a parents' familiar song-and-dance routine: The collective groans when one of us mentions that our son or daughter has just turned thirteen, the joking comments about raging hormones, about shipping teenagers off to a desert island "'til it's over." It's harmless enough, an outlet for our frustration. But, like most jokes, it masks some real fears and anxieties — ours, not theirs. Yes, raising a teenager can be hell. Yes, they do turn into "other people." And, let's be honest about it: Most days they're a lot harder to love than they were when they were little. But we have to keep reminding ourselves of one crucial fact: It's precisely what's *supposed* to happen at this stage of life. Teenagers really *are* in the process of becoming "other people" — namely, adults. The misunderstood teen is a cliché, but also a reality, and the misunderstanding is largely ours. A large part of the "problem" of adolescence lies less in teens' behaviour than in adults' reaction to it.

The Tribe of Adolescence

A big part of the problem is that, as a society, we're still getting used to the whole idea of adolescence. Throughout most of Western history, the distinction between childhood and adulthood was not nearly as sharp as we make it today. In former times, becoming an adult had more to do with taking on the trappings, especially marriage and childbearing, and the onset of puberty was largely synonymous with "adulthood." In his landmark work *Centuries of Childhood*, the cultural historian Philippe Ariès argues that the notion of childhood and adolescence as distinct stages of life took hold only in the past couple of centuries. The word "teenager" doesn't even make an appearance in English until the 1920s. The peculiar character of adolescence began to emerge during the Romantic period, in the person of such popular idols as Werther and Siegfried. The protagonist of Goethe's eighteenth-century novel *The Sorrows of Young Werther* suffers the mood swings, suicidal thoughts and tortured romantic longings that we now regard as typical of modern-day teenagers. And Ariès himself calls Siegfried, the hero of Wagner's famous opera, the "first typical adolescent of modern times."[1]

Ariès also characterizes our era as "the century of adolescence," which seems particularly apt. The twentieth century, after all, has been witness to the rise of the mass media and the consumer society, both of which have been integral to the evolution of a distinctive teen "culture." This teenage lifestyle — ways of dressing, tastes in pop music, and so on — is so much a fact of modern life that it's easy to forget that it has existed only for the past few decades. The teen "uniform" of the late '40s and '50s, with its brush-cuts and bobby sox, looks awfully quaint to us now. But back then parents were just as appalled by Elvis as parents in the '90s are by gangsta rap. Teens nowadays are somewhat chagrined when they discover that they actually share some of the same musical tastes as their aging baby-boomer parents. Fortunately for them, they've managed to come up with some new ways to mark the generational divide, such as tattoos and body piercing.

Since the mid-1950s young people have turned to this common teen culture for validation of their lives and acknowledgement of what they're going through. *Rebel Without a Cause*, starring James Dean, pioneered an entire genre of movies about high-school life and adolescent angst which extends right up to the present in movies like *Heathers*, *Fast Times at Ridgemont High* and *Dazed and Confused*. There is a deep well of despair coursing under many of these teen movies, the despair of a generation with no one to guide them into adulthood. In *Rebel Without a Cause*'s most famous scene, Dean's character turns to his utterly insensitive, constantly harping parents and screams, "You're tearing me apart!" The anguish of his outburst is echoed in the harsh melodies and raw lyrics of another, more recent generational martyr, Kurt Cobain.

One theme that runs through all of teen culture is its decidedly jaundiced view of adults. Even in the farcical teen movies of the mid-1960s like *Muscle Beach Party* and *Beach Blanket Bingo*, the adult characters are routinely depicted as ridiculous, ineffectual and none too bright. In the dark comedy *Heathers*, Winona Ryder's character offers a standard reply to her father's rhetorical inquiries like: "Why do I read these spy novels?" "Because you're an idiot," she replies sweetly, but, as we clearly see in her face, she knows it's all too true. And in latter-day "slacker" comedies like *Dazed and Confused* and MTV's *Beavis and Butthead*, adults are not only useless, but practically non-existent.

Of course, teen culture hasn't exactly been monolithic. There have always been very real differences between Black and white youths, between middle-class and working-class kids. But, in its earlier days, this teenage world was far more coherent and homogeneous than it is now. Today, there is no single teen culture, but many subcultures within the larger tribe of adolescence. And these various subcultures are largely defined by preferences in pop culture. Where you shop for clothes, what kind of music you listen to — these are what determine which adolescent "tribe" you belong to. This fragmentation of teen culture is a reflection of what's happening in society at large, in this age of niche marketing and the five-hundred-channel universe.

I once watched several teens on a TV talk show argue that this banding into tribes is precisely what's wrong with teen culture. "Why do we always have to be part of a group?" one complained. "Why can't we just be individuals?" It seemed to me that these kids were being a bit hard on themselves and their peers, and I suspected they were feeding back the kind of phrases adults had thrown at them: "Why do you have to follow the crowd? Be yourself!" Adults tend to see this strong need to identify with a group or tribe as some kind of moral failing in teenagers. But if separation from parents and family is the major "developmental task" of adolescence, it makes perfect sense for teens to have strong drives to form new bonds, to find other ways to "belong" outside the family.

It's ironic, then, that as it grows more and more splintered on its home turf, the culture of North American teenagers has become such a global phenomenon. Kids all over the world crave jeans, watch the same rock videos, and use a lot of the same slang words no matter what their mother tongue. And this is the first generation to have largely grown up with, and in, cyberspace. With instant communication via the Internet and with rock concerts simulcast on the World Wide Web, some new-media enthusiasts even argue that this generation of young people are the first to think of themselves as truly global citizens.

To others, this new global culture adds up to little more than a global marketing opporunity for multinationals like Coke, Levi Strauss and Sony to hawk their wares to teenagers from Main Street to Malaysia. And it's undeniable that, in large part, teen culture is itself a creation of marketing. In the late '40s and early '50s, a whole new sector of the economy was created as advertisers began to "discover" teenagers as a distinct group of consumers with their own styles, their own products and, most importantly, their own money to spend.

We may not like to admit it, but being a consumer is a large part of what defines personhood in our culture. To teens, having their own money and the power to decide how to spend it is a highly valued mark of their own self-determination. Adults criticize teenagers for spending a small fortune on running shoes, and being so obsessed with having clothes from the "right" stores (while we conveniently overlook our own consuming passion for new cars and stereo equipment). The prevailing adult view is that teens are gullible sheep being led meekly into the marketplace, eager to buy whatever's hot at the moment. But it's not that simple: Teenagers aren't just consumers of pop culture, but "creators" of it as well. Social theorist John Fiske points to blue jeans as an example of how the typical consumerist scenario can get turned around. Levi Strauss and Guess can manipulate teens into buying a product like jeans. But, by a variety of gestures — tearing their jeans, proudly wearing them low-slung or oversized — kids find a way to put their own personal stamp on the product, and rebel against homogenization and corporate authority.[2] And it's a good fit in more ways than one, because, in the popular mind, rebellion against authority is what adolescence is all about.

Squeegee Kids versus Superheroes

"They have execrable manners, flaunt authority, have no respect for their elders ... What kind of awful creatures will they be when they grow up?"[3]

Those words read like yesterday's news story on youth crime. But Socrates wrote them in the fourth century B.C. Even then, there was a widespread belief that rebellious youth were causing the downfall of civilization, and Socrates' rhetoric echoes down through our own century in periodic waves of panic about out-of-control youth. During the '40s and '50s, this panic manifested as alarm over rising rates of juvenile delinquency. A number of experts, most notably psychiatrist Frederic Wertham, blamed comic books as the cause of this epidemic of youthful lawlessness. In 1954, Wertham published *Seduction of the*

Innocent, which documented a whole slew of violent crimes supposedly committed by teenagers after reading comics.[4] Much as parents today call for a crackdown on violent rap lyrics or TV shows, most adults in the '50s thought the solution to juvenile delinquency was a total ban on comic books. A couple of years later, as millions watched Elvis swivel his hips on *The Ed Sullivan Show*, adults thought they'd discovered a new demon leading youth astray. A entire genre of "teen rebel" movies grew up during this period, typified by *The Wild One*, in which Marlon Brando plays the sullen leader of a motorcycle gang. When asked, "What are you rebelling against?" he replies with a threatening sneer, "What d'ya got?"

Today, the terminology has changed. We don't hear a whole lot about "juvenile delinquency" anymore. But we're still gripped by the same fear and loathing of our own young people, which nowadays takes the form of widespread hysteria over youth crime. We're fed a daily diet of headlines about teenage violence. Many people are convinced that our high schools are seething cauldrons of violence, that roving gangs of teenagers terrorize shopping malls, and that the system is hopelessly lenient on young offenders. The latest manifestation of this demonization of youth, at least in large urban centres, is the so-called "squeegee kid" phenomenon. Street youths in Toronto and other larger cities have taken up the practice of cleaning windshields for money as an alternative to panhandling, which has led to calls for a crackdown on the practice. Some drivers complain that squeegee kids are too aggressive in their tactics, but what adults find even more disturbing is the very sight of these tattooed youths wearing eyebrow rings and work boots, grouped on street corners, wielding windshield cleaners that look uncomfortably like weapons.

Teenagers scare the living daylights out of us. They separate themselves off from the rest of society, hanging out in malls, going to all-night raves, joining quasi-formal gangs. Even their taste in movies and books is terrifying: horror novels by Christopher Pike and R.L. Stine, "slasher" films like *Prom Night*, *Nightmare on Elm Street*, and the recent hit *Scream*, which manages to be scary and send up the genre at the same time. One reason for the persistent appeal of horror stories lies in the fact that they provide a powerful metaphor for the physical changes of adolescence, for teens' deep-seated fears of their bodies going out of control. Horror stories also frequently link sex with danger. Adults have managed to find an accommodation with sexuality, a way of taming and fitting it into domestic life. But teens are encountering sex for the first time, and for them, it really *is* scary, and retains a kind of a primal power.

Teenagers are our collective cultural nightmare. We're terrified of these barbarians at our gates, and so we try to reduce them to walking catalogues of "problems" — drug abuse, unwanted pregnancy, high-school drop-outs — which we then earnestly seek to solve. But, while the adult impulse is, understandably, to maintain order and stability, the teenage impulse is toward excitement and experience, toward *instability*. Teens flirt with danger because it's in their cultural DNA, maybe even in their biological make-up, to do so. And as I'll argue a bit later, there may be better ways to deal with adolescence, ones that take these raw, wild energies and try to work with them.

There are a few positive voices among the doomsayers, however. Some observers of demographics trends argue that the offspring of the baby boomers, most of whom are just now entering their teenage years, will be a "generation of altruists" — more co-operative, socially active and environmentally aware than any generation preceeding them. Even crime statistics give quite a different picture from the public perception. The so-called epidemic of youth crime is, in fact, largely a myth. The relatively small increase in crimes committed by teenagers is largely the result of contemporary zero-tolerance policies and more stringent reporting procedures. In other words, behaviours that used to be tolerated as youthful hijinks or were dealt with privately, within the school or the family, now are put through the criminal justice system.

In some arenas of pop culture, teenagers are even depicted as powerful forces for good. It's fascinating to look at the Teenage Superhero genre in this regard. In TV shows like *Mighty Morphin' Power Rangers*, *Teenage Mutant Ninja Turtles* and *Sailor Moon*, as well as popular comics like *GEN-13*, the characters are teenagers who "morph" or transform themselves into beings with superhuman powers. In these stories the teenage superhero is actually a metaphor for the coming-into-power that's *supposed* to happen at adolescence. In a very real sense, teens are undergoing a metamorphosis into another "life form" altogether. Consider the young "mutant" teenager Jubilee, a character in the *X-Men* comics and TV series. Jubilee frets over her inability to control the changes her body is going through as her special powers begin to assert themselves. The process of morphing or mutating is actually a wonderfully apt way to describe the enormous physical and emotional changes of adolescence. Jubilee feels like an outcast and longs to just be normal. "I didn't ask to be a mutant!" she cries. It could also be the lament of any adolescent who feels robbed of the body and the "normal" life she or he knew before.

Different kind of powers take hold of the teenage girls in occult-themed movies such as *Buffy the Vampire Slayer* and *The Craft*. In the latter, a quartet of girls decide to delve into traditional witchcraft practices, and discover powers they didn't know they had. The protagonist of *Buffy* is informed by an otherworldly mentor that she has been "chosen" to fight the vampires that are slowly taking over her school, and must undergo a rigorous training process. Her mentor even informs her that her powers are specifically related to her menstrual cycle. ("Great," Buffy responds ruefully. "My secret weapon is PMS.") It's interesting that these mentoring figures — characters whose explicit role is to provide sympathetic but challenging guidance to teen superheroes — are so prominent in these stories. Besides Merrick in *Buffy*, there's Zordon, the gigantic talking-head, in *Power Rangers*, and the kindly old rat Splinter, who tries to help the Ninja Turtles develop self-discipline and control their constant craving for pizza and other junk foods. These mentors, and in fact the whole Teen Superhero genre itself, are inspired by ancient myths and age-old initiation practices, which embody a very different approach to adolescence than our own.

Rites of Passage

Becoming an adult is more than just a matter of acquiring certain physical characteristics. It requires a profound change in the way young people see themselves, and in how they're viewed by those around them. Without any of our modern scientific knowledge of hormones and the physiological changes of puberty, tribal cultures understood that adolescence is a time of great physical and emotional transition. For generations, tribal societies have provided a social mechanism for dealing with this major transition in the form of initiation rites.

These initiations or rites of passage are variously known as "visions quests," "walkabouts" and other names. Their content differs considerably from culture to culture, but there are certain common elements.

The young people are isolated for a period of time from the rest of society. Typically, they are given difficult, sometimes life-threatening, tasks to perform, and in the process of overcoming these difficulties they can experience extreme emotions. The rituals may involve the use of herbs, drugs or fasting, which is meant to evoke altered states of consciousness. Much of our knowledge of these rites involves the initiation of young males, but in many tribal societies girls also undergo initiation, often on the occasion of menarche, or first menstrual period. We tend to regard these practices as inherently sexist, because so many seem to treat menstruating women as dangerous or unclean. But, in another sense, these forms of intiation also convey an implicit acknowledgement of the power of menstrual blood and of the female body.

Interestingly, this description of traditional initiation bears a lot of similarity to the behaviour we observe in modern teenagers — the danger-seeking, the separation from adult society. It also helps explain why teens are so drawn to drugs and alcohol, and why the "Just say no" approach has been so ineffective. There's no doubt that substance abuse can cause severe damage in kids' lives, and no responsible adult would advocate a totally *laissez-faire* approach. But teens are keenly aware of of their parents' hypocrisy when they gloss over their own past experiences with drugs and blithely advocate a philosophy of "Do as I say, not as I did." Without a deeper understanding of the appeal of mind-altering experiences, and of the spiritual role they play in the initiation process, adults can't help kids identify what it is they're really looking for when they take drugs. Similarly, with anti-smoking campaigns, evidence is mounting that the "danger" model is singularly unsuccessful with teenagers, and it's not hard to see why. Kids often greet these ads with hoots of derisive laughter, because they feel they're being condescended to, that adults aren't levelling with them. Playing on fears isn't effective with teens precisely because they're not afraid of the things we think they should be.

Virtually all cultures that practise adolescent initiation regard adult involvement as absolutely crucial to the process. Initiation is not seen as something young people can do for themselves, but something through which they must be *guided* by adults. Indeed, in most societies the process is considered too fraught with dangers — both physical and psychological — to be left to the young themselves. Adults are supposed to provide structure, boundaries, a kind of safe container for the extreme emotions young people experience during the period of initiation.

But it's important to point out that the process of initiation isn't at all the same thing as what we think of as "parenting." In many ways parents are the *least* appropriate people to guide young people through initiation. To achieve true adulthood, kids have to leave home psychologically, to break away from the influence of their parents and find their own way in the world. Traditional societies view initiation not as a private, family matter, but as a social mechanism for which the entire community takes responsibility. And implicit in this is an acknowledgement that nothing is more vital to a society's well-being than the task of helping each new generation take its place in the world.

Unfortunately, in our culture there's a vacuum where this responsiblity should be. Despite all the accumulated wisdom that's been handed down to us from tribal cultures, adults in the contemporary world are largely abdicating their roles as guides in the process of initiation. Like the grown-ups in those teen movies, many of us are no help, or absent altogether. But in abdicating this responsibility, we're abandoning young people to their own devices, and effectively forcing them to try and initiate themselves. This is what a lot of teens' danger-seeking behaviour is really all about. They feel an inner drive to push things to the edge; they need to do so in order to make the transition into adulthood. But, tribal wisdom tells us they can't do it alone. The process really *is* dangerous. They need our guidance.

What's an Adult to Do?

So how can we help them? Many well-meaning adults, influenced by New Age ideas, argue that we should take our cue from tribal cultures, and adopt their traditional rites of initiation for our own children. But, lifting these rites out of their cultural context and transplanting them into ours usually doesn't work. New Age feminist mothers may go all warm and fuzzy at the thought of ceremonies to mark their daughters' first menstrual periods, but the girls themselves usually head for the hills as soon as the subject comes up.

As with so many aspects of modern life, we're in uncharted territory here, trying our best to cobble together a new way of dealing with adolescence — one that fits in with contemporary realities but still draws on ancient wisdom. Much as we might wish our kids would just "stay out of trouble" and avoid all those risky behaviours, to some extent we have to stand back and let them go through it. As in traditional initiation, our job is not to block the process, but to provide some safe boundaries for it.

At the very least, we need to keep reminding ourselves that we used to be teenagers ourselves. This is doubly true for baby-boomer parents, many of whom think that their style of adolescent rebellion was the only "right" one, and who, ironically enough, are often far more critical of the younger generation than their parents were. We need to become aware of how dealing with teenagers brings up our own fears, our own unfinished adolescent business.

In the end, initiation is the responsibility not just of parents, but of the whole society. And if we began to deal with our young people differently, we might end up with a very different kind of society. What if we viewed adolescence as more than a way station on the road to adulthood? As more than a stage to be endured or a problem to be solved? What if, instead of giving into our terror of teenagers, we took our cue from Teenage Superhero stories, and celebrated their emerging strength instead?

Notes

1. Philippe Ariès, *Centuries of Childhood* (New York: Vintage Books, 1962), pp. 29-30.

2. John Fiske, *Understanding Popular Culture* (London: Routledge, 1989), pp. 18-19.

3. Socrates, in *The Penguin Book of Childhood*, Michael Rosen (ed.) (New York: Viking, 1994), p. 6.

4. Maria Reidelbach, *Completely Mad: A History of the Comic Book and Magazine* (Boston: Little, Brown & Co., 1991), p. 12-13.

An Ounce of Prevention: Adolescent Drug and Alcohol Use and Misuse

Cheryl Littleton

Drugs and Alcohol Are Here to Stay

For many thousands of years, alcohol and certain drugs have been used by people of almost every culture in their religious, ceremonial and healing practices. Alcoholic beverages such as wine and mead were incorporated into religious ceremonies in the cradles of civilization; opium was used in Ancient Egypt to alleviate pain, and indigenous persons in pre-Columbian Mexico carved stone idols of psychedelic mushrooms 2,500 years ago. In late twentieth-century North America, we are deceiving ourselves if we think we can eliminate the use of substances by advising people to "Just say no."

To assume that the problem of drug and alcohol misuse can be solved by simply making the right choice when faced with temptation is ignoring much of what we know about the problem. It discounts the part played by poverty and unemployment; the availability and low cost of alcohol and many drugs; family example; emotional needs, such as depression, for feeling "high"; and the role of self-esteem, peer pressure and culture.

In the 1960s, a great deal of attention was focused on a new phenomenon, the teenagers who "turned on and tuned out." Widespread use of drugs such as marijuana, LSD and "speed" by the youth of developed countries was targeted by critics as contributing to the breakdown of society. During the late 1970s, a whole industry was spawned to identify and treat those youth involved in "chemical dependency," later called "substance abuse." The substances being abused covered the whole spectrum, from alcohol to cigarettes to heroin. Psychiatrists, social workers, psychologists, nurses, teachers and many other professionals and non-professionals have been trained to assess, educate and counsel those who abuse drugs and alcohol. Treatment programs, journals, seminars and research institutes have been developed that are devoted to issues of substance use and abuse.

Why Is Adolescence a High-Risk Time?

Adolescence, as with any transition period of life, can be a time of bewilderment and conflict. More changes are taking place physically, emotionally and socially than in any other life stage except infancy. Becoming comfortable with these changes can be difficult for even the most well-adjusted and supported teen. Those teens with special circumstances, such as a history of abuse or neglect, a learning difficulty, a chronic illness, adoption issues, sexual-orientation confusion, family dysfunction, emotional distress or alcohol-/drug-addicted parents, may be especially attracted to drug and alcohol use as an easy means of stress reduction. Coping with the search for personal identity, assuming sexual roles and breaking away from the dependent-child position can catapult the teen into some risky situations. The desire for the freedom to try every possible experience, when coupled with the innate curiosity and enthusiasm of youth, can be a thrilling stage for kids but a time of anxiety and frustration for parents.

When children are in early adolescence, which starts at about age twelve, many parents describe a feeling that their teens are starting to pull away from them. They no longer share after school confidences; kids may resist going places with their parents and seem to spend a lot of time on the phone, and in the bathroom, gazing into the mirror. Around this time, many kids start going to parties and hanging around in groups. Most younger teens still have curfews and limited allowances, so their social activities are usually centred at school or someone's home, but for those determined to experiment, alcohol is easily obtained, either from parents' liquor supplies or from older teens. A limited number of young teens get involved in glue sniffing, as this solvent is cheap and readily available at corner stores. The early teen years are a prime time to start to experiment with smoking cigarettes, especially for girls who are concerned with body image and might start smoking as a means of appetite and weight control. By middle adolescence, fifteen to sixteen years of age, teenagers enjoy more freedom, more money and more temptations. At this stage, many teens will have experimented with marijuana in the form of smokable weed or hash, and perhaps with hallucinogens such as LSD (acid) or "magic" mushrooms. This seems to be the highest-risk age for sexual involvement, entry into the criminal justice system, "bad trips" and visits to the hospital emergency department for alcohol poisoning and related injuries. By the time their kids reach late adolescence, most parents can breathe a sigh of relief. The age of experimentation is over; education takes on more importance, along with a more realistic view of future employment goals; and teens have usually settled into more mature peer relationships.

In the past, parents of teenagers were sold a bill of goods that proclaimed they could not expect — indeed, should not even try — to influence their children as they would be totally ignored in favour of peer values. This idea has now lost credibility as experts in the field have come to believe that the best-adjusted and happiest teens are from families where parents have stayed very much involved in their teens' lives.

Is Drug and Alcohol Use by Teens Inevitable?

The answer to this question depends on whom you ask, and varies from region to region and country to country. One answer is illustrated by the studies conducted by Addiction Research Foundation (ARF) in Toronto. Every few years, for several decades, ARF has administered a confidential questionnaire to thousands of high-school students from four regions of Ontario. Dr. Reg Smart of ARF has examined the trends in teenagers' reported use of drugs, including tobacco and alcohol, and found the highest peak in the 1970s, then a small but steady decline in use until 1993, when the figures failed to show any decline; the 1995 study demonstrated an alarming increase in almost every category. In that year, reported use of marijuana at least once over the past year increased from 12.7 to 22.7 percent and LSD use from 6.9 to 9.2 percent. Heroin, cocaine (including "crack"), solvents (such as glue and gasoline) and amphetamines (stimulants such as speed, Ritalin and Ecstasy) all had a higher rate of reported use.[1]

Despite the reported increase in the use of illegal drugs, the substances still most frequently used by teens are alcohol and tobacco, both sold legally (at least, to adults) and still considered by many to be socially acceptable. However, the ARF studies have shown that 42 percent of Ontario high-school students report never having used alcohol and 62 percent have not smoked cigarettes. The majority of teens do not view their use of alcohol and tobacco as a problem. Often, the only problem they see is getting caught by their parents, teachers or the police. Naturally, the quantity used, the frequency of use and the choice of substance vary greatly. Tobacco is most commonly the first substance used by teens, followed, in order, by alcohol, marijuana and LSD; some teens may then progress to cocaine and heroin. This is often referred to as the "gateway theory" of drug use. Some purists even suggest that caffeine is the original gateway drug!

If you are concerned about your child's use of drugs and alcohol, the following observed behavioural differences among experimental, regular, early addicted and addicted users may give you some perspective:

- First experiences, referred to as *experimental use*, are usually spontaneous and happen because of an opportune set of circumstances. Usually, these experiences are with same-age peers, are the result of curiosity and do not interfere with school or other areas of life. For example, kids may try alcohol and get sick or hung over and either never drink again or learn to decrease their intake.
- A certain percentage of teens will progress to *regular use*. This usually takes place on weekends and is associated with social activities. Some planning is required to obtain the drugs and alcohol. Students may experience a drop in grades and change in friends. Conflict at home may develop.
- Reports from students and teachers suggest that approximately 5 to 10 percent of any high-school population will fall into the category of *early addictive use*. At this level, the substance use occurs almost daily, and tolerance, or the need to increase

amounts to get the same effect, continues to increase. The teen has less control and choice over use and may be having serious problems at school, with parents and with the law. You may notice a withdrawal from responsibility. The teen's energy becomes primarily directed toward obtaining, using, and recovering from the effects of the drug and alcohol use.

- A small number of youth reach the *addictive stage,* which occurs when the person needs drugs to feel normal and is unable to control use. Health problems such as infections may become serious due to poor nutrition and neglect. Personal appearance and general hygiene deteriorate. Teens who are using "crack" cocaine or heroin often feel hopeless and associate only with others with addiction problems. At this stage, users commonly engage in criminal activities such as car theft, house break-ins, prostitution or drug dealing to obtain money for drugs.

Of course, very few teenagers progress from experimental use through to the addictive stage, and it is certainly not true that every teen who smokes a cigarette or has a drink of alcohol will end up as a drug-crazed and homeless person. The people who do become addicts did start somewhere on the continuum, however, and not just parents, but all concerned members of society, have a responsibility to prevent, monitor, intervene and help as much as possible anyone who might be spiralling into trouble. As we approach the end of this century, we cannot be complacent about the potential dangers facing our young people as new and stronger drugs become available.

Is Concern about Drug Use Valid?

Many parents who grew up in the 1970s think that the alarmist reaction of the media and politicians to drug use by today's teens is unwarranted. Maybe they experimented with the occasional "toke" or "hit" themselves and it didn't do them any harm. The strength and composition of today's drugs are much different from those of drugs in common use twenty years ago. New and improved methods of marijuana growing, such as the use of hydroponics (rooting in water), result in a concentration of THC (the active ingredient) as much as six times stronger than in old "weed."

Drug dealers often "lace" marijuana by adding PCP (a potent hallu-cinogen also called "angel dust"), crack, acid, and even rat poison to increase the "jolt." There is no quality control of street drugs, and no way to know what dangerous additives buyers might be exposed to.

Concerns about the increased use of drugs by teenagers are not just about the legal issues, as serious as these can be, but also about the all-too-real risks to physical and mental health; the injuries resulting from activities such as driving, diving and fighting; and the possibility of sexual assault. We are aware of the increase in infectious diseases such as hepatitis and HIV among intravenous drug users; permanent brain, liver and kidney damage in solvent abusers; alcohol poisoning; more respiratory infections, emphysema and, of course, lung cancer in cigarette and marijuana users. Many young women who use drugs and alcohol do become pregnant, and if they continue to expose the developing fetus to these substances, the effects can be very serious. Fetal alcohol syndrome (FAS) or the less-severe fetal alcohol effects (FAE) can result from alcohol ingestion during pregnancy. The babies can experience physical and mental developmental delay and require patient and constant special help. Smoking during pregnancy can result in premature labour and low-birth-weight babies. The use of cocaine during pregnancy can result in premature separation of the placenta, and haemorrhages in the brains of the babies, leading to brain damage or possible death. Heroin and morphine use, particularly in the last trimester, can result in an addicted baby abruptly separated from his drug supply and requiring special care for withdrawal symptoms.

In the last decade, a new area of teen drug use has developed in a place parents may have least expected — the world of sports. A dramatic increase in the use of steroids by both male and female teens from many countries to enhance athletic performance, and the desire to attain a more muscular appearance, has raised concerns about the negative physical risks, ranging from hair loss to aggression, and the increased risk of HIV exposure through shared needles. This trend is illustrated by a Canadian study in 1993 that estimated that 80,000 youth aged eleven to eighteen years reported using steroids.[2] Steroids which are legitimately prescribed as topical ointments and asthma treatment, and for other therapeutic uses, should not be confused with the illegally obtained, injectable cortisone meant for veterinary use but prized by body builders. So, if your teens start sporting impressive new muscles, and experience hair loss, aggressive behaviour and an increase in acne, consider asking them about the use of steroids.

The frequent use of drugs and alcohol seems to go hand in hand with a decline in school performance. Kids report a higher incidence of skipping classes, an inability to concentrate and short-term memory loss. Often, these kids are just too busy living a "druggie" life to fit school, and especially homework, into their schedules. They have to plan how they are going to get the drugs, and how they will have enough money to pay for them. Then they have to decide who they are going to do drugs with, where they will be safe, how to leave the school, what lies to tell parents and teachers about where they have been. They may have had to "borrow" money from parents' wallets or siblings' piggy-banks. They might have to explain red eyes, slurred speech or the "munchies."

What Makes Kids Decide to Do Drugs and/or Alcohol?

"Peer pressure" is often named as the major cause of teen's involvement with substance use. Many parents would like to believe that their child has been pressured by "the wrong crowd" or that horrible kid down the street. All teens like to think of themselves as competent to make their own decisions, and often see their choice to do drugs as a mark of rugged individualism despite saying that "everyone does drugs."

Although teens may be attracted to a drug-using group for a variety of reasons, they never identify a desire to conform or the need to give in to repeated offers as influencing factors. The most commonly cited reasons for younger teens to start using drugs and alcohol are curiosity, boredom, being seen as "cool" or older. Parents may feel that these reasons are forms of peer pressure, but teens don't identify them as such. They always interpret peer pressure as having someone hold a bottle or cigarette to their lips and forcing them to partake, or as the fear of lack of approval from a group if you decline to join in their activities, and this is just not their experience. In fact, most kids tell me that, rather than pressuring them to try drugs or alcohol, older teens will often warn them, "You don't want to get involved in this because it is too hard to quit." For kids who have been using and then quit, there is a lot of envy and encouragement from their friends. Kids who do continue to use drugs say they use them to feel high, forget their problems and be able to enjoy social occasions more.

Research in the area of adolescent substance use suggests the following "markers"[3] can help predict which teens are more likely to start using drugs and alcohol on a more than casual basis:

- *A family history of substance abuse* appears to be a significant marker. Whether you believe the nature (inheriting "bad genes") argument or the nurture (exposure to a "bad environment") argument, the child with a family tree studded with alcohol and drug abusers is at higher risk of developing problems with substances.
- If the teen has *friends who use drugs and alcohol regularly*, it is very difficult for that teen to resist being "one of the gang." The users have convinced themselves that they are "cool" and that non-users are losers.
- Another marker seems to be the *early use of tobacco or alcohol.* Teens who report drinking alcohol and smoking cigarettes before the age of ten seem to advance more quickly through the stages of other drug use.
- *School problems*, particularly those due to learning disabilities and attention deficit disorder, already make young people feel different, and often they feel "stupid." Since they earn few positive strokes from peers, teachers and parents for academic achievement, they feel accepted into drug-using groups, which place value on other forms of achievement.
- *Family dysfunction* is considered to be another marker. Having a parent who is mentally ill, a criminal, a substance abuser, or absent due to death, divorce or desertion increases the chaos in the teen's life.
- A *history of physical abuse, sexual abuse or emotional abuse* can cause the teen to turn to drugs and/or alcohol to deal with the painful memories and current feelings. The psychodynamics which develop from neglect or abuse in the children of alcoholics or other abusers are most commonly low self-esteem, self-blame, and feeling stigmatized, angry and confused.
- *Sexual-orientation issues* often surface in the adolescent period, when sexuality in general is being sorted out. The gay teen dealing with confusion, anxiety and very real fears for safety and acceptance may turn to drugs and alcohol as a way to cope. Places where the teen may feel accepted, such as gay bars, often seem to encourage heavy alcohol consumption.
- *Poor social skills* can make shy teens feel tense and uncomfortable in social situations, and so they seek the disinhibiting effects of alcohol and drugs.

- *Depression* is estimated to be clinically identified in a large number of teens in counselling for substance abuse. Many teens report that some drugs act as antidepressants, and they do not get "high" but just feel normal on drugs. Due to the very real danger of suicide attempts by teens, depression should be taken seriously.
- Teens with a *chronic disease*, even when invisible (such as diabetes), have been observed to drink alcohol and do drugs at a higher rate than their peers. They are often dealing with feelings of resentment, anger and low self-esteem all tied into their self-perception of being "different" from their peers.

What Signs Might Tell Me My Kid Is on Drugs?

Parents often begin to scrutinize their children more closely as they enter the teen years, fearing that the media reports about the horrors of parenting teens will soon be enacted within their own walls. I would caution you to avoid jumping to the conclusion that your child is involved in drug or alcohol use if he or she begins to exhibit changed behaviours and attitudes — they may well be just a normal manifestation of adolescence.

Teens who are falsely accused of "bad" behaviour often feel their parents don't trust them, and trust is a very important issue to teens. They may also consider such an accusation to be a sign that the parents don't care about them, and don't really realize what they are doing. They then rationalize getting into trouble by saying to themselves, "They think I'm doing this anyway, so I might as well really do it." On the other hand, do not ignore your gut reactions. After all, you know your child better than anyone else, so you are best positioned to pick up signs of a "troubled teen." I usually advise parents to stop, look and listen. Trust your instincts and ask lots of questions if you have any concerns about your teens' friends or activities.

Several years ago, a parent support organization called Parents Against Drugs (PAD) published a list of signs that might indicate involvement with substances:[4]

- *Physical changes* such as weight loss, particularly with the use of cocaine and/or amphetamines (i.e. speed), bloodshot eyes from marijuana use, and a runny nose from snorting cocaine.
- *Psychological changes*, which can include becoming more withdrawn, often becoming angry and irritable and seeming to get less enjoyment out of life.

- *Social changes*, such as acquiring a new group of friends, usually older, and spending less time doing activities previously enjoyed.

If you find substance-abuse paraphernalia, such as rolling papers, tubes of glue, pipes, baggies, marijuana plants, or tablets, or bottles of alcohol, in your child's room, you have the right to ask for an explanation. Be prepared to be called a snoop. ("I can't believe you read my diary or listened in to my phone calls or searched my room!") Be prepared for denial. ("How could you think that of me? I'm only keeping these for a friend.")

For a variety of reasons, many parents do not feel that they can talk to their child about their suspicions, and might be tempted to enlist the help of a friend, relative, school counsellor, help line, or even the police, for advice and reassurance. My advice is, as in any conflict resolution, discuss the problem first with the principal person involved, and then, if there is a need for further action, turn to other avenues of support. Imagine the anger and embarrassment the teen would feel when the first inkling she had that her parent is concerned is when she finds herself behind the closed door of a "helping professional" on an invented excuse. Naturally, this common situation is non-therapeutic for all involved.

What Kind of Treatment Is Available?

Even though most people automatically think of teenagers when drug problems are mentioned, the substance-abuse treatment field has been slow to respond to the unique needs of this age group. Most treatment models have merely adapted adult models, without consideration of the very different developmental changes teenagers are going through, both physically and psychologically and their special needs for education, socialization and recreation. It is only in the last decade that there have been programs developed specifically for youth. There is still a great deal to be done to fill the gaps in services for adolescents.

"Risk reduction" was the term for a new approach in the early 1990s, welcomed by those in the drug and alcohol addiction treatment field who had realized that many of the expensive campaigns to warn kids of the dangers of substance use were not at all effective. There were some people who would experiment with drugs despite dire warnings to dissuade them, and perhaps our responsibility was to inform them of the risks involved. This evolved into a relatively new movement within the field of substance abuse called the "harm-reduction approach." The term "harm reduction" applies to strategies which recognize the need to address the harmful consequences of drug use rather than the prevalence of consumption. It started in Europe and has been embraced by Canadian public health agencies at the provincial and federal levels. It is not yet a popular movement in the United States. The basic premise is that, instead of demanding total abstinence from drugs and/or alcohol before help can be offered, it is assumed that use may continue and, if this is so, that the person deserves to be educated as to how best to reduce personal risk. Individual, group and day treatment programs can be based on this philosophy. Condom distribution to prostitutes and clean-needle exchanges and methadone clinics for heroin addicts are some initiatives that demonstrate this principle.

There is still a place for abstinence-based models, particularly in residential programs for those whose use is extensive, increasing in scope and severity, and, in many cases, possibly life-threatening. Many therapists in the field of addictions still employ the twelve-step approach, used for decades by the Alcoholics Anonymous movement. This approach advocates cure of addiction by giving up control to a higher power and acknowledging that one is struggling with an incurable disease. It has had a traditionally male, adult and Christian focus, which did not appeal to most teens, although those who welcome structure seem to respond well. Recently, more flexibility has been introduced. For example, a spiritual power need not necessarily be Jesus but could even be Mother Nature. Hail the Goddess!

What Can I Do to Prevent Problems?

There is no fail-safe way to prevent your child from becoming involved with drugs and/or alcohol, but in my experience few teens who feel valued, loved and supported within their family get into serious trouble.

In a small number of cases, parents who do everything right still end up having kids in trouble. Do not blame yourself and do not hesitate to ask for help.

Talk It Over

It is a cliché to say that maintaining good communication within a family is a crucial cornerstone to reducing the likelihood of serious problems developing. But, like many clichés, it has its roots in truth. Being able to talk openly and honestly with one another strengthens families.

Try to initiate conversations about drugs and alcohol before there is a problem. Don't be afraid to state clearly your own attitudes, values and beliefs. Many parents who tried drugs, and perhaps still use them, may be reluctant to bring up the subject as they fear their children will think they are giving them permission to experiment or that they are being hypocritical. Some experts suggest that the best approach is to say, "Yes, I did try drugs, or used to smoke or drink, but I'm glad I didn't continue and I hope you won't." Role-play with your children what to do or say if offered a cigarette or a drink. Advise them that, when they are of legal age, they can make up their own minds about cigarettes and alcohol, but that, until then, you will not fund or condone illegal and unhealthy practices. Other experts suggest providing a safe place for some experimentation somewhat before they reach legal age, such as serving wine with meals. This allows the teen to consume alcohol in a relaxed social atmosphere, thus diminishing the "forbidden fruit" mystique.

Develop Support in the Family

Build confidence and self-esteem, starting when your child is very young. Be generous with praise and encouragement, and miserly with criticism, teasing and put-downs. Frequently say things like, "You are great. You are wonderful. I love you. You are funny. You are talented." Show your love. Don't be stingy with hugs. Listen and follow through on promises. A bored child is more likely to get into trouble. Enrol your children in as many activities as you and they can manage. Team sports, in particular, seem to have a beneficial effect. Try to have realistic expectations of what they can accomplish, and recognize achievements.

Studies of why some kids from difficult situations still do well in life suggest that resilience can stem from having at least one person who believed in them. It might be a parent, grandparent, a teacher or a friend. Avoid making comparisons among family members. Try to make your love unconditional by not withdrawing your affection if your child does or says something of which you do not approve. Remember what you said to your child at age four: "I love you, but I don't love what you are doing." When there is a problem, try to keep things in perspective. If you are feeling under stress, lying awake at night worrying about your child, or find that you have become preoccupied with looking for signs of a problem, it is time to share your anxieties with a relative, friend, counsellor or spiritual adviser.

Establish Guidelines

Don't be afraid to set up rules and regulations for your family — in a democratic way, of course. Your family life shouldn't resemble boot camp — the authoritarian model — but rather should be based on a cooperative model, where rules are discussed and agreed on by all family members. Many studies find that children feel more secure in families where the boundaries are clearly understood by everyone. Family rules and responsibilities should be updated on a regular basis to reflect growth and changes.

Set a Good Example

Children notice and imitate the way their parents handle alcohol, tobacco and other drugs. It is important to be a good role model. Develop non-chemical ways of handling stress. When you drink or use drugs, don't drive. Don't send your kid to the fridge to get you a beer, or to the corner store to buy your cigarettes. Show your family that you don't have to use drugs or alcohol to have a good time.

Ask about Feelings

Encourage family members to talk about their feelings. Choose a time to talk when people are relaxed, not angry or tense. Let your teens know how much you care for them. If they know how you feel, you can often avoid misunderstandings.

If Prevention Fails

What if you are faced with indisputable evidence that your child is involved with substance use? Perhaps you have had a call from the school, the police or the hospital, or you have found drugs or drug paraphernalia. Parents' most common reactions are shock (How is this possible?), anger (How could you be so stupid?), denial (There must be some mistake), a sense of betrayal (After all we've done for you), self-blame (Where did I go wrong?), fear (Has there been physical or mental damage?) and shame (What will the neighbours say?). If your teen has obviously gone beyond the experimental stage, or if he is underage and you have been clear about not condoning illegal practices, you might go through all the stages of grieving over a loss, as indeed you *have* experienced a loss — one of trust. When trust has been broken, a great deal of work by both parent and child is required to re-establish it. Your efforts are important if the teen is to believe that she is still welcome to come to you for guidance. This is sometimes referred to as the "building bridges, not walls" stage.

Teens often resent being asked to change their behaviour, which they usually do not see as a problem, or to give up associating with certain friends. Teens are often fiercely loyal to their friends and will usually find ways to continue to see them, particularly if there is a romantic involvement. Avoid confrontation when feelings are running high. Wait until things have calmed down. Avoid hostility and blaming.

Try to establish or maintain communication by allowing the teen to explain his side of the story. Through dialogue, arrive at a mutually acceptable list of consequences that are appropriate for his behaviour, and then stick to them. Suggestions such as going for counselling should be broached because the parents are concerned and are involved out of love, not out of an attempt to control or punish. Do not be reluctant to tell the teen that her choices have had an impact on the family. Most teens are so self-centred that they see their lives only in terms of individual freedoms and never think of the worry and disruption their behaviours cause other family members.

In an ideal situation, when parents are concerned about their child's involvement with drugs and alcohol, they should be able to have timely access to an experienced substance-abuse counsellor. This person should, in a supportive and non-judgmental way, assess the extent of use, educate the teen and parents about risks, and initiate counselling or refer you to someone else, as appropriate. The counsellor should recommend support groups for the family as well as for the youth. Many schools have peer and/or mentor programs to assist kids who have experienced substance-abuse problems.

Don't ignore the problem. Don't blame yourself. Don't give up on your kid. Get help. Join or start a parent support group. Get political and lobby for more treatment programs for kids or banning cigarettes or raising the drinking age or getting drug pushers out of your neighbourhood.

It is important for parents to remember that the majority of teenagers choose to abstain from the use of drugs and alcohol or, if they do get involved, it is a brief and experimental flirtation. All the values you have taught your children and the good advice you have given will eventually prevail, and your teen will weather the turbulent, but time-limited, period of adolescence safely and confidently. And you, the parent, will uncross your fingers, sleep more soundly and celebrate the transition of your teen to young adulthood.

Notes

1. E. Adlaf et al., *1995 Ontario Youth and Drug Survey* (Toronto: Addiction Research Foundation, 1996).

2. Canadian Centre for Drug-Free Sport, *The National Survey on Drugs and Sport*, conducted by Price Waterhouse, 1993, quoted in Steve Newman's article in *Canadian Medical Association Journal* 151, 6 (1994), pp. 844-6.

3. Deborah Lindsay et al., "Alcohol and Substance Abuse by Adolescents: A Statement of the Canadian Paediatric Society," in *The Canadian Journal of Paediatrics* 1, 3 (1994), pp. 94-5.

4. These points are listed with the permission of Parents Against Drugs, a Canadian organization with chapters across the country.

A is for Advocate: Parenting through Secondary School

Carol Ricker-Wilson

It's not just what you know ...

It's Tuesday, 1:40 p.m. and your fifteen-year-old is in school, right? Not bad, given a daily absentee rate at some high schools approaching 20 percent.[1] But assuming she's bodily present at her desk, does she want to be? How safe and self-confident does she feel at the moment? What exactly is she doing in that classroom that might engage her, emotionally and intellectually, to the degree required for her to aspire to academic success, which might mean anything from obtaining her grade-twelve diploma to securing the 92 percent average needed to vie for a university placement in Pharmacy? And how might you, her parent, best be her advocate as she charts her complicated course through the often rocky terrain of secondary education? An advocate supports, defends, espouses the cause of or pleads in favour of another. Your secondary-school child needs you to advocate for her now as much as she did in elementary school.

Profound transformations in every sector of the workforce currently compel students who once would have moved straight from graduation into jobs to strive instead for a postsecondary education. Downsizing, relocation, automation and cutbacks mean it's no longer enough to simply graduate. Today, academic achievement is more necessary than it's ever been. Nonetheless, a significant number of thoughtful and articulate young people across the ethnocultural and socio-economic spectrums continue to underachieve, disengage or drop out, often in increments, skipping an increasing number of classes until they've lost a credit or a year. Others hang in but take little pleasure in the seven-hour-a-day, ten-month-a-year confines of compulsory education. They have reached the critical point at which disaffection with schooling, by which I mean the dynamic interactions of the school environment with its inhabitants, activities and materials, overrides the desire to learn and the compulsion to obtain that diploma. What is it that so disaffects them?

Academic achievement depends on motivation, and motivation is inextricably linked with self-image. But self-image is undermined when students find the process of becoming educated a boring, alienating, demoralizing or punitive experience. Schooling's hierarchical structure, its heterogeneous student body, and the curriculum itself interact in numerous and complicated ways to affect a young person's self-image and level of motivation. Because children enter school with diverse values and experiential and cultural knowledge, becoming educated is never simply about processing and reproducing the material teachers pour into their presumedly receptive brains. It's about perpetually negotiating a relationship to the particular knowledge being presented to them. It's about attempting to negotiate safe and reasonable interactions with those who determine, very prescriptively, what they learn, and measure, always subjectively, how well they have learned it. Becoming educated is also about negotiating multiple and unpredictable interactions with peers, some of whom are intolerant of difference as a specific individual might represent it for them. In short, becoming educated, for many young people, is a complicated and constant struggle for dignity and autonomy in circumstances that don't easily lend themselves to either.

I write this as someone who knows how much is at stake when students become disaffected with schooling. I'm a former student "underachiever," a parent of two preadolescents, and a teacher of twenty years. These lengthy experiences with schooling, in conjunction with my research, have led me to recognize that academic success depends largely on some combination of five inextricably linked factors:

- The more sensitive parents are to their children's specific emotional and educational needs, the more children want to please them.
- The more comfortable children feel in the learning environment itself, the more risk and responsibility they are willing to take.
- The more committed the school is to addressing equity issues such as plurality in learning styles, multiple abilities and cultural diversity, the more comfortable the learning environment.
- The more empowered parents are to advocate for their children's specific needs, the more compelled the school is to address them.
- Finally, the more access families have to material and cultural resources, the easier it becomes to reinforce and ensure their children's academic success.

… but who you are

Historically, the learning environment in developing countries has been most comfortable for white, middle-class children. Critical educational theorists Samuel Bowles and Herbert Gintis, in the United States, Paul Willis in Britain, and Bruce Curtis, David Livingstone and Harry Smaller in Canada, describe the Western phenomenon of compulsory education as a decidedly undemocratic process in which the hard work of many students has not been ultimately rewarded by social mobility and economic success. Rather, these critics argue, schooling has systematically produced a workforce in which students learn to take their place, after graduation, on the same rung of the socio-economic ladder as did their parents. The myth that the poorest child can some day become bank manager has been just that. Historically, when girls, children of colour and working-class students did make it into university and high-paying sought-after jobs, it was more a fortuitous anomaly than the norm.[2]

It wasn't academic ineptitude, for example, that shunted Alice, a truck driver's daughter, into the secretarial track in her Buffalo, New York, high school. Her speech, home address and other subtleties enabled teachers to classify her as a working-class girl and, in the early 1960s, bright, white, working-class girls became secretaries. It was that simple. When my father, himself a teacher and her great-uncle, visited

Alice's family and heard about the gap between her grade-point average and her "pink collar" placement, he marched straightaway to her school guidance counsellor, whom he none too gently queried as to why she was in the vocational program. Alice was subsequently "reassessed" and has long since obtained her Ph.D. Alice and her parents did not believe, given their social status at that time and place, that they could successfully challenge her placement. It was my father's middle-class mannerisms, knowledge and position that enabled him, ironically, to challenge the school's middle-class biases, to advocate to Alice's benefit.

Not every child is so fortunate. Some studies have documented how the deliberate or unwitting biases of schooling's predominantly white, middle-class teachers and administrators have systemically operated, through formal or informal, subtle or overt mechanisms, to stream students into non-academic or academic courses with little reference to their potential or actual school performance. Working-class children and children of colour must constantly address the fact that, to their detriment, their own values, cultural experiences and ways of speaking and acting are not considered the institutional norm.[3]

Bias also permeates the curriculum. Academic performance is profoundly affected by the manner in and degree to which students see themselves represented in the curriculum. A curriculum that presents all knowledge from a male and Anglo-European perspective has historically denigrated, ignored or marginalized the lives of all other peoples. A considerable body of research indicates that, where girls and children of colour are underrepresented in texts or depicted in subordinate or stereotypic roles, their self-image and academic performance deteriorate. It's hard to imagine oneself in a profession from which one has historically been barred, due to gender, class or race — which may be why, in the late 1990s, in North America, it's still disproportionately white, middle-class males who make it into many of the highest-paying professions and the institutional positions of power they are thus ensured.[4]

So much for the bad news. The good news is that, in the thirty years since Alice graduated, departments and ministries of education, school boards and individual schools have begun, albeit unevenly and sporadically, to respond to calls from parent advocates and progressive educators for more equitable education for all children. So, even though secondary schools, with their multiple players, will never be uniformly safe, engaging, enabling spaces, this awareness has translated into some wonderful initiatives, programs and policies which have encouraged a wider variety of children to achieve academically. In the narratives below, parents and young people from diverse backgrounds relate histories of resistance to and engagement with schooling. In each case, you can see the degree to which the five factors noted above have interacted to enable or disable children from acquiring positive self-images and academic achievement.

Lindsay

Lindsay is in grade nine at a school with an applied-science and technology focus. The family bible, passed down through her seventeenth-century Norwegian paternal forbears, is displayed on one of several venerable and graceful carved wooden chests in her home. Floor-to-ceiling bookshelves are stacked with old favourites and current acquisitions. A lovingly nurtured and economically privileged child, Lindsay has found little, at home or at school, that did not support her.

"We've always tried to help our children cultivate a positive self-image," says her mother, Deirdre, a social-housing planner and professional partner to her architect husband. Lindsay's parents have been energetic, thoughtful advocates of their children's education. When Lindsay briefly required academic remediation, her parents could afford a tutor. When what they perceived to be an overly zealous teacher suggested Lindsay had a learning disability, her parents felt empowered to challenge this. On their own, they took her to a specialist, who determined there was nothing to warrant such a designation. "You choose your battles," Deirdre declared. "We worried about the message it would send Lindsay if she had to go to a learning centre."

Through familial and professional contacts, they become aware of opportunities from which Lindsay might benefit, such as the Ontario Legislative Page Program, the only one of its kind in Canada, in which middle-school students may participate. By grade eight, Lindsay's self-discipline, high marks and engagement in extracurricular activities helped win her a coveted spot in this program. "It was spectacular!" Lindsay exclaimed. "I was able to meet all of Ontario's political leaders. I felt important, like I was part of something that made a difference."

Her frequent visits to a highly educated extended family, members of which are located throughout North America and Europe, have given Lindsay first-hand knowledge of geography and other cultures that most children acquire only passively from maps and texts. On one trip to England, her family visited only specific sites they'd read about in children's books. She remarked, "My teachers never fussed if my parents wanted to take me out of school for a trip. They really liked me and gave me breaks. They even accepted excuses when my homework was late."

In short, a substantial number of Lindsay's learning experiences contributed to her self-confidence, which in turn contributed to her motivation to achieve. She has rarely felt discomfort in any learning environment and, when she did, it was quickly redressed.

Given her variety and wealth of experience, it's not surprising that Lindsay, at fourteen years old, is already focused on selecting the best university at which to major in math, education or psychiatry. She plans to fast-track through high school, graduating early, and to travel around the world after university.

Although Lindsay may change her mind more than once in the next four years, and will certainly be subject to life's vagaries and tensions, there is little to suggest, given her past experience and present drive and inclinations, that she will not continue to achieve the kind of academic success which assures her an intellectually rich and occupationally rewarding existence. Should her parents' financial futures be uncertain, Deirdre noted that there's money invested for the children in registered education plans. Having enjoyed a fortuitous configuration of caring parents who possess the creative bent and savvy to access community resources and opportunities to her benefit, material privilege and comfortable school environments, Lindsay has responded to the demands of school with self-discipline and assurance.

Miriam and Stephanie

Miriam, fourteen, attends the same school as Lindsay, but it's not been such a favourable environment for her. Nor did she recollect any of her earlier Canadian schooling experiences very positively. She came to Canada in grade six from what she described as a radically different school system. "In Catholic school, in Trinidad, the work was extremely challenging. Teachers gave detailed explanations for what we were supposed to do, and there were straightforward, strict consequences for bad behaviour. There we were doing about grade-eleven math in class; when I came here it was at about grade-one level."

A strong student throughout elementary school, Miriam was able to choose her present secondary school not just because of its science and technology focus, but because "it expected a lot from you; you'd be pushed hard to do more work than usual. Also wearing a school uniform would save money."

Saving money is extremely important in Miriam's life. She is one of four children, and her self-employed father is finding few home-renovation projects in these harsh economic times. Her mother, Paula, has recently been dismissed from her job in a nursing home, so the family has moved into subsidized housing in a low-income area of the city, with the result that Miriam now commutes three hours a day between home and school.

Eventually Miriam would like to become a photographer, and Paula hopes to help her purchase a camera. But, for now, Miriam's simplest material desires are on hold. A prolific and diverse reader in a school where talk of college and university is the norm, Miriam, aware of her family's financial constraints, hasn't even considered the subject of further education. "It's pretty far off yet," she commented. "At this point I hope to find a part-time job so I can get a camera."

Furthermore, even though her present school is challenging, it's not an altogether comfortable place for her. Somewhat hesitantly she described how race affects her comfort level in a school where about 15 percent of the students are Black. She described the behaviour of one teacher who ignores Black students when they put their hands up to answer questions, and concluded, "Mostly it's hard to define. It's how some people look at me when I'm talking to a white person, like 'What do I think I'm doing?' It's how some move away when they're near me. Then there's one girl who says really bad things about Black people."

When I asked if Miriam was aware of her school board's policy to address racist language and actions, she replied, "It wouldn't solve anything by talking to teachers about it. It won't solve how anyone feels."

As Miriam is clearly aware, the school by itself has a limited ability to regulate behaviour. Furthermore, in such a site of perpetually unequal power relations, it is not easy for students to risk protesting the behaviour of those evaluating them. When school is a contradictory place in which those supposed to be protecting students from discrimination are the very ones students perceive to be practising it, this can have a profoundly negative effect on minority students' motivation, performance and prospects.

Stephanie, a Black grade-twelve student with an 82 percent average, is no more economically privileged than Miriam. She lives with her grandmother, a retired factory worker, who supports Stephanie solely by her pension. But Stephanie attends a school that provides her with an emotionally greater comfort level. Thanks to its extraordinarily diverse student population, a mélange of Somalis, Serbs, Tamils, Vietnamese, Turks, Jamaicans, Tibetans and Portuguese, there is no visible majority. Stephanie sees this as positive.

"The students are accepting. They're all mixed around in class, but at lunch the Blacks all hang out together, and the Chinese do, and so does everyone else. I don't know why, but it's comfortable."

Black students often find themselves in what Black American educational theorist John Ogbu believes is an uncomfortable and paradoxical position. Ogbu argues that, although Blacks historically struggled "for education and equality of educational opportunity as a form of opposition against white people who denied them access to [it],"[5] and although they continue to desire an education which might broaden their prospects for meaningful work and economic security, many tend to associate the behaviours required for academic success with the white, middle-class system which has barred them from the possibility of obtaining these very aspirations. Consequently, to engage in what they perceive to be "white" and "middle-class" behaviours such as being punctual and exerting academic effort, to succeed by the very standards of those who have marginalized them, is to compromise Black students' ethnocultural and, frequently, class identities. Those who fail, skip and drop out might be signalling both their disaffection with and resistance to an educational system which they feel marginalizes them. Those who practise behaviours of achievement may be subject to their Black peers' criticism. For these reasons, it can be very alienating to be Black and do well in school.[6]

However, what might be considered a critical mass — a third to a half of all students — in Stephanie's advanced-level classes are Black.

Stephanie is not only part of a sociocultural community in which she's "comfortable," she's also part of a supportive academic community of Black students and several Black teachers who, by their very presence and interactions with each other in the larger school environment (where most of those in authority are white), create a space where it is, qualifiedly, permissible and comfortable to succeed. Although Stephanie does not find the curriculum itself especially sensitive to the interests of students of colour, she does find it meaningful to participate in Black history assemblies and an after-four Black Studies program run by the Black teachers at her school. Here both cultural pride and academic achievement are continually nurtured.

As well, attuned to the fact that its low-income Portuguese and Afro-Caribbean students are among those least likely to succeed, Stephanie's school has taken a particularly novel measure to address the problem. It has initiated a "Steps to University" program, a school board initiative in which students unlikely to imagine pursuing higher education are encouraged to take an on-site university credit course in social science to get a taste of what is possible. More than half the students who take the course enrol in postsecondary programs the following year. Were Stephanie not already considering postsecondary education, she has the profile to be nominated by her teachers for the program.

Like Lindsay, both Stephanie and Miriam enjoy emotional support at home. "It's hard to explain," Stephanie mused, "but my grandmother is my life. She's raised me since I was three months old and has enormous influence on me. I do things to make her proud and make myself proud as well. She couldn't always come to parent-teacher nights and stuff because she did shift work. But now, since she's retired, she's at every assembly I'm in and any event I'm part of at school. She's always there. She'll cancel appointments to be there."

"My mother pushes me hard," noted Miriam. "She believes in working hard physically and mentally and she taught me to believe in myself. Try hard. Do your best."

Added Paula, Miriam's mother and the first in her family to attend college, "We came here [Canada] to better ourselves. We want our children to achieve something higher. When I first came here I only could bring two of my children. I worked night and day to make a living for them and went to nursing school at the same time. I sent for the others once I got immigrant status and could afford to bring them. We represent the Canadian dream."

Obtaining the dream of higher education will not be easy for either young woman in the present economy, where it's hard to find even a minimum-wage job that might enable them to earn tuition. Said Stephanie, "Tuition fees are getting higher. I'll have to get a student loan for college. There may be no jobs. But even if there isn't right away, it'll still be worth it. If you're good you just better yourself. The money you spend just can't compare to your talents and education."

Mike

Mike, eighteen, is excelling in his final year at the same school Stephanie attends. A peer counsellor and big brother to a disabled child, he comments, with pleasure, "At the beginning of last year, I kept ending up in the vice-principal's office because of my lates and absences. Now I'm in there 'cause I'm on the School Safety Committee."

"In grade eleven in my old school," Mike recalled, "I started to hang out with the wrong crowd. I began skipping a lot and my grades slipped. At the end of the term, me and my mother met with the guidance counsellor. It was either stay and get no credits, or change to a semestered school."

"I know in this society you need a diploma," remarked his mother, Teresa. "Mike keeps telling me there are no jobs, but a diploma at least gives you a better chance."

Nineteen years ago Teresa came to Canada from the Azores with a grade-six education. "I always wanted to be a teacher," she said. "My teacher sent my father a letter begging him to let me go on for teacher's training, but he was old-fashioned. He said, 'No, school's for boys.'"

Now Teresa works mainly as a home and office cleaner, and Mike's Portuguese-born father is an industrial cleaner. "I don't like my job, but I had no choice," declared Teresa. "I wanted Mike to have a choice."

"My mother would have let me get a job if I'd wanted to," added Mike. "If school hadn't been my thing. If it'd made me really unhappy. On the other hand, I knew how important school was to her. With her help and the guidance counsellor's, I decided to change schools and not quit until I found a job.

"I was a good kid, but quiet," Mike continued. "I'd never really applied myself. I started skipping because I was bored. But I was bored because I didn't pay attention. I realized that I had to make a choice. I asked myself what I really wanted. A minimum-paying job?" Mike's first-hand experience helping his mother clean offices and occasional stints as a dishwasher and cook gave him a sense of the tedium of such labour. Gradually his priorities changed.

"At first, it was hard. I began skipping again and I'd end up seeing the guidance counsellor. But because he was a friend of my uncle's, I felt there was extra support for me. I felt a sense of belonging in this school. He really listened when I talked. I liked his style."

By increments, over the next sixteen months, Mike began attending to his course work, obtaining better grades and gaining the self-confidence to risk more. "I started to accomplish something," he recalled. "Teachers started saying good things about me. Some encouraged me to become a peer; another pushed me at math to the point where I was helping others with it."

Mike's own personable manner was certainly a factor in his ability to acquire these numerous mentors. But Mike attributes a lot of his success to his mother. "She never yelled at me. She gave me options. She would talk to me and was always involved in what I was doing."

"If I see a problem," added Teresa, "I want to solve it. I would try to get a tutor or find extra help for the children if there was a problem."

Teresa's own thwarted aspirations made her a strong and sensitive advocate to Mike's academic needs. Attempting to negotiate a balance between birth and adopted cultures, and to give Mike an edge, she encouraged him to speak only English with her at home, although he speaks Portuguese with his father. Once Mike found a supportive learning environment, he thrived. Finally, he has reason to be optimistic about the future. His own willingness to contribute, combined with savings from his parents' years of hard work, will ensure his partial tuition for postsecondary school.

"If I fail, I can always say I gave it my best shot," declared Mike, who hopes to pursue a college or university program in computer programming and design. "I can't look down on myself. Right now I don't think I've reached my potential. I've got more to do."

Nor has Teresa reached hers. She says, "I'm not in the right job. But I'm not going to stay there my whole life."

Jenn

You might have noticed that three of the four young people described thus far live with both parents. Stephanie's narrative challenged simplistic, conservative notions about the "dysfunctionality" of the single-parent family, and so does Jenn's. She's twenty, a second-year university student in civil engineering. Before Jenn began grade school, her mother, Marjan, an early-childhood educator from the Netherlands, separated amicably from Jenn's father, a Dutch-American immigrant who has held a variety of jobs, mainly in the garment industry. Today both parents pay a portion of their two daughters' university tuition.

"In postwar Holland, money was fairly tight," noted Marjan. "But there were lots of activities that didn't cost a lot, and from my parents I learned how to budget, to invest."

Early on, Jenn embraced her mother's money-management techniques, saving her summer earnings, and expects to have no debt when she leaves university. "Since I help pay for it, I have a different attitude from some of my friends whose parents even pay their credit-card charges. I attend all my classes. I work really hard. I want to get my money's worth. I save for when I need it."

There were several factors in the school system itself which enabled Jenn to achieve academically and made the environment welcoming to her. During her childhood, she received no private lessons and had few of the material trappings of the middle-class life, but she became involved in many school-based extracurricular activities. "These made all the difference in keeping school fun and interesting," she said.

She also benefited from special education. Although there is considerable controversy concerning who gets designated as "learning disabled" (a term disproportionately applied to working-class and minority children) and to what degree this label benefits them, academic support for children so designated is now widely available in urban and rural areas throughout the English-speaking world, and sometimes such special attention can be a blessing. Jenn was identified as needing a remedial program in grade four.

"I couldn't read or write very well, and I spelled terribly. I also had an attitude of resistance to learning how to do these things." As her learning-centre teacher helped Jenn learn writing strategies and increased her comfort level with the material, her motivation increased.

Although Jenn continued throughout school to experience difficulty with the mechanics of writing, her teachers didn't penalize her unduly for this; recognizing her analytic skills, they tended to value content over style. As well, having two articles published which she wrote during high school made a huge difference in her attitude toward her ability. "I still can't spell and my handwriting is sloppy," she declared, "but the computer has made life much easier. I can move blocks of copy, my work looks much neater and I spend a lot of time using spell-check."

Jenn has also benefited from feminist research on education which has determined that girls across the socio-economic spectrum lose confidence in themselves as they progress through school and tend to fare poorly in maths and sciences, the very areas in which they might hope to acquire a measure of economic and social equity with men. Sensitive to historic gender-based inequities, for two decades Jenn's school board has employed full-time Women's Studies consultants, who have, with teachers, coordinated numerous initiatives to enhance girls' esteem and academic opportunities. Consequently, Jenn twice enjoyed in-school opportunities to attend presentations by and about women in non-traditional careers. What she heard on these occasions was encouraging as she moved toward the decision to major in engineering.

In the aftermath of the 1989 Montreal Massacre, in which fourteen women, thirteen of whom were engineering students at École Polytechnique in Montreal, Quebec, were systematically separated from their male peers and executed by a psychopath who contended that "feminists" had ruined his life, Canadian universities, in conjunction with professional associations, have made efforts to create a more positive climate for women in science and technology.[7] That 30 percent of the engineering students in Jenn's university are now female indicates the profound inroads feminism has made in young women's lives. Jenn believes both that some of her male peers are conscious of their own historic privilege and that others "know it's unacceptable to make any negative comments about women."

The financial constraints of Jenn's family have derived, not primarily from its single-parent status, but from the historic and ongoing systemic undervaluing of those, generally women, professionally engaged in child care. But Marjan's modest salary was counterbalanced by her emotional resources and her adaptation of attitudes and behaviours acquired from her own parents. She used this knowledge to empower Jenn.

Peter

Like Jenn, Peter also has a learning disability. Age twenty-four, this Canadian-born son of Yugoslavian immigrants is in his last year of a community college program to become a child and youth yorker. After he failed grade three, he was diagnosed as dyslexic. "I was in special ed. classes for one or two periods a day for about as long as I can remember — right up until grade ten. I felt different. About then I started to believe they weren't helping me anymore and that to be designated 'l.d.' was a self-fulfilling prophecy." Peter asked for decreased support and subsequently withdrew from the program. But the strategies he learned there have served him well in university.

"I became adept at listening and memorization. I have excellent attendance, and photocopy other students' notes since I can't write fast enough. I begin my papers well in advance [of the due date] and do them on computer."

About the time Peter was feeling confident enough academically to forgo special-education support, he was forced to address a major assault on his identity. If, historically, female students have not fared as well as they might have in school, gay and lesbian students have faced such absolutely virulent homophobia from their peers — and lack of protest against it from their teachers — that it's amazing any of them make it through the system with their self-image intact. Indeed, a disproportionate number commit suicide.

"Out" as a gay male since grade eight, Peter increasingly became the object of his peers' homophobia. In grade eleven he suffered continual harassment and, one day, was gay-bashed by ten older students from his school. Friends offered to help him get back at his assailants, and one acted as his body guard, protecting Peter during a second assault, but it was exceedingly stressful. "I felt so isolated. My grandmother died that year, my best friend didn't speak to me again after I told him I was gay, I was seeing the school psychiatrist and contemplating suicide. I didn't finish the semester."

Fortunately, Peter benefited from a unique educational initiative. He began to attend and receive support from a lesbian, gay and bisexual support group, the only board of education-based one in Canada. This helped him feel less isolated and more secure in his identity. As well, like most of the students described here, he had easy access, in his urban venue, to diverse learning environments and finally found, in alternative schools, a place where he could feel safe and comfortable. "Both the alternative schools I attended," he stated, "were gay-positive environments. In the second school, the one I graduated from, people were very matter-of-fact when I told them I was gay."

Each alternative school has a student population that's nearer to 100 than 1,000, and while these schools have diverse programs and student populations, their teaching staffs tend to share and espouse consciously progressive agendas. Teachers and students actively discourage sexist, racist and homophobic behaviour. Hierarchical interactions as well are diminished by various strategies. Students and teachers are on a first-name basis, students have a say in determining who gets hired, and they often deliberate, with teachers, about course offerings and disciplinary measures. Finally, size itself enables these schools to be more nurturing, personable environments than is the norm.

Peter recalled, "I realized I could be myself there, and the other students actually started to socialize me. They accepted me but wouldn't let me talk about my gayness all the time. At the same time, I could do a gay monologue in drama and be applauded. I enjoyed coming to school. I felt safe. It was fun." Once Peter found a comfortable and supportive learning environment, he had the energy to focus on academics.

Throughout his difficulties, Peter's mother, a teaching aide, supported his decisions. "My dad's a school custodian. He wasn't really into my schooling," Peter stated. "But my mother was always involved in my education. Since my reading was slow, she'd help me select and cut out articles. She'd read to me when I had trouble. But most importantly, both my parents supported what I wanted to do. When I wanted to stop special ed. they supported me. Even though they had reservations about me dropping out and attending alternative schools, they still supported me. They gave me lots of independence. They trusted me. If I had any advice to give parents as a son and youth worker, it's this: If your kids want to do something, you don't necessarily have to know why. They have a purpose and need to do it. You have to give them room."

Brad and Naomi

While students in North America have reasonable access to remedial education programs, whatever their geographic location, most of the other initiatives and resources described throughout this essay are primarily available in urban settings, where a greater number of parents and educators have demanded them. It's relatively simple to transfer schools if you live in a city of 2 million, but what do you do if you live in a village of 700?

Brad and Naomi, from, respectively, rural and small-town settings, recalled the relatively limited support services and initiatives their small schools offered and their dependence on individuals and out-of-school support for academic encouragement.

Brad, whose family hails from rural Quebec, related how teachers and schools "read" their class identity and discouraged their academic efforts. "My father was dirt poor, from a family of eight. He was overweight and constantly teased about it. One day the gym teacher, who picked on him a lot, called him 'Pudgy' and my father punched him. He was immediately expelled. He eventually tried to complete high school but never did. He had a strong work ethic though. He put in sixteen- and eighteen-hour days driving trucks, in construction, as a meat packer, to support us so my mother could stay home with us. I'm the first in my extended family to finish high school and the first to graduate from university. And I did it in style; I graduated with high distinction."

It was not easy for Brad, twenty-seven, recently hired for his first teaching job, to get to this point. A voracious reader, he was easily bored in school. Primarily to "keep him out of trouble," one teacher kept giving him more challenging math texts, so that he completed grade-nine math in grade five. He has no recollection of any formal enrichment or gifted program offered in his school, but had there been one he doubted he would have been selected for it. By his own definition he was "a clown. I distracted everyone. My family had a reputation as troublemakers and, since we were visibly poor and I acted up, none of my teachers gave me the time of day. Except for one I had in eighth grade when I was getting wretched grades. One day he said, 'You're talented and wasting it.' He took a lot of time to talk to me. From that point on I got straight A's." About the same time Brad joined a local church and found it instrumental in changing his life. "I found good friends there who sustained me. I'd been getting into minor trouble before. But between my new faith and new friends, my whole attitude and direction began to shift."

While Brad, in his words, "broke the chain" of poverty and its vicissitudes, his siblings haven't fared as well. He believes that, because of how the school understood his family, a "learning disability" diagnosis was wrongfully applied to both his brother, now a talented but self-destructive electrician who dropped out of high school, and his sister. His experience with schooling's biases have shaped his own understanding of teaching.

"All during my practice-teaching experiences," reflected Brad, "I've looked for the quiet kids. The troublemaking kids. The kids with tons of talent and no money. They're the ones that need coddling. If you can make them feel good about themselves, it will carry them for years."

In contrast, Naomi, a twenty-two year old divinity student from a town of 700, acknowledged how advantageous was her own family's social standing in her community. When her middle-class parents, both educators, advocated for her to receive individualized enrichment activities in school in the absence of any formal program, the school was quite receptive to it. When they related Naomi's need for a time management program, that, too, was provided her.

She relied, as well, on efforts of individual teachers and her church to acquire what she needed. She recalled her response to a relatively simple action on the part of her male Physics teacher to make a space in his class for gender equity. "He showed a film featuring women in non-traditional occupations. This reinforced my own interest in science and encouraged my sister to become an engineer."

Subsequently, through her church's youth-group network, Naomi and her sister both found families to board with so that they might attend an specialized urban science school in their final secondary-school year.

But students shouldn't need to rely solely on the highly arbitrary efforts of individual teachers to nurture them. Many students may never establish any such personal connections, which is why it is crucial that schools envision themselves as learning communities, in which institutional initiatives to create equitable and supportive climates are available to all.

Advocacy begins at home

The caregivers mentioned here knew when to push and when to give their children space. But they also took actions, long before secondary school, that contributed significantly to their children's prospects of achieving academic success. In every family I interviewed, reading was highly valued. Several parents mentioned frequent trips to public libraries and reading with their children.

"Books were very important to our family," declared Deirdre. "Her dad read to Lindsay every night until she was nine. We'll buy them pretty well any book they want as long as it's not hardcover."

"As a child," Miriam noted, "I found it easy to read. My dad used to read to me a lot. Reading expands my mind."

And Brad recalled how, in a family of TV watchers, his mother's reading encouraged his own.

Parents were also involved, in ongoing and active ways, with their children's homework. Miriam recalled, "My mother would get me to do my homework before I watched TV. So now, even if I don't have homework I'll pick up a book instead of watching TV."

Marjan remembered her own mother making tea for her and her siblings when they'd return from school, then talking with them about their day. "Then we'd work on our homework at the table. My mother would work on the same math problems along with us. We were sharing. She showed us that she was interested in us and made it fun." Marjan employed similar strategies with her daughters. "Since I didn't know Canadian history, I'd ask them to tell me about it and had them leave their books out so I could read them after they finished. I'd get the kids to show me how to connect the VCR and learn to use the computer."

"It really helped that she was involved," added Jenn. "And later on she knew when not to harass me about doing my homework."

As a teacher, I've advised parents that their teens who shun homework might simply need a kick start. Even though we expect them to behave as adults, they still might require their parents to direct them to a place to do it. They might enjoy being within close proximity to their parents or siblings while they study. Many young people don't study well in silence and isolation. They need to ask questions, to talk before they write, to share what they're doing, to be gently reminded to stay on task. Even if you can't help with that math problem, you can see that it's done. If your child can't do it, you know where she needs more help and can respond accordingly by writing a note to the teacher pointing out the need for more support. Many students are reluctant to ask for additional help on their own.

While their children were growing up, the majority of mothers, fathers and grandmothers described here worked outside the home part- or full-time, in a variety of physically and mentally demanding positions. But far from resenting or perceiving them as neglectful, their children gained from working parents an understanding of what it was possible to become and achieve. Indeed, one Canadian study initiated by educational theorists John Porter, Marion Porter and Bernard R. Blisher illustrates this point: the daughters of mothers employed in lower-paying jobs were more likely to aspire to university (23 percent compared with 14 percent) than those whose mothers were unemployed.[8] In each case I've described here, it was these working parents' nurturing and advocacy that encouraged their children to strive to do their best.

Failure is a place you visit

In twenty years of teaching, I've never met a stupid child. Certainly some can't write well or solve quadratic equations, and many never will, but, with time, proper strategies and encouragement, many can learn far more than they ever anticipated. Sometimes, when it seems a student can no longer open a book or put pen to paper, I have recommended to families that dropping out could be of immense value if students drop in to a job or volunteer activity which might nurture self-image and give them the time, space and experience in which to think about what they want and need from school. The term "drop out" should not suggest someone who forever drops off the face of the educational planet into failure. Today students drop out and back in to school all the time. In one particularly articulate and motivated grade-eleven class I taught, one-third were former "drop-outs"! Many former drop-outs and underachievers re-enter education in night school or adult-education classes. Having learned how much they don't know, mature students are almost invariably motivated. It's astounding how well people do in courses when they choose to be in school and have a real goal based on lived experience.

The mind is never static. People learn when they need to, when they feel it matters, when it's safe. No one can predict the number of times your child will visit failure. But the more familiar you are with the educational terrain, the greater the chances of finding a path through it if it looks like your child is stuck. And since your child is only one of many who is experiencing difficulty, consider the measures you might take, as a member of your learning community, to widen the path not only for him or her, but for all of its children. No child can ever have too many advocates.

Notes

1. Daily absentee rates have long been a problem, vary widely, depend on environment and parental income level and, in general, increase with grade level. Joseph Adwere-Boamah's American study, *Project MACK: Final Evaluation Report* (Oakland, CA: 1974-5), documents successful efforts to decrease the 23 percent daily class-cutting rate in an Oakland, CA, school to 7.2 percent. The National Council for Education Statistics, U.S. Department of Education, in *The Condition of Education* (1990-1), noted, on average, an 8 percent daily absentee rate for rural schools and a 12 percent rate for centre-city schools.

2. See: Samuel Bowles and Herbert Gintis, *Schooling in Capitalist America* (New York: Basic Books, 1976); Bruce Curtis, David Livingstone and Harry Smaller, *Stacking the Deck: The Streaming of Working Class Kids in Ontario Schools* (Toronto: Our Schools/OurSelves, 1992); and Paul Willis, *Learning to Labour: How Working Class Kids Get Working Class Jobs* (New York: Columbia University Press, 1977).

3. Bruce Curtis, David Livingstone and Harry Smaller.

4. For example, a report on the economic and demographic trends for U.S. women during the 1980s found that, while the number of women completing college doubled over the previous two decades, those with the same years of higher education made substantially lower incomes than their male peers. In the specific occupations of educational administration, "minority women lagged behind their white counterparts" proportionately in both job acquisition and income level (Cecilia Ottinger, "Women in Higher Education: Where Do We Stand?" in *Research Briefs* 4, 2 {1993}).

5. John Ogbu, "Class Stratification, Racial Stratification, and Schooling," in *Class, Race and Gender in American Education*, Lois Weis (ed.) (Albany, NY: State University of New York Press, 1988).

6. Subtle and overt streaming by dominant-culture educators of minority and lower-income students into non-academic courses, in conjunction with these students' resistance to and disaffection with such streaming, may account for such statistics as the following. For example, the 1991 Board of Education for

the City of Toronto *Every Student Survey* (Toronto: Board of Education, 1993) indicates that Black students are disproportionately overrepresented in "basic" and "general" secondary-school-level courses, which significantly affect their prospects for postsecondary education and bar them from eligibility for university. Representing 9 percent of the student population of Toronto, they comprise 16 percent of basic and 18 percent of the general programs. The board has made efforts to address this concern.

7. To learn how women in Jenn's program fared after graduation, I perused *The National Report of Workplace Conditions for Engineers, 1994* conducted by the Women in Engineering Advisory Committee of the Professional Engineers Ontario. A greater percentage of male than female respondents were in managerial positions and made salaries above $65,000. However, in 1987, the *Canadian Engineering Student Enrollment and Degrees Awarded, 1991-1995* report by the Canadian Council of Professional Engineers showed that 10 percent of engineering undergraduates were female; by 1995 this proportion had risen to 19 percent. At the professional level, a host of organizations have instituted outreach programs to encourage girls to pursue careers in science and technology, in Canada, under the umbrella organization of the Canadian Coalition of Women in Engineering, Science and Technology.

8. John Porter, Marion Porter and Bernard R. Blisher, *Stations and Callings: Making It Through the School System* (Toronto: Methuen, 1982), p. 217.

Travelling Uncharted Waters: Mothering Aboriginal Teenagers

Gail Winter

Mothering an Aboriginal teenager differs from mothering other "types" of teenagers because of the world we come from. Six generations ago, counting my daughter as generation one, Native people in Northwestern Ontario had Indian names only. Therefore, five generations have been born since traditional times prevailed (the sixth generation is now being born), not a long time when you think about it. When my daughter's father was born — in the forest, in a moss-covered structure, the traditional winter dwelling — most people spent their winters trapping in family units, and their summers in larger groups at summer gatherings. Then, during the mid-1960s, the Department of Indian Affairs constructed on-reserve day schools, which disrupted the traditional means of livelihood when, "for the sake of their children, parents gave up their semi-nomadic, family centred, independent lives as trappers"[1] to settle in permanent communities. This settlement caused social upheaval, which is still ongoing, because people were raised to be interdependent in a family, not a community, situation. In addition to the upheaval caused by the educational system, European religious, political and economic systems, as well as community infrastructure development and the mainstream media, disrupted traditional culture. The end result is that the

170

world the Elders grew up in is not the world the youth are growing up in. This causes communication problems, and is especially problematic because the Elders are the traditional teachers, conveying "responsibilities, loyalty, and proper codes of behaviour"[2] to the children and youth. The cultural erosion has undermined family relationships, "and teachings are no longer strong. Patterns of parenting have, in many cases, been broken."[3]

The degree of variation concerning social recognition or non-recognition of adolescence as a distinct life stage is perhaps more pronounced than for any other stage of the human life cycle.[4] As with other North American Native traditional societies, the people of Northwestern Ontario did not recognize a teenage phase of life because "the group's survival depended on everyone's working together and sharing ... Children were expected to contribute to their group, as soon as they were mature enough to do so."[5]

The transition from childhood to adulthood was rapid; with the attainment of social maturity and adult responsibilities roughly coinciding with puberty.[6] Because everyone shared the same value system and means of survival, young adults did not rebel against their way of life, as that would have been counter-productive in terms of their own and the group's survival. Everyone had a meaningful role and contributed to the group's well-being.

Today, the attainment of early adulthood remains strong in Northwestern Ontario. Most youth leave formal schooling between the ages of fourteen and sixteen, and many wed and/or become parents soon after. However, as the work needed for physical survival diminishes and other forms of employment fail to fill the increased free time, many people, especially the youth and young adults, find themselves in limbo. With no meaningful role in the community, they tend to stay home during the day and go out at night. As the Royal Commission on Aboriginal Peoples reported, "Many Aboriginal youth feel socially and psychologically isolated, that their families and communities do not care about them."[7] It is possible that some youth may interpret non-interference, a traditional sign of respect, as a lack of parental and community interest, leading to social and psychological isolation. The ethic of not speaking of personal feelings in public may also contribute to their feelings of isolation. Some youth exhibit deep apathy and feelings of hopelessness for the future; they feel their everyday life is bleak, and they are confused about their identity.[8] Many refuse paid employment in the community; feeling socially and psychologically isolated, they are not disposed to contribute to the community's well-being. The increasing number of youth suicides, a negation of the future, is profoundly demoralizing and plunges communities into shock and pain. Because most suicides occur between the ages of fifteen and twenty-four, it seems that entering adulthood, rather than leaving childhood, is a traumatic event. More males than females commit suicide. Some reasons for this may be that the intergenerational transfer of women's work has been less disturbed than men's, that women marry at a younger age than men and so have fewer years "in limbo," and that, in our community, there was an Anglican minister who sexually abused young boys who are now teenagers.

There is little or no organized "teenage culture" in Northwestern Ontario; people of all ages, from infants to Elders, attend community events such as dances, bingo, feasts, church and movies. However, the youth suicide epidemic is beginning to contribute to an elaboration of an adolescent stage of life, and some communities now have Youth Councils which bring the concerns of youth to the community at large. That is, in some First Nations, the youth are beginning to break the protocol of maintaining emotional silence.

Like Aboriginal peoples the world over, the people of Northwestern Ontario have lived through, and are living through, radical fundamental changes in their way of life. These changes make life very difficult for everyone, especially for the youth who seek a firm future in the shifting sands of change. The communities need to foster an atmosphere in which their youth can build a secure sense of self-confidence, self-esteem and self-respect, and in which youth can see they are valued and can make meaningful contributions to their families and communities. But, because of rapid societal changes, the Elders and parents are travelling uncharted waters.

Our Story

Our story contains elements of single parenthood, of poverty, of alcoholism and of racism, as well as common human experience and the experience of being an Aboriginal Canadian. Aboriginal people and their parenting practices are as varied as those of any other race of people, and so I caution the reader against creating stereotypes based on our idiosyncratic story.

My husband, my daughter, Grace, and myself left the North for a six-month stay in Toronto, a large multicultural urban centre in Southern Ontario, when my daughter was three years old, because my husband had to conduct some business. The differences between life in our First Nation community and in a city are profound and pervasive; trying to convey them in a few words "is like compressing a caribou herd into a single bouillon cube."[9] In a city there is electricity, running water, television, roads, cars, traffic lights, and noise and air pollution. There is time pressure, and you live and move among strangers in a segmented society. My husband and I were accustomed to urban life but it was a shock for my daughter to move from our log home in the woods to an apartment on a busy city street. Because I started working, she attended daycare, which was another shock, especially as she did not speak English. However, being resilient, she adjusted quickly. My husband and I separated during these six months, and my daughter and I remained in Toronto. My daughter was accustomed to her father's frequent absences (as a result of both business and drinking), but she did expect his occasional presence, so his subsequent two-year absence was initially difficult for her. After her father re-established contact, she moved easily between his home in our First Nation community and Toronto, and appeared to be a happy, secure child. I let my daughter adjust to the mainstream environment in her own way rather than insist she comply with Native social protocol, because I thought doing so would court an identity crisis on her part. Because she visited up north, I assumed she would develop a bicultural identity, which she did. I gave my daughter freedom to learn and explore the world in her own way while ensuring physical safety, which is consistent with the autonomy given to children up north. Many people commented favourably on our closeness and harmony.

At school, I judged Grace's progress by northern benchmarks and thought she was doing fine. However, in Grade Five, her teacher criticized her disorganization, which had been a problem for some time, and I noticed her increasing disorganization at home. I tried to help by setting little schedules and writing lists of things to be done. Looking for a quick fix, I thought I could teach her how to take control of her life and reduce her increasing anxiety about forgetting things. Although she said nothing about my actions, she saw it as taking away her control. I was succumbing to the parenting demands of mainstream society as reflected in the school system, where parents are expected to encourage and, if necessary, force their children to succeed. This is at odds with traditional Native parenting practices, where children are allowed to develop at their own pace without excessive interference or pressure, and parents demand little but that their children be themselves.[10]

In Grade Six, when she was eleven years old, we moved to Thunder Bay, a small city in Northwestern Ontario, for one year so I could collect data for my doctoral dissertation. My daughter found school more relaxed, because the school board had a no-homework policy. In Toronto she had been in after-school daycare; in Thunder Bay she was free to roam with her new friends. I was happy for her; her life came closer to my ideal of childhood — freedom from excessive rules, restraints and time demands, freedom to explore the world on her own and with her friends in a safe environment. Her days reflected my own childhood memories and were consistent with the free movement allowed in our First Nation. Her independence from me and her closeness with her peers increased. It was all in the natural order; however, there was foreshadowing of later rebellion. She lied about doing a school project and was found out. She received her first grounding and I cut off the cable television. I wanted her to understand the seriousness of lying. She understood the seriousness of getting caught in a lie.

I wanted to remain in Thunder Bay because of its friendlier environment, but economic considerations made it necessary to return to Toronto. My daughter, now twelve, became close friends with a girl one year older and one grade ahead (a Palestinian visiting from Israel) and they spent most of their waking hours together. I tried to retain much of the freedom she had known in Thunder Bay. For the first time in Toronto, she freely roamed our downtown neighbourhood with her friend. My nervousness over potential dangers abated as I saw her arriving home safely. Her friend talked to my daughter and me about her difficulties with her parents; she brought issues of personal independence and parental control into the open. At the end of the school year, they were caught shoplifting. I will never forget the look on my daughter's face as two police officers escorted her through our door. I had no need to rant and rave, because the police had done a thorough job of intimidation. I also knew that shoplifting at their age is very common, almost a rite of passage, and a one-time occurrence — which is what it turned out to be.

During the summer her best friend moved away, and my daughter hooked up with a new friend, who had some Aboriginal ancestry and infrequent contact with the Mi'kmaq community in Newfoundland. I felt uneasy about her new friend. I thought she dressed too provocatively for a twelve-year-old, and the brittle sheen in her eyes made me feel I was not seeing the real person but rather some fabrication that she hoped would pass muster. That summer was one of unease and worry, a summer of missed suppers, broken curfews, lies and evasions. At first I let my daughter and her friend roam the neighbourhood at will, as I had permitted her to do with her previous friend. However, as she missed suppers and came home late, I laid out rules and curfews. One night, about ten minutes after her curfew, my daughter had not returned, so I went downstairs to get her. She was not there (she was supposed to tell me where she was going if she left the downstairs area). Some children told me that she and her friend were last seen walking away with two guys. I searched for about an hour, becoming increasingly frantic and angry. As I walked, I kept thinking of a woman in our First Nation who used to go looking, with a stick in her hand, for her teenaged granddaughter. When I returned home, my daughter was there. I found out later that they had gone to the apartment of one of the boys. I phoned his mother and he was punished for having girls in his home when no adult was present. In my daughter's and her friend's eyes, I turned into an enemy, a squealer. During this summer I viewed my daughter as the innocent; I was in the "it's the other kid's fault" phase.

Grade Eight began, and my daughter, now thirteen, joined the "in crowd." In this group were some teens with mixed Aboriginal ancestry, but they were not connected to any Aboriginal community. She left her summer friend behind. She made a reasonable effort at school and spent most of her free time "hanging with her crew" in the schoolyard. For a few months she neglected her grooming, and then she became super-clean and began experimenting with make-up. She became a hip-hopper, wearing baggy jeans or long baggy shorts, long shirts and a Walkman. I had already decided not to make clothes, make-up or music an issue of contention, as I wanted her to have as much autonomy as possible. I held to my resolve, even though some adults considered her appearance disturbing, and I wanted to protect her from censure. She also began having long conversations on the phone with many friends. I was bemused — she had become a "typical" teenager. However, although she was (and is) immersed in hip-hop culture, she is a Native hip-hopper — she has a strong sense of Native identity and is proud of her heritage. Most people think she is Spanish or Asian, and she is quick to correct them.

During her Grade-Eight graduation, her class was discovered in a collective lie — my first encounter with a group "rebellion." They told us that they were planning their graduation party with a teacher; the teacher thought they were planning it with the parents. After the graduation ceremony, their chaperons arrived, looking like a hybrid motorcycle gang and extremist religious cult. Needless to say, some parents refused to let their children attend the party. Others did some fast negotiating, setting a midnight curfew and getting one teacher to chaperon. Some mothers, including myself, went to check out the hall and then left. My daughter had a magical time and arrived home on time, with stars in her eyes. During the summer holiday, I kept her busy. She spent the first part of the summer up north with her father. Then she spent the rest of the summer figure skating (from her earliest days she exhibited strong athletic abilities, and after trying a number of different sports, she settled on figure skating). The skating used up her energy and kept her out of trouble, but she complained about not having time to spend with her friends and began to hate skating.

My daughter and her friends from Grade Eight joined a larger group in the new school. Teens of colour, hip-hoppers and teens from single parent-families predominated in this group. She told me that the teachers and staff disliked her group and discriminated against them. However, I felt asking her to leave her group would have been counter-productive. It was impossible to restrict her in her choice of friends but I supported her learning about various cultures from the safe anchor of home. Besides, she was not getting into serious trouble. Now, two years later, she tells me she stays with her group because "it's easier"; she does not have to prove herself. They group together because they are surrounded by teens of European descent who are afraid of them. Socio-economic status also separates them. This discrimination at school is very painful for them. I need the support of a healthy community to raise a healthy adult, and racism does a lot to negate that support. I am proud that she speaks up in class when she sees inaccurate portrayals of Indian people in her school books or when her teachers gloss over Native voices in her textbooks.

Grade Nine is emblazoned in my mind as the year from hell. Three days before school was to start, her father failed to show up for her birthday as promised and did not phone with any explanation. He had started drinking again. Although I had told her he had a problem with alcohol abuse, she had never seen it (that she could remember) because he had been sober for ten years. Her sense of security with her father was shattered. I reached an unprecedented depth of fury against her father as I watched her struggle with the pain of her abandonment. She saw my upset, which added to her distress. She rebelled almost immediately. A coincidence? I think not. If her father had been there to continue to encourage and support her as she entered high school, things might have turned out much differently. I also think it is easier to rebel when only one parent is in the picture. She adopted a hard attitude.

School was a disaster. Before school started, I had discussed strategies for academic and social success in high school and she had listened. Once school began, she told me she had no homework, which surprised me, but I believed her. Her first report card contained failing grades because of incomplete homework and assignments. She vowed her next set of grades would improve; they did not. My continued propounding and encouragement fell on deaf ears because she knew of the school board's ruling that all grade-nine students would pass. When the school board rescinded this wacky rule toward the end of the school year, she tried to bring her marks up, but it was too late.

My daughter and her friends commenced Grade Nine with a declaration of "war on all mothers." They compared maternal injustices, and sometimes my daughter unfairly accused me of some other parent's actions. They read us very well, and when they wanted to do something they knew would not be permitted or would involve a lengthy hassle, they concocted a web of lies and strategies to circumvent rules. The lying destroyed my trust and I looked for the lie in her every outing. My imagination spun more devious lies than the reality, and when I think back, I am glad I kept my mouth shut as often as I did.

Some mothers, including me, discerned untruths and we telephoned each other to verify the particulars of various outings. Many mothers were also in "it's the other kid's fault" stage. Once, when I was uneasy with my daughter's explanation of an outing, I went to phone a parent only to discover my daughter had blacked out all the parents' numbers in my phone book. As we parents became more comfortable with our teens' outings, checking with one another lessened, and our teens' subterfuges diminished dramatically. I had always thought that my daughter and I would negotiate her greater independence — I never thought that I and her peer group would perform that negotiation.

Her rebellion encompassed all adult authority figures. Figure skating was a disaster. She was in constant rebellion on the ice, refusing to listen to her coaches and making no progress. She disliked the other skaters because they were not hip-hoppers and because their parents, mostly their mothers, and their coaches controlled their lives. She also saw them as conceited and phony. Because she had loved skating and was at an advanced level, I kept her on the ice, hoping things would change. However, I realized she was not soon going to change her attitude and I was wasting my money. She left figure skating at the end of the school year.

The initial board ruling that all Grade-Nine students would pass was only one reason for her poor school performance. She could not tolerate any adult telling her what to do and, of course, teachers are forever telling students what to do. She refused to do work for any teacher she disliked, and she disliked most of them. Although I sympathized with some of her personality conflicts with her teachers, I also tried to make her understand that she would end up only hurting herself. However, she could not "play the game"; she believed it was honest to have only one way of acting. I also saw her behaviour at school as attaining the personal strength to overtly challenge things that had bothered her for a long time. She had always been unhappy with the rigid structuring of school; for example, she would be engrossed in math and then she would be forced to move onto reading. She had also developed a strategy in earlier years where she slacked off for the first part of the year and then worked hard to pass. I told her that strategy would not work in high school because of the marking system, but she seemed to think it would. When I received her final school report card, I had a good cry as the report encapsulated all that had gone wrong during the year. I made the very difficult decision that she should repeat Grade Nine, hoping she would thank me later if she graduated with all her postsecondary education options open.

During this year I had a moment of great insight. My daughter was arguing with me on some now-forgotten point and I looked in her eyes and saw, behind the frustration and anger, a deep sadness and a silent plea. She wanted me to understand what she was doing because she did not. I floundered; I was not the wise parent, who could take control and guide her, that she wanted and needed; I was travelling uncharted waters without an oar. For all her insistence on total freedom, she also wanted parental control. It was a scary time for her too. Striking a balance between freedom and control is very difficult. I began to deal seriously with the reality rather than distressing myself with imaginings. Rather than upsetting myself and trying to change her behaviour, I tried to view things from her perspective and help her work things through as quickly as possible. I tried not to do anything that would intensify and prolong her transition to independence. I was happier with my facilitative role than with my earlier controlling role.

With my heightened sensitivity, I soon noticed that a hot topic of conversation among her friends was the proper degree of parental control and discipline. I often heard the comment: "Her parents don't care what she does" when a teen could do anything without receiving punishment. It was clear they did not want total freedom. I have always been strong on curfews. I think they are important in maintaining health, by regulating eating and sleeping patterns, allocating time for school work, sidestepping late-night mayhem and influencing who becomes a close friend. My daughter's preferred choice of discipline for broken curfews was grounding, so I went along with it, even though I felt I was "shutting the barn door after the horse was gone." However, she saw it as a sign of my concern and support, and I found it gave her time to regroup.

I saw the changes in her, but she did not see the changes in me. To her I was still the parent of the dependent child. She saw me as much stricter than I really was, and this hurt — my daughter thinks I am an ogre. Her friends told her that I was funny and nice, much to her consternation. She spent most of her time in her room, which was off limits to me. I was hurt, I was weary, I missed our happy relationship. My winter of discontent had arrived; times were tougher than I had ever known, not only with my daughter, but also with other aspects of my life, and I had no meaningful support as the people I spoke to had little empathy and tended to judge. I broached the subject of professional counselling for us, but she said that would only make things worse. I also considered and rejected a support group for children of alcoholics. I took her to her physician and discovered she was severely anaemic, which explained her lassitude. I dredged up the personal strength to act positively and worked doggedly on my dissertation, knowing my graduation was the key to a better life.

Toward the end of the school year, clubbing (going to all-age nightclubs) came into the picture. Her friends reassured me that it was not dangerous and they gave me a mother's phone number to call (but was it a mother I was speaking to?). I nervously let her go, after setting a curfew and ensuring she would not be travelling alone. I also gave her a quarter so she could phone if she was going to be late (a simple phone call goes a long way in alleviating parental stress) and taxi fare in case of an emergency. Later she negotiated outings, suggesting punishments for broken curfews that were much harsher than those I would have asked for. Because she created the punishments, I conceded, but in fact they were never needed. Because of rampant groundings, her entire circle of friends could rarely get together that summer. Clubbing continued unabated. She spent many evenings in parts of town where I would not dare to venture. I had to let her go and I prayed that she would be all right. During this year, a youth-suicide epidemic began in our First Nation and I dared not push her too hard because of its large contagion effect. Although none of my daughter's closest friends or cousins up north committed suicide, the suicides shocked us and were a salient part of our lives.

My daughter believed I would change my mind about her repeating Grade Nine. When I did not, it was a harsh awakening for her; her first serious failure. Her other friends, even those who had failed Grade Nine, entered Grade Ten at the general level (parents have the final say on where their children will be placed) and my decision shocked them. Surprisingly, as the year progressed, my daughter defended my decision. Her first report card was poor. She said she would work harder and I should trust her. Her second report showed no improvement and she said her education was of consequence only to her, so I should not care. She wanted me to detach completely, something I could not do. Her dismal academic performance continued and I thought she might do better with someone else. Obviously I was not doing a good job or these things would not be happening. Although the thought saddened me enormously, I was prepared to suffer the emotional pain if it made her life better. She passed Grade Nine, barely.

Early in the school year, clubbing ceased abruptly because my daughter had a falling-out with one of her clubbing friends and her favourite club closed. My daughter stopped ignoring me and started communicating. She pierced her nose and added multiple earrings. I said nothing but did object to proposed tattooing. I had never objected to her appearance, so perhaps for that reason she agreed to wait for tattoos until she was on her own. Although she hung out at a mall with her group every day after school, she observed her curfews and stayed home on school nights. On one occasion I became genuinely fed up with my daughter's histrionics. I was deep in thought and the tone of my response conveyed that I had more important things to think about than her boring childishness. Unintentionally, I had shocked and hurt her. For a moment she stood back and saw her actions objectively, and what she saw was unflattering. This fleeting exchange had a powerful effect; it helped her mature. I don't think this is something that can be staged; it just happens.

When school finished, against her vehement protests, I sent her for a week-long visit with her father. They fought constantly. He thought of her as the relatively obedient child he had last seen two years earlier and she gave him a crash course. During the remainder of the summer, she spent most of her time lying on the couch, watching television. She refused party and dance invitations. She made a few tentative attempts to find a job but felt no one would hire her. She dyed her dark brown hair blonde.

On the first day of Grade Ten a new person emerged. Obviously she had been doing a lot of thinking on the couch. She was organized. She began doing homework and studying. She forbade me to tell her what to do and I complied (although I gently encourage her when her energy for school work flags). This year I found out that she thought she was a young offender because of her earlier shoplifting. When I assured her that wasn't the case, she seemed relieved and regarded herself in a more positive light. Her relationship with her father, who phones often, is slowly healing. She regulates her bedtimes and phone calls. She has begun to reflect rather than simply react. She considers extenuating circumstances rather than thinking in terms of absolute right or wrong, and her insistence on acting one way in all situations is fading. She selects her friends and outings carefully. I enjoy our conversations and her ideas. This is turning into the winter of my content. Lecturing has given way to a few well-chosen words in the course of normal conversation, and she listens. I have learned to let her go. Of course, it's easy to let go when nothing awful is going on. I am lucky. My daughter has many wonderful personal qualities that I respect and admire. She never refused to attend school, she has no drinking or drug problem, she does not smoke, she is not promiscuous, and she is not in trouble with the law. She has steered clear of or distanced herself from teens in serious trouble.

One ongoing concern I have is the glamorization of violence in hip-hop culture. Violence worries me and excites my daughter. Her hypothetical responses to situations and peers she dislikes are invariably violent — this from someone who never had a temper tantrum; who had an extraordinary sense of social justice during childhood; and who cried when an after-school daycare worker instructed her to hit a child who had been bullying her. That is, aggression is at odds with her basic personality, and I fear she is arresting the development of her true self. A counterbalance to violence is to enter into a personal relationship with spirituality, which provides inner strength and guidance. However, she believes that developing such a relationship would have major personality and social consequences, and she is not willing to go through that at this time. Many parents up north echo my concerns over the lack of a spiritual base among the Native youth.[11] In Toronto, Christianity lacks a connectedness to the land because the spirits of the land are faint. In the North, the spirits of the land are strong, and the spiritual and secular blend. In our First Nation "being Christian is part of being Native"[12] and traditional Native ceremonies are not accepted. I respect all forms of spirituality and will support her if she wants to become involved in Native spirituality. Her father would also support her, but most other people in the North would object strongly.

In mainstream society, my daughter is in the heart of her teenage years, having left childhood behind and not yet entered young adulthood, although she is considering issues such as a vocation. When she next visits our First Nation, she will have young-adult status. Her father told her she was an adult when she turned fourteen, but he soon realized his judgment was premature. He conferred adult status on her sixteenth birthday. This was a very important event for him, but, even one year later, she feels she is a teenager, not a young adult. She recognizes the dichotomy between her status in the city and her status up north, but it does not cause her dissonance. She also recognizes the other differences between life in mainstream society and life up north. For example, she likes our First Nation because, she says, "life is natural." People do not hide their real selves behind masks, they do not rush around, and there are few restrictions placed on personal independence. She especially likes that she can walk into her relatives' homes and help herself to food. In spite of that, she would not like to live there right now, because she feels alienated and says there is nothing to do (agreeing with what teens who live on First Nations in the North say). However, she wants to teach on her First Nation when she is an adult.

We would prefer it if we could interact with other Native people on a daily basis instead of our having to make a special effort. However, such interaction is not possible because Aboriginal people do not live in communities in Toronto — they are widely dispersed and we are surrounded by non-Natives. This is very different from up north, where there is continuity with kin relations. My daughter goes to the First Nation House at the University of Toronto twice a week for tutoring, where she sees many Native university students (her tutor just recently obtained his Ph.D. in mathematics). Sometimes she expresses an interest in the Toronto Native Centre, a short walk away from our home, but will not go alone. She willingly accompanies me when I attend events (she will seldom go anywhere else with me). She reads our regional newspaper and knows, and is comforted by the fact, that I can answer her questions on Native issues and historical facts. Her father keeps her informed on happenings in the North.

Unlike in our First Nation community, my daughter has to deal with racism on an almost-daily basis, even though Toronto is a multicultural city and people are generally tolerant of each other. As mentioned earlier, racism is most apparent in her school. In the city at large, racism is reflected in subtle actions and discriminations rather than overt expressions. Belittling and uncomplimentary media portrayals of Aboriginal peoples irritate us. However, she has not internalized negative stereotypes, nor does she view herself as a victim of society. Issues of Native identity and oppression may become more salient when she enters adulthood. For now, though, she knows of many successful and strong Native adults, both in the city and up north.

Reflections

Much of the stress we have experienced arises from living in a large city. I feel autonomy for teens is facilitated when parents perceive the environment to be safe and familiar. However, in Toronto, during her child-to-teen transition, my daughter moved among strangers in unfamiliar surroundings. This is much different from a First Nation community, where you know the other teens from birth and there are no unfamiliar areas. Another stress arises from the education system. Educational achievement in the city is strongly emphasized, yet "teachers have less of a vested interest in the achievement of students that are not of their community, or have less of an idea of how to educate them."[13] Up north, parents tend to be detached from their children's education (the fact that most teens must leave their communities to attend high school also contributes to this detachment) and there is little or no excessive pressure to succeed. The average educational level is less than grade nine. My daughter continues to struggle in high school and I continue to encourage her because she has the capability to do well. However, I find myself alone in encouraging her; up north her present level of educational attainment (grade ten) is considered sufficient.

Another stress is that, as a single parent in a large city, I missed the benefit of extended family and community support in parenting, which is prevalent up north. Because my daughter and I were alone, we developed an unusually close bond during her childhood. This closeness made her rejection extraordinarily painful for me. However, the strength of the bond also helped during our difficult times; it twisted and tensed but never broke, and is stronger now, although of a different quality. Our bond is also unique in that we alone among all our acquaintances in the city understand life up north. I see that the first cuts toward independence were the deepest and drew the crudest responses, and slowly evolved into delicate negotiations. I am thankful that my daughter's rebellion did not escalate to dangerous dimensions and that my love survived. Most important, I learned that empathy, however difficult the situation, is crucial. But our story cannot be complete. We have almost three years to travel before she leaves her teens. However, I catch glimpses of the emergent woman and I am pleased at what I see.

Notes

1. B. Minore, M. Boone, M. Katt and P. Kinch, "Looking In, Looking Out: Coping with Adolescent Suicide in the Cree and Ojibway Communities of Northern Ontario," *The Canadian Journal of Native Studies* 11, 1 (1991), p. 19.

2. Carol Locust, "Wounding the Spirit," in *Facing Racism in Education* (Cambridge, MA: Harvard Educational Review, 1990), p. 116.

3. Nishnawbe-Aski Nation Youth Forum on Suicide, *Horizons of Hope: An Empowering Journey* (Youth Forum final report, 1997), p.viii. Available from Nishnawbe-Aski Nation, P.O. Box 755, Station F, Thunder Bay, ON, Canada, P7C 4W6.

4. Richard G. Condon, *Inuit Youth: Growth and Change in the Canadian Arctic* (New Brunswick, NJ, and London: Rutgers University Press, 1987).

5. Carol Locust, p. 115.

6. Richard G. Condon.

7. Royal Commission on Aboriginal Peoples, *Choosing Life: Special Report on Suicide among Aboriginal People* (Ottawa: Canada Communication Group Publishing, 1994), p. 31.

8. Nishnawbe-Aski Nation Youth Forum on Suicide.

9. Clare Brant, *Understanding Your Native Patient (Inmate, Student, Pal, etc.)*, p.1. Available from The Sioux Lookout Program, University of Toronto, P.O. Box 1500, Zone Hospital, Sioux Lookout, ON, Canada, P0V 2T0.

10. Richard G. Condon.

11. Nishnawbe-Aski Nation Youth Forum on Suicide.

12. Lisa Philips Valentine, *Making It Their Own: Severn Ojibwe Communicative Practices* (Toronto: University of Toronto Press, 1995), p. 13.

13. Imani Perry, "Public and Private Schools," in *Facing Racism in Education* (Cambridge, MA: Harvard Educational Review, 1990), pp. 4-8.

Racism:
Sharing Experiences,
Taking Action

Pat Watson

Somewhere, at all times, someone is being wounded by racism. Some are even being killed. For the most part, those who are the objects of racism are experiencing the kind of stress akin to existing in a war zone with no ceasefire. Its pervasiveness holds us between states of high- and low-level turmoil, interwoven with numbing shock. None of us is specially designed to withstand this form of antagonism: therefore, we manifest the characteristics of those suffering from post-traumatic stress — except that the trauma is ongoing.

Racism, like other social conditions, is inherited from our past. It continues to make itself known in various incarnations. As a testament to its endurance, it can be observed that the term "racism" has only recently been coined, replacing the older terms "colour prejudice" and "racial discrimination." In South Africa it is called "apartheid," which, according to the regional pronunciation, sounds like "apart hate." Whatever contemporary form it takes, the spirit of racism exists among us almost invisibly. Often we see it only in retrospect.

What is racism? Essentially it stems from the fear, and consequently the dislike, of another group of people whose appearance is different from our own — from whom we feel apart. We aren't willing to identify or empathize with "the other." It starts with stereotyping, the belief that "they all look, think, act" in a similar predetermined, frequently negative way. The next level is prejudice, where one decides or accepts without investigation or previous association that an individual belonging to a particular group will act in a stereotypical manner. Add to that mix, discrimination — actions based on those beliefs. Racism is more than ugly graffiti and rude remarks about skin colour or racial origin. It is more subtle than that. It can also grow out of the lack of awareness of the diversity that is our society today and out of the assumption that we are all alike — or should be.

But racism becomes even more troubling when it appears in our social structures and institutions; that is, when it goes beyond the personal feelings of individuals and becomes part of the fabric of society. Sadly, no society is free from the influences that can lead to systemic racism. The outcome is that it handicaps some members of society, preventing them from fully and freely participating, as do others.

The Adolescence/Racism Mix

The teen growing up in such a society faces many hurdles. It is generally accepted that the years from twelve to eighteen are a time of transition between childhood and adulthood. The landscape of the teen's emotional and social growth is one of trying to balance her increasing awareness of her own identity against all the images of the roles she is expected to play. She wants to fit in, and she also wants to be her (new-found) self, whoever that may be(come).

Expect her to continually challenge the family status quo in the process of establishing that individual self. Weary adults will call it "rebellion." She suddenly does not *need* to told anything because she *knows it all.* Yet she has bouts of feeling inadequate and unsure as she tries to establish her own values and questions the world around her at a deeper level than in earlier years. She feels at times uncertain about her role in society and within her family. Her body is changing, and so there is the conflict between growing up and not wanting to grow up. She begins to need more privacy — an expression of her new-found sense of control and autonomy.

Her relationships with other teens are also changing. The strong emphasis on separating from adults is balanced by a strong pull toward being with other teens. She begins to relate to boys differently than when she was younger. Expression of hostility and/or increased attraction to the opposite sex also become more evident. In some situations they are also treating her differently.

Add to this potent mix the growing awareness that now she will have to begin handling issues of racism without the level of protection that parents have to offer to younger children, and it makes for a very challenging period.

A visible-minority teen has to contend with her maturation process as well as the role racism plays in her life. She faces some teachers in the school system who hold racist views and may express them consciously or unconsciously. She will find that she faces lower expectations from society at large. She may have to deal with the contradictions of differing or opposing cultural expectations and practices. Some people in society will react to her based on their notions of stereotypes that conflict with what she knows or is beginning to know about herself. She may not understand why these stereotypes exist, or their origins. She may struggle with knowing that racism has absolutely nothing to do with her since she didn't start it, but that she will have to contend with it throughout her life.

The feeling of apartness that a racist environment generates can lead to dropping out, not just from the education system, but from mainstream society. Black teenagers, noticeably young Black men, are tellingly affected by racism in their midst. Young Black men are overpoliced by law officers. Consequently, in Canada, their presence in jails is proportionally higher than their numbers in the larger population. The only other minority group that has a higher proportional representation in jails in Canada is Aboriginal women in the Prairie provinces, where they *are* the majority in some jails.[1]

As racism plays itself out among young people, unemployment figures, while high for youth in general (16.5 percent in Ontario in October 1996 compared with approximately 10 percent of the general population),[2] is higher for minority youth. Subsequently, many minority youths find themselves becoming members of an underclass that is engaged in what anthropologist Frances Henry describes as alternative employment[3] — income-generating activities that are illegal.

Given that youth must seek employment in the current economic climate of cutbacks and menial jobs, parents may consider encouraging the entrepreneurial side in their teens. Help them to identify skills or avenues that will allow them to be self-employed, to form cooperative groups, to run their own businesses. Begin with local government employment agencies or organizations whose focus is to channel teens and young people into starting their own businesses. Help them to find mentors who will give them the apprenticing experience they need, as well as introductions to industries that match their interests and aptitudes.

Encourage then to look at alternatives outside the mainstream and to explore particular niche skills, services or products. If they exhibit an inventive nature, encourage them in this. As much as it is possible, find the means to allow them to extend their inventiveness — for example, support that could enable them to attend exhibitions and workshops.

In the School System

One important arena for teens contending with racism is the school system. The minimal representation of teachers from groups outside the majority affects minority teens. The Canadian Alliance of Black Educators found that 40 percent of Black high-school drop-outs went to schools where there were no Black teachers.[4] Additionally, little attempt is made to include histories and contributions of those other than the majority's. The result is an unbalanced view of the total value of our diverse society.

Minority teens face the growing knowledge that they are valued differently from the majority; that expectations for them are not the same as for other youths; that they may not be rewarded for showing equal or better aptitude compared with their classmates or workmates. They are not expected to succeed in the same arenas. They are often streamed into more vocational, less academic courses of study.

In many cases they are penalized for the same qualities for which other non-minority youths are rewarded. If a Black teen likes to take initiatives, her actions may be interpreted as aggressive. If she challenges information, she may not be seen as questioning but as argumentative. If she is quiet, she may not be viewed as introspective or thoughtful, but may instead be viewed as sullen. These conditions result in a higher-than-average drop-out rate from formal education institutions.

According to the 1996 Progress Report of Canada's Children:

> Black Nova Scotians, aged 15 to 18, are at much greater risk of becoming drop-outs than their non-Black counterpart. The

drop-out rate for young Black men is 57 percent, compared to 42 percent for non-Black males. Young Black women are 25 percent more likely to leave school than non-Black women ... Many drop-outs spoke of an alienating school environment where they received little or no encouragement and guidance, and had to deal with insensitive and sometimes prejudiced teachers.[5]

Nova Scotia, a province that until the 1960s had segregated schools, offered in June 1995 to spend $1 million to establish programs to try to end systemic racism that prevented many Black children from receiving an education there. The province promised to adjust its education curriculum to include Black history, culture and traditions. Additionally, five scholarships were offered by 1996 to Black students pursuing careers in teaching. A scholarship program was also promised for Black students entering studies in medicine, pharmacy, dentistry and engineering. In 1995 Nova Scotia's unemployment rate averaged 15.8 percent, while its Black population's unemployment rate was 35 percent. These rates have been directly linked to the school drop-out rate that result in low-wage jobs or unemployment.

Some Statistics

According to a December 1995 article in *The Globe and Mail*, the study done by the Canadian Alliance of Black Educators on 334 Black dropouts found that 56 percent were suspended from school at least once. Eighteen percent had been expelled. Twenty-nine percent had repeated a grade. More than 50 percent of young Black women who dropped out had unplanned pregnancies. Racially motivated conflicts were experienced by 20 percent, and approximately 33 percent had run-ins with the police.[6]

Most students who needed help did not go to their parents, turning instead to other people. What they most liked about school was friends, and they disliked teachers most. The article cites this conclusion from the study: "Social and educational systems (i.e. home and school) are continuing to reproduce a sizable population of Black youth who are disenfranchised, disaffected, and at risk to society and themselves." In other words, many Black youths are in trouble and need support in this society.

What we have are teens who are experiencing emotional suffering due to racism. They have a strong sense of powerlessness and despair, with even less hope for the future than other teens. The institutions of authority do not treat them with real respect, so they have no respect for authority, showing mistrust instead.

It is important to note that the study was done with drop-outs and so did not focus on those who are surviving in the mainstream. However, my own experience in the Toronto school system echoes aspects of these conditions. For example, many years after leaving high school, I had a chance meeting with one of my former teachers, a teacher of English, who showed real interest in her students. When I told her that I had studied political science at university, she expressed considerable surprise that I had not gone on to pursue a career in writing. Years later, after having written professionally, I remembered that chance meeting. Her expression of surprise suggested to me that she had been aware of my aptitude but had never mentioned or encouraged a career in writing. It led to me recall other oversights and insensitivities of a racist nature.

Parents and teachers are partners in educating teens. The providers of this formal education are in a 50/50 partnership. With particular reference to African heritage, find out how much information teens get in school about Africa and African achievements and contributions to the world. Actively participate in parent/teacher groups to address cultural, educational and social issues in your teen's school. Involve your teens in the process. This will generate a feeling, for your teen, of being connected to the school and community that cultural difference could otherwise prevent. The amount of interest parents contribute to their children's school, and therefore their education, affects the level of the children's success.

Racism Creates Communities

Being the object of racism is, tellingly, the single common characteristic of African Canadians. It forces individuals to identify with each other. This uniting experience is their common ground.

In a 1995 study, anthropologist Frances Henry found that Blacks do not, excepting racism, identify themselves as one homogenous group. Divisions among Blacks exist along national, cultural, regional and class lines. Moreover, in the case of Caribbean immigrants, the gap between adults and their Canadian-born children is also quite distinct, and not just because of the traditional generation gap.[7]

According to Henry, immigrants from the Caribbean are more focused on their culture and motivated to be in Canada, and do not identify as strongly as their Canadian-born children with the Black/White issue. As one first-generation minority youth put it, she felt a sense of not belonging. She stated that, if she is in a social situation or school setting where she is the only visible minority, she feels uncomfortable — as if she does not belong. She feels more reassured if she is "not the only one." If possible, try to choose a school setting where your teen is not the only visible minority. Teens experience significant feelings of loneliness and alienation as a result.

Henry's study finds that Black teens today see themselves as existing in opposition to the larger society precisely because it is seen as overwhelmingly White. Consider also that the information they receive from its most influential voice, the mainstream media, is almost unfailingly negative in the images it offers them of themselves.

What Media Do

Although a few newspapers report on specific minority communities, and a smaller number report on youth culture in those communities, minorities often turn to mainstream media to see themselves.

What they are presented with are stereotypes — jocks or criminals, math whizzes or devout fundamentalists. A local Toronto tabloid paper, *The Toronto Sun*, for example, is well documented as a media outlet with an unhealthy habit of portraying Black youths in a negative light. But neither are other sectors of the media without their insensitivities. Youths are not portrayed by the powerful media as they really are, nor as they see themselves.

A steady stream of photographs depicts young Black men in handcuffs. When these images cannot be found locally, they are imported. Stories in the press highlight alleged Black involvement in petty crimes involving illegal drugs and assault, or focus specifically on racial heritage and the attempts to improve social conditions within troubled communities. "Positive" images are usually of male athletes from basketball, track or baseball. Then there are the endless stories about war and famine in African countries. There is very little deviation from these themes. Add to that the near total exclusion of visible minorities from the "good life" touted in advertisements, and the landscape depicted becomes extremely bleak.

The relentless presentation of negative stereotypes and the meagerness of realistic or positive information sometimes results in children struggling with these images and attempting to resolve the distress by wishing they were white. Clearly the discrepancy existing in the social climate that accommodates majority youths and negates minorities, is, for impressionable youth, often glaring. (And this is so although teens are generally regarded as being outside the mainstream — as a subculture.)

The route to dealing with this aspect of racism lies in changing the composition of the media force. The media population is largely made up of people from the visible majority, many of whom have little in-depth experience or understanding of minority issues. So parents who see that their teens have an interest in media participation should certainly encourage it. Kids are never too young to write letters to the editorial pages of newspapers and magazines. Encourage them to counter these negative images by submitting their own articles to those outlets. Refuse to watch television shows that present negative and stereotypic portrayals of minorities. Write to television stations and television and movie producers, making them aware of your disapproval and offer them alternatives to the negative images they choose to portray. All parts of the media, whether radio, television or print, have regulating bodies that look into complaints, whether about racism or other concerns. They are there for everyone.

Also seek out alternative media that are more in keeping with your understanding of your community. Support them by using what they offer, by subscribing to them and buying advertising space through them.

In this age of the Internet, teens who have access can form groups and set up web sites and chat rooms that make public statements about their experiences and methods of coping with situations unique to minority teens. In these ways teens will begin to have the experience of contributing to the truth about who they are and a sense that they are not powerless in these situations.

Who Cares about Racism?

Recently I was watching a left/right television debate[8] about employment equity in which a lawyer representing the "right" stated repeatedly that "yes, racism was a factor in the world of employment, but it was *not significant*." I found myself wondering, not significant to whom? It's clear that many of those who perceive that they do not suffer from the stresses of racism, those who enjoy the privilege of being a member of the majority/power group at least in part, view racism as "not significant."

Yet I know that this "insignificant" thread that runs throughout the fabric of our society has affected my life since the first full day of my being in Canada. At the ages of nine and eleven years, respectively, my sister and I visited Canada as a prelude to moving here permanently. On our first morning in Toronto, having arrived by plane the night before, we walked along ahead of our mother to see the city. We became aware that two boys were shouting about something, but we did not realize that they were shouting at us. Our mother, however, did realize it. She became very agitated as she caught up to us. She went over to the house where the boys had been standing, rang the doorbell and explained to the woman who came to the door what had happened. She warned the woman — apparently the mother of the boys — that, if they continued this behaviour, there would be serious consequences.

My sister and I were somewhat confused by the whole incident. It was the first time we had heard the word "nigger" and we did not know what it meant. Coming from the Caribbean, we had never had such an experience before.

This type of blatant racism continues and can be present through harassment in school, difficulties getting jobs and other social interactions.

There is certainly an arguable advantage in growing up in a culture that allows you to feel accepted, to be a part of it instead of apart from it. I have had the experiences of living both as an insider and as an outsider. The feeling of being an outsider may at times be connected with originating from another country, but for visible minorities born in Canada, with families here for a generation or more, constantly being asked what island you are from can be alienating. A Black teen quickly goes from being an insider to being an outsider.

To Parents

If you are the parent of a visible-minority teen, then you already know that many issues you deal with concerning your child must be dealt with at two levels. In common with other parents, you deal with the specific issue, whatever it may be. And although not always the case, "race" frequently factors into the equation. For example, take the regular parent-teacher meetings to discuss and assess your child's school career. Questions hang over the encounter that are absent for parents of the majority of children. Is this teacher evaluating my child fairly based on her skills, achievements and abilities? Is the teacher consciously or unconsciously grading her based on cultural bias or skin colour? Is my child receiving fair treatment? Is she being overlooked or judged differently for the same things other children also do? Understanding how pervasive racism is, do I need to acknowledge that racism and its effects are of real concern for my child and our family? My own experience tells me that any discussion of racism across racial lines rarely approaches the personal acknowledgment of racist behaviour to any degree. This exercise, therefore, will serve to alert others to your own sensitivity to the issue and may make them somewhat more conscientious when dealing with your child, although this is not always the case.

The parent wonders how soon before childish innocence becomes lost to the painful personal experience of racism in some public or private setting. No minority parent can totally shield her child from this sad encounter. Many have asked why the children must also suffer. What's important is to provide support to our children. For those of us from other cultures, it may be difficult to connect our earlier experiences to today's youths. Nonetheless, our teens ask of us what other teens do of their parents: that we attend school events to which we have been invited, neatly dressed (this matters even to the grungiest teen); that we respect their emerging adulthood; that, despite their messages to leave them alone, we do not abandon our role as parents; that we let them know in clear terms that we value them; that we regularly acknowledge their strengths and not just their weaknesses; that we listen thoughtfully when they speak and wait until they have completed their thought before responding.

When issues of race and racism come up, as they inevitably will, of course share them. Do not deny the experience, thinking it will spare your teen some pain. It is vital to every minority teen that parents work with her to develop practical strategies for dealing with racism. Given a circumstance of racism, your discussion may include asking your child, "What do you think is a good way to handle the situation?" You will discover your solutions arising from such a beginning. It allows your teen to participate in creating strategies, and therefore to own them. It is reasonable to have some preparedness for these situations, since not doing so is akin to going into battle totally unarmed. For minority teens, racial socialization, that is, engaging in encouraging cultural pride and preparing for race discrimination, is necessary for their well-being and survival through the adolescent years. Include spiritual and religious strategies. Consistently include the extended family in your life activities. Reinforce cultural pride when the opportunity arises, but avoid cultural chauvinism. Even if teens sometimes seem not to care or not to be paying keen attention, still give them cultural information. Talk to them about family members of old or who are far away to aid in continuing the feeling of connectedness.

About Culture

One of the features of adolescence is "cliquing." The clique in this context plays a twofold role. It brings together young people attracted to one another because of the easy familiarity of common culture, in this case Black youth culture. It also acts as an insulator, protecting them from the trauma of racism.

Since the American civil-rights movement of the late 1950s and the 1960s, people of African descent have been reclaiming their lost histories. Afrocentricity, therefore, is a part of today's Black youth culture. It has generated a notion that today's African descendants are the latter-day sons and daughters of African kings and queens. This speaks of a need to reclaim African cultural esteem in the Diaspora, as well as self-esteem for individuals. It is in part a reaction to negative portrayals and an attempt to fill the void of information about Black history and relevance. There is an emerging African-Canadian youth culture that is an interesting hybrid of disparate African cultures. This youth culture, however, still takes its lead from the powerful (African) American influence.

Black teens and other youths live with the beat of hip-hop music and culture, today's reigning influence. Sounding its arrival in the late 1970s, many claim it's the new standard. Hip hop frequently describes the sometimes harsh, sometimes glamorized environment of the ghettoized Black underclass. And like Rastafarian influences in reggae music of past years, it gives voice and information to teens about conditions within their community and the larger society.

Hip hop will do for Black teens what they will not allow their parents to do — that is, pass on valued information to them. Many teens display a resolute resistance to hearing about their histories from their (immigrant) parents, viewing such information as irrelevant to their lives. They are more accepting of Black culture clubs or other such programs in the transfer of this information. Sociology professor Carl James of York University, himself the parent of a teen, recommends that parents place the current Black youth culture within the context of today's changing society, that is, set it within the economic and political reality. For parents who experienced their adolescence living in another culture, it helps to be conscious that you are raising teens in a different context — the times and the location have changed.

Another aspect of the buffer effect of culture is the perception of physical beauty. Since there are few Black models in the popular fashion milieu, where the ideal of extreme thinness is largely emphasized, that (thin) beauty image doesn't have any notable effect on Black teens. They don't see themselves in those images. Beauty in Black teen culture has more to do with being consistently well dressed and having well-groomed hair in keeping with the day's hot fashions and — very importantly — projecting a positive attitude about oneself. The ideal places a heavy emphasis on being respected. To be "dissed" — as in "disrespected" — is to be made to feel ugly. It infringes on a teen's pride and self-esteem; these are essential survival tools for dealing with racism. Interestingly, many Black teens who drop out of mainstream institutions were found to have fairly high self-esteem.[9]

Churchgoers — a community within a community — also serve to maintain a tangible identity. Religion has long been a support structure of hope for Africans in the Diaspora. There are churches that are exclusively Black, with very active community lives. Members pray and socialize together, and in this way are somewhat insulated from the goings-on outside of their social/religious sphere. Some churches regularly spend entire weekends praying, meeting, eating and socializing. Because of the churches' strong cohesiveness, teens who are part of this milieu stand a good chance of making it through the trying teen years without dropping out. In contrast, reaching outside Black culture can be seen as a rejection of one's peers. Sean Henry writes, "I was never

Black enough for the standards of my Black peers. Just because I didn't 'walk the walk' or 'talk the talk' I was considered as acting white. My clothes were different and most of my friends were white."[10] To "act white" is seen as a questionable practice of voluntary exclusion from Black adolescent communities. A Black teen may be seen to be giving up her culture — an act of betrayal. "Black" and "White," therefore, are not only racial descriptions, but also attached to culture. Henry goes on to ask, "What is 'acting black'? What is 'acting white'? What are the rules and who made them"?

As parents, we begin to help our teens work through this situation by repeating the question Henry asks — What is "acting Black"? Help her to see how she views herself as a member of the African-Canadian community. Ask her to identify what things she does that tell her who she is in her community. Look for positive experiences to discuss that remind her, as well as yourself, that you are part of the African-Canadian community. Continue to encourage her to look for ways that remind her that, even if the larger society views our community negatively, we are valuable and valued.[11]

To Teens

Racism is not a two-way street. Of course members of visible minorities also engage in the discreditable action of prejudging individuals and groups, and pandering to ridiculous stereotypes. Coming from minorities, who are comparatively powerless, these acts of prejudice rarely have the same impact as those from the dominant culture. The relative size of the majority ensures that.

Racism in any situation, from any source, is morally unacceptable. If some person or group chooses to behave in ways that are harmful to you because of your culture or skin colour, remember it is a completely separate issue from who you really are or anything you have done.

The truth is that such actions are a clear statement about that person or group. It is important to know that, when we have negative feelings about others, it's not because of who they are, but because we see in them the qualities we dislike about ourselves. It is somehow easier to see our weaknesses and flaws in others than to see them in ourselves. It is a characteristic of our society and, some would argue, of human nature. Nevertheless visible minorities are paradoxically called upon to solve the social disease of racism.

In order to engage your teen in continuing to deal with this challenge, ask her what solutions she envisions to stop racism. Moreover, support the considered steps she takes in dealing with it. Encourage her to think about what is important for the African-Canadian community. This will play a part in moving her toward understanding and appreciating her connection with her community. It will also help her to find ways of being involved. Since her personal identity will, to a significant degree, come from her cultural connection, it is a very necessary exercise.

Notes

1. Ministry of the Solicitor General, Government of Canada, *Annual Survey*, 1994.

2. Statistics Canada, *Unemployment Statistics*, October 1996.

3. Frances Henry and Carol Tator, *Racism in Canada: Social Myths and Strategies for Change* (Toronto: York University, 1985).

4. Canadian Alliance of Black Educators, *School Leavers Survey*, 1991.

5. Canadian Council on Social Development, *Progress Report of Canada's Children*, 1996.

6. "A Look at Black Dropouts," *The Globe and Mail*, December 26, 1995, p. A16.

7. Frances Henry, *The Caribbean Diaspora in Toronto* (Toronto: University of Toronto Press, 1995).

8. CBC Newsworld, *Face Off*, December 10, 1996.

9. Canadian Council on Social Development.

10. Sean Henry, *The Montreal Gazette*, March 17, 1996, p. F8.

11. For further reading on raising minority teens, see: Gail Christopher, *Single Parent's Guide: Providing Anchors for the Innocent* (Noble Press); Susan Kulkin, *Speaking Out: Teenagers Take on Race, Sex and Identity* (Putnam & Son); Dr. Alvin F. Pouissaint, *Raising Black Children* (Plume); and Deborah Prothrow-Stith and Michael Veissman, *Deadly Consequences: How Violence Is Destroying Our Teenage Population and a Plan to Begin Solving the Problem* (Harper Perennial).

Raising Teens: A Class Act

Martha Fleming

A decade ago, you might have found me at the local wading pool, an active five-year-old and toddler in tow. Fanned out around that pool were other women from the middle class poor; we shared the values and the upbringing of the middle class, but not the cashflow. We considered ourselves to be "starting out" — with babies, second-hand furniture and low-budget meals. At that time, my husband and I and our two children lived in a housing co-operative, which was cheap and safe and embraced socialist views. We supported a women's shelter, sent our children to a co-operative camp and sat through endless meetings, working out the details of living in a community together. Ten years later, my son is well into his teen years and my daughter is not far behind. I have completed my education as a teacher and we have moved from that co-op to a small, postwar house. Unlike many of my friends of that time, I am still married, and so have not slipped into single-parent poverty. By sheer luck, our family has not been hit by the massive layoffs and downsizing that are pushing many others into unemployment and marginal working conditions. You could say we have struggled our way up the middle-class ladder a rung or two. Nonetheless, I have not found full-time employment and the odds of joining the marginally employed are not decreasing. My husband has a relatively well-paying and secure job, and it is his income which provides the financial stability in our household.

Those of us who were teaching our toddlers to swim in the '80s were also going to school, working part-time and preparing for a return to the workforce. We thought that the jobs we left behind in order to raise our children would still be there when we were ready to return to the paid work force. I have friends who never expected to be juggling two or three jobs while raising kids. I certainly did not anticipate working as a supply teacher with little possibility of full-time employment for so many years.

My parents came from a generation that saw an increase in their standard of living over the course of their lives; my generation is contending with increased taxes, frozen wages and reduction in services. Even while juggling this economic ball, struggling middle-class families like mine are determined to give their children the experiences that wealthier friends and relatives take for granted. We want our children to have the chance to do things we didn't and hope to prepare them for work in a highly competitive world. We believe that our kids need challenges in order to grow. These convictions form the backdrop for many families raising middle-class kids as this century draws to a close.

I was one of seven children in a Catholic family growing up in a conservative, Protestant area of southern Ontario. My father was an accountant with a struggling business and my mother worked as a secretary. My parents valued education and the arts and were active in their church community. Finances were a concern in our large family; children were expected to earn money for spending and clothing. We were encouraged to perform well academically and were expected to pursue higher education. My family formed part of the growing middle class of that time.

My husband Marcel comes from a solid working-class family; his father joined the military at a young age, learned a trade and retired from the military thirty years later. A strong work ethic, the ability to fix anything and a more *laissez-faire* parenting style form part of his working class legacy. Our differing class backgrounds have come to the forefront in raising teens. Our differing beliefs come as a bit of a shock; my husband and I have generally agreed on issues concerning younger children. Marcel lets the kids stay out later and go to places that I see as potentially dangerous. I am still checking on school work and suggesting productive summer activities. My inclination is to guide and protect; Marcel's is to let them loose. The children benefit: I usually agree to activities that I see as worthwhile and their father allows more freedom. My husband and I have had to determine what is acceptable to each of us with regards to parenting teens; my bottom line usually has to do with safety and Marcel's with reasonable expectations. For example, my daughter recently wanted to learn to ride a horse, an expensive and rather upper-class notion. As part of my middle-class credo, I could see the value in this activity. My husband just rolled his eyes. Together, we decided that she would try it, with no expectation for continued and ongoing lessons. If my daughter decides she wants to pursue this activity, we will discuss how she can make a contribution. We encourage and pay for our kids to try most things that fall into the educational category, such as music and sports. Horse riding pushes those boundaries; if my daughter is really committed, she will simply have to come up with some means of contributing, perhaps through her allowance or babysitting.

We give our teens a generous allowance. Marcel simply smiles when they spend it all on French fries, while I lament the waste. He wants them to figure out things on their own, such as how it feels to have no spending money later in the week. While I agree in principle, I have found it hard to bite my tongue when our son spends all his money at the school cafeteria. Some lessons take a long time to learn but our son has recently started talking about part-time work, so perhaps Marcel's strategy is bearing fruit. We have learned to avoid pay-in-advance requests and have made clear exactly what the children are responsible for with their allowances (entertainment, gifts and expensive clothes). While there has been some creative gift-giving and going without, handling their own money is working well with our children. We want our kids to figure out their financial priorities.

As my children reach their teens, they request more and more freedom. My husband and I have had the most discussions on this issue. His background dictates a lot less parental supervision; he had opportunities to roam much further afield than I, and to be much less accountable to his parents. Marcel thinks that kids need to be in situations where they will develop sound judgment, such as at parties where there may be drinking and experimenting with drugs. My tendency is to be informed about the details of my kids' whereabouts and to set guidelines and time limits. I am concerned that there will be situations that they are not able to deal with and may put them at risk.

We deal with these scenarios as they arise. As the children are successful at making sound judgments, we give them more freedom. We have found that we can avoid some confrontations through an open dialogue; if the kids know why I have reservations about hanging out at a downtown mall, they are more likely to respect the boundaries.

In spite of living close to the poverty line, or living with the threat of job loss, we make it a priority to create opportunities for our teens. In the past, we have relied on the public school system to pick up the slack. I have always been a firm supporter of the public school system, a system that provides the same opportunities for all kids. I am seeing many of those opportunities eroded in subtle ways at the high-school level. For example, my son goes to the local arts high school, which provides specialized learning in visual arts, drama, music, literary arts and dance. In order to be accepted, he needed a portfolio of work; we had sent him to art lessons the preceding year to increase his chances of being accepted. Now we need to be able to afford fees for supplies and provide transportation — a city bus pass or personal chauffeuring — if our children are to attend this kind of school. This kind of "pay for privilege" is difficult to maintain, and is not possible for many people in my circle. Consequently, many kids get locked out of the opportunities available to the middle class; for talented teens from poorer families, funding is available, however, the confidence required to apply to special schools is significant. Much of this confidence comes from success at trying many things in the early years. Middle-class parents have been successful at procuring those confidence-building opportunities. Struggling middle-class parents are frustrated by knowing what opportunities are out there and not quite as available for their children. In the housing co-op where I lived, many families are from the working class. Their children attend the neighbourhood schools, whereas the more middle-class parents send their children to French Immersion, specialized high schools and alternative programs. Working-class parents are often unaware of the possibilities that exist and couldn't afford the extras that invariably accompany these programs. This year, my son has enrolled in an Outdoor Education class that is, ostensibly, available to all students in Grade Ten. Yet, there is a substantial fee, and I'm sure there will be costs along the way. Challenging and fun courses like this one keep high school students engaged in their learning and more likely to complete their education. I think about the families who can't afford these kinds of extras and wonder if the inaccessibility is a subtle barrier to completion of high school.

My daughter will be attending a French Immersion school this year. In theory available to all students, French Immersion is a stronghold of the middle class in Canadian schools. It is seen as an enrichment and future employment opportunity. Since the school is not in the neighbourhood, we will be paying the transportation costs, for her to attend — my family will be tightening the belt in other areas to provide this educational advantage.

Our local school board is well known for its programs for special needs students. In the last few years, class sizes have increased and resources have been pulled. The waiting list for assessment of children with learning difficulties has grown. Many parents who can afford it are choosing private testing and private schools. The two-tiered system that could result scares me. Will we end up with a public system that teaches less fortunate kids and private schools filled with families who can scarcely afford the fees? Middle-class children with learning difficulties who might flounder in the public school will receive the kind of academic attention that may secure their futures: additional computer technology training, science education and sports. Upper-class children will never experience the struggles that families from other classes face in order for their children to have a reasonable education. A wealthy friend has a child with learning difficulties; in addition to private school, my friend is providing her daughter with specialized tutoring. This child will learn strategies to achieve success in school.

With the promise of opportunity comes the pressure to perform. Middle-class children have been given music lessons, sports camps and ballet lessons. To parents, the teenage years look like the right time to shine; many teens, however, want to lie around all day and listen to music, talk to friends on the phone for hours and avoid adults. Parents want them up and doing something, not "wasting their time." My middle-class son has no compunction about hanging around doing nothing and doesn't really understand why this should be seen as a problem. It helps me to think of my fifteen-year-old son as being in a chrysalis: sleeping, eating and getting ready. As long as family and school obligations are met, I try not to intervene. Although there is a temptation to compare my son's idle hours to my teenage years of part-time jobs, I have found this to be less than productive. The poster on my son's wall sums it up, "When I was your age, I walked twenty miles to school, uphill both ways." Conversations with other parents have confirmed that their teens go through the same stage. This ability to hang out is another middle-class luxury that working class kids can't afford; they often have part-time jobs or more responsibilities within the family.

There is so much depression among teens; waiting rooms for guidance counsellors are full. While middle-class kids may suffer from depression as a result of pressure to perform and a sense of inadequacy, many more poor teens are experiencing the struggle their parents have to survive, and are affected by a kind of hopelessness about the future. They may be working and trying to complete school; they may feel disenfranchised by a system that effectively although not overtly locks them out of many academic opportunities. Young women are particularly at risk for depression. A guidance counsellor at my son's school told me that the anorexia of the '80s is being replaced by self-mutilation in the '90s. Young middle-class women who have been offered the same opportunities as their brothers are now struggling to be taken seriously in a world that suffers from the cult of youthful beauty. They invariably find themselves lacking and are devastated by their loss. The contrast for middle-class girls between what they have been led to believe and what now seems to be true is stark. How they look is more important than what they think and do. As a parent of a middle-class teenage girl, I am well aware of the potential "dumbing down" of adolescent girls and try to balance cultural pressure by providing outlets. Engaging my daughter in girl-only activities is a way I have found to de-emphasize the desire to look good. One benefit of the horse-riding episode is that it seems to only attract young women. They sweat, muck out stalls and have to take control of the horse.

In my home, the television and I have been at war for years. In addition to its mind-numbing nature, I object to its stereotypical portrayal of young women. Happy and successful women are beautiful and under twenty. No wonder young girls don't want to become adults — they need to stay young in order to fit the cultural norm. Our television has a comfortable shelf in the garage where it lives about 50 percent of the time. When the television does make it's way back to the house, there is much discussion generated about what does or doesn't represent reality. Closely connected to the problem — how young women are portrayed on TV — are teen magazines. My daughter brings them home, and hides them from me so that I won't give lecture #31, "Beware of Teen Magazines." These magazines feature infuriating articles such as, "Get Sexy: 101 Ways to Look and Feel like a Total Babe." They give the impression that any worthwhile life is dependent upon catching a boy. As a way of countering the effect of these magazines, I have purchased more progressive and proactive magazines. Her response is dubious — she wants to know what is expected of her in the culture represented by teen magazines. She wants to be able to discuss articles in her teen magazines with her friends. I try to overcome my reaction and offer other views; my daughter has learned to highlight articles that I would not object to, and is quick to point out ads that show young women in a negative light. I also realize that this seems to be a stage that does not necessarily have long-term effects. My daughter has been reminded of my "boy-crazy" youth on many occasions by her well-meaning aunts. This has elevated my daughter's opinion of me and allowed me to see this interest as a stage young women go through. Nevertheless, I don't remember feeling that my body type would never measure up to the norm. My daughter and her friends talk about anorexia and bulimia casually and with some knowledge. They want to know how thin girls can be without being considered anorexic. Middle-class girls are particularly susceptible, since most of the young women represented by the media appear to be from the middle class. They don't question the media driven stereotype of women so I consider this my job, and take the opportunity to point out strong and active women whenever I can.

Teens from poorer families have added pressures, such as how to maintain their sense of self-worth when there is so much emphasis on wealth. They are constantly juxtaposed against their peers. Thankfully, many teens have found ways to minimize some of these class differences. My son's friends buy their clothes from second-hand stores, regardless of their finances. Appearance, which is so important to the identity of these kids, becomes less of an issue. I try to remember that when I see my teens wearing torn and baggy pants. It is a fashion driven by the need to spend as little as possible on clothes and the desire to reduce class differences among themselves. I guess it is not that much different from some of the clothes sported by teens of the '60s and early '70s. My husband wore an army coat that his father saw as an insult to the military but was really just an attempt to look like the rest of his peers. When middle-class parents are sacrificing so much to be sure their kids have all the opportunities for success, blue hair and pierced noses can feel like a slap in the face. The outer manifestations of teenagehood scared my parents: long hair and beads were just plain weird. Now as a middle-class parent, I struggle to remember that and breathe deeply when my children choose styles that I don't like.

I don't think middle-class parents of a generation ago worked so hard to understand and influence their teenagers. They had more confidence that their children would find work and a place in the future. They also had more children to worry about and focused on the family as a unit rather than on each child's needs. Middle-class parents today, especially those who are really struggling, feel the need to secure their children's place in the future. My son often tells me that I am overly interested in his affairs; what he sees as nosy is my attempt to make sure his grades are kept up and that he stays on the right track. Teenagers seem to want to make their own choices and many parents feel that those choices can sometimes be dangerous. Many parents today need to know more about their children's lives than our parents did in order for them to be safe. Fear of AIDS and other STDs, drug addiction and depression leading to suicide are real concerns. Teens feel that as they are maturing, parents should have less of a say in their lives. Whereas my parents gave a lot of free reign to experiment, I try to keep a close eye on what my teens are doing. Many of my daughter's friends who are eleven and twelve spend a lot of time alone; their parents are working shifts or working at two jobs to make ends meet. They do homework, make meals and entertain themselves without supervision. They gain independence in these tasks, but I know their parents are worried about the cost of being alone. It seems that the job of middle-class parents today is to protect kids from the culture at large rather than let them discover the larger culture. In homes where parents are working two or three jobs, where teens are working to help the family, where the stress of layoffs and unemployment dominates, the job of helping teens secure a future while trying to keep them safe is all the more difficult.

Middle-class parents of the '50s and '60s had a firm and united view of the place that teens held in the family and society. That place was subordinate to the authority of the parents, in particular, the father.

Much rebellion was done without parents actually knowing anything about it. As children of those authoritarian parents, many middle-class parents of today are determined to do things differently. We allow choice, we devote much of our income to provide opportunities and we let our children express themselves (excessively). We want to make sure they make their mark in the world. As a middle-class parent, I have let myself in for more negotiating than I would have believed possible, and less respect than I would have liked. Mothers that used to hover over toddlers at the pool, are now reading "How To Parent Teens" articles on the bus home from work. Our middle-class determination to raise our kids remains unshaken. The economic climate has changed however, and parents who are really struggling to maintain a standard of living for their children feel resentful when their kids question and rebel.

The world seems to have become more stressful in that intervening decade between toddlerhood and teens. Work prospects look grim for teenagers, (not to mention parents!), the standard of living has dropped for many of us, the public school system is eroding, the social safety net is being pulled out and family configurations are changing at a dizzying rate. Many families are struggling with marginal incomes and are burdened even further. We have a button kicking around our house that dares us to "Question Everything." It's an apt expression of teen sentiment — this is their time to start looking at the world around and their place in it. In the face of a shrinking middle class, will my children find their middle-class upbringing something to question? Is their access to computer technology, horse-riding camp, French Immersion and art lessons evidence of an affluent lifestyle that doesn't really match the world around? Truthfully, it doesn't even match our pocketbook and it isn't just our family — friends who live on less income than we do are driven by the same unspoken desire to provide their children with the advantages of the middle class. I worry that we are setting our teens up to anticipate an adulthood that drives them where they want to go. On the other hand, I believe that middle-class children of this generation have been given many gifts: the confidence that comes from success at a variety of things; concerned parenting; advocacy on their behalf; and protection. As a teacher at inner-city schools, I see the effect that poverty has on children every day. I recognize that many of the struggles to learn and socialize are a result of class position. I think about my children sitting in their classes, well-fed and competent in their environments. The contrast between these two images is startling and disconcerting.

Families struggling in this shifting, competitive world are looking for stability and hope for the future. Parents sense that they are up against formidable odds and share some of the same worries that their teens have; worries about the future and finding their place in a confusing society. With this in mind, my husband and I strive to let our kids have fun and enjoy this part of their lives, to experience everything, to feel good about themselves and to be armed with confidence and skills for whatever fate blows their way.

When the Family Breaks Up

Rachel Giese

A few years back, my nephew's grade-three teacher thought that it would be "cute" to stage a mock wedding. A bride, groom and attendants were selected; costumes were put together; and there, in the cloakroom with crayon drawings for decoration, two eight-year-olds promised to love each other until death did them part.

When I asked him a few weeks later how he felt about the event, my extremely sage nephew replied that the happy couple had divorced. "He just wanted to play trucks and she didn't like him anymore," he said. "She's in a new relationship now."

Despite fearful hand-wringing over the state of today's family, the kids are obviously all right. Since the first Canadian Divorce Act became law in 1968, the incidence of divorce in Canada has increased 500 percent and has involved more than one million children. Canada's divorce levels, the numbers of divorces in a year measured against the number of weddings that year, are almost as high as those in the United States. In 1987, in Canada, there were 477 divorces for every 1,000 weddings, and in the United States, 485 couples divorced for every 1,000 who married.[1] But the experts are hardly in agreement over what this might mean. Research into the effects of family breakdown on children and adults offers contradictory messages.

In fact, according to research cited in Stephanie Koontz's extremely good book, *The Way We Really Are*, divorce in and of itself has far less of an impact than "family values" advocates would lead us to believe. "Many of the problems seen in children of divorced parents," writes Koontz, "are caused not by divorce, but by other frequently co-existing yet analytically separate factors such as poverty, financial loss, school relocation, or a prior history of severe marital conflict."[2]

Of course, while increasingly common, family breakdown and divorce are never easy for children. (For the sake of convenience, I use the term "divorce" to refer to the breakdown of all family units. The term "marriage" can also be seen as referring to mixed-sex and same-sex common-law unions.) Divorces, even the most amicable, are extremely stressful. They divide the loyalties of family and friends; they cause tremendous upheaval; they break hearts; they disrupt routines; and they can cost a considerable amount of money. And teenagers, already dealing with a variety of personal transitions, have their own particular issues related to divorce. They may have a troubled relationship with one parent, making custody proceedings more difficult. They may seem apathetic to the parental break-up because they are already preoccupied with personal issues: sexuality, school, or peer relationships. They may blame themselves or their parents. They may cope wonderfully or behave miserably. Or, if they are in the throes of adolescent rebellion, they may simply add "divorce" to an already long list of parental faults.

Parenting a teenager during a break-up can be extremely tough for mothers, and it remains mothers who do most of the parenting during and after separation and divorce. In Canada, women obtain sole custody of the children in 75 percent of divorce cases, compared with the 12 percent of cases in which men receive sole custody, or the 11 percent of cases in which some kind of joint custody is granted.[3] And not only are mothers responsible for a disproportionate amount of childrearing during and after divorce; they also experience a disproportionate amount of blame.

The troublesome single mother who looms so large in the imagination of political conservatives has become a scapegoat for every social ill under the sun, from increasing high-school failure rates to teenage pregnancy. In actual fact, the family today is no more diverse or unstable than it ever was. In the past, marriages ended through early death or desertion, and high infant and maternal mortality rates, war, famine and disease made family life precarious.

The family of today barely resembles the mythic "perfect" unit of the past — the large Victorian family headed by a strong but loving patriarch, or the 1950s nuclear family safely ensconced in the suburbs. Of course, neither of these family units was an option during their own time for the many people excluded from them by class or race. And for those who were involved, these kinds of family units maintained by strict and separate gender roles were often miserable.

The rapid social change of the last fifty-some years has seen a tremendous increase in the number of women in the workforce, a loosening-up of sexual morals and a decrease in the size of families. People are waiting until later to marry, or are opting to live in common-law relationships. Women are insisting on more equality within their relationships with men. Gay men and lesbians are demanding that their diverse family units be recognized. Infidelity is increasing. Teenagers are becoming sexually active at a younger age and with more knowledge. Divorce rates are up, and fewer people are willing to stay in relationships that no longer make them happy just because "they ought to." As feminist journalist Katha Pollitt puts it: "Why shouldn't society adapt? Society is, after all, just us."[4]

Of course, not all these changes have positive results. Shifting socials norms can make people feel alienated or lonely. Divorce, for many women, remains a ticket to poverty. But often, when trying to deal with these dilemmas, it's the wrong problems that get tackled. Instead of addressing the increasing rates of sexually transmitted diseases among teenagers by providing them with better sex education and access to medical services, school boards recommend chastity programs. Instead of being provided more access to daycare and better working conditions, single mothers are attacked for living off the state. And instead of recognizing that our notions of family have changed, divorce is viewed as a social crisis of massive proportions.

One of the reasons the divorce rate has increased is that people are living longer. One or two centuries ago a lifelong commitment may have meant only ten or fifteen years of marriage; today, people are less willing to remain in a joyless relationship that can last forty or fifty years. As well, our laws have changed significantly in the last thirty years, allowing "no-fault" grounds for divorce that have simplified the process and eliminated its stigma. In addition, while the expectations of women have changed, and few still expect or want to stay home and be fully supported by a bread-winner, the structure of marriage and the relations between men and women haven't caught up. In the United States, the majority of women cite their husband's unwillingness to help with domestic chores as a significant reason for their divorce. Women today are far less likely to stay in a bad marriage for economic reasons. More women work and are economically independent, but most still experience financial hardship following a marital break-up, which is one of the reasons social and economic conservatives dislike the idea of divorce so much: In their view, intact nuclear-family units support themselves and look after each other. Single-parent families might require some public support, such as free daycare, or breakfast programs in schools, or subsidized medical care (though with massive job losses, an increasing chasm between rich and poor and a high unemployment rate, many two-parent families are in need of public support as well).

So what does family breakdown mean to teenagers and their parents today? Well, it means that teenagers are less likely to live in homes watching unhappy parents make each other more miserable. The break-up may cause temporary trauma, but it may also end a whole lot more day-to-day tension and hostility. There's no denying such an upheaval is difficult to launch and difficult to experience, but few childhoods and adolescences are without difficulty. In many circumstances, the experience provides children the opportunity to watch their parents struggle, change, become independent and start new happier lives, which is a powerful life lesson. And, so far, the increased incidence of divorce hasn't deterred people in their twenties and thirties, including, and sometimes especially, those from divorced families, from marrying or entering into common-law relationships. (In fact, divorce doesn't seem to turn most divorced people off marriage. Three-quarters of Canadians who divorce remarry within five years, though "second-time-rounders" have a higher incidence of divorce than those on their first marriage.)[5]

Still, the relationship between parents and teenagers can change dramatically during family breakdown and divorce. Unlike younger children, who have somewhat simpler needs, and perhaps a less-fraught relationship with their parents, teenagers may already be experiencing conflict with their parents and the divorce may exacerbate this. For younger children encountering family upheaval, reassurance, physical comfort and emotional support are often easier to provide. Teenagers react in more complicated and indecipherable ways, though they may be hurting as much or more. On the cusp of seeking their independence from their family, they may feel suddenly abandoned because of the emotional and temporary physical absence of one or both parents. Mothers may be made the scapegoat by children ("You made Dad leave!"), teenagers may act out their unhappiness by rebelling, breaking household rules, fighting with parents and siblings, and so on, or adolescents may shut down emotionally.

When my parents broke up, I was sixteen, the younger of two daughters and the only one still living at home. Wrapped up in my own life, my first sexual relationship, school work, friends and social activities, I very much resented (and felt guilty about) my mother's pain and grief. And I wished that she would just get over it so that I could get back to the business of being a teenager.

It's common for children, even older ones and adolescents, to find it difficult to face their parents' frailty and struggles. Divorce, particularly an acrimonious one, makes parents temporarily unable to parent at full capacity. Ending a relationship is difficult enough; add to it the other possible aspects of divorce — moving, expensive legal fees, a drop in standard of living — and the demands of parenting can seem impossible.

Often adolescents will step in and assume some responsibility for the mother's well-being, creating a parent-child role reversal. They will do more household chores or work more diligently in school. Sometimes a teenager, particularly a girl, will become the mother's confidante, or become the go-between for two feuding parents. Sometimes a teenager winds up stepping in for the absent parent as an escort or a sympathetic ear. Or the teenager may be bribed by one or both of the parents with gifts or money or a loosening of rules. It's easy for a teenager to play off of this.

If teenagers are already experiencing troubles with one parent, they may use the divorce to lash out, refusing to visit the non-custodial parent, for instance. Teenagers may choose to live with their father following a divorce because they see him as more lenient and less emotionally involved than their mother. Because Dad tends to do less of the practical aspects of parenting (setting curfews, chauffeuring, helping with homework), kids see him as the "nice guy" and the parent they can more easily live with. Unless they were very involved before the divorce, men may find single-parenting a big challenge. It may be difficult for them to get their kids to open up, or they may be at a loss when attempting to decipher the problems of their teenage daughters. Women have been coping with the "double shift," working full-time and performing the lion's share of the domestic and parenting tasks, for quite some time now. Men may not be used to the colossal amount of work involved in single-parenting. It's important that single dads learn to cope, without being too indulgent or without demanding that kids step in too much for the absent mother.

It's easy for parents to want to give in to kids or to place high expectations on them during a period of family break-up. The parent's own feelings of sorrow, loss or abandonment may make him or her want to pull children closer. This can put an awful strain on teenagers, especially if they feel caught in the middle. It's important that parents who are breaking up seek support from other adults, turning to a friend, a sibling or a counsellor instead of confiding in their kids. It's also essential that parents do their best to resolve custody and support issues quickly, so that kids regain a sense of stability and routine. This isn't often easy, however. Many parents, both mothers and fathers, will use issues such as custody and support as a bargaining chip or as a form of punishment ("You left me, so you can't see the kids" or "You had an affair, so you don't deserve support").

Parents must be honest with teenagers when they explain their decision to divorce. Teenagers are very aware of what goes on between their parents and, if the family's dysfunction is extreme physical abuse, chronic infidelities or alcohol addiction, the reasons for the break-up will be apparent. But when the problems are less visible, parents need to decide the best way to tell their kids. Age plays a large role in deciding how much information is appropriate. With teenagers, it's best to be as upfront as possible, while at the same time avoiding blame and hostility. Kids need to be told the truth. They don't need to be told that Dad thinks Mom is a "slut" or that Mom thinks Dad is a "big loser."

Sometimes, however, despite parents' best efforts, teenagers still feel that they must take a side, or feel unable to discuss their feelings and needs with their parents. Children of all ages need to have the opportunity to be upset. It's natural for them to be angry at one or both of their parents. Occasionally, parents can feel so guilty about their divorce's effect on their kids that they don't give their kids the space to be unhappy. It's important to keep the lines of communication open, and perhaps this is another situation in which it's useful to turn to a family member or friend whom the teenager trusts to provide some additional emotional support and attention.

Commonly after the initial crisis of break-up, things seem to quickly return to normal. But parents and kids will have a considerable amount of grief and anger to work through. Kids are not over it, just because six months have passed and they seem fine. Certain events may open up old wounds. For instance, watching parents date is extremely tough. Teenagers find their parents' sex lives as gross as parents find their teenagers' sex lives alarming. And teens may resent their parents' dating, not only because it seems disloyal to their other parent, but because it encroaches on their teenage territory of crushes and sex and flirtation.

Remarriage and the formation of new, blended families is also extremely rough on teens. The optimum time to integrate a step-parent into a family is when the children are very young, or when they are grown and beginning their adult lives. Adolescence is the worst time for children to acquire a step-parent. And, indeed, teenagers can hardly be expected to be thrilled suddenly to have a new authority figure in their lives. Step-parents are wise to adopt a friendly or avuncular attitude, rather than a parental one. Kids do not want to feel as though someone is trying to replace one of their parents, but they also need to find a way to deal with the new step-parent. Early on, before the new spouse begins to live with the family, the parent, the new step-parent and the children need to discuss how the new family will operate. The parent should be prepared to be put in the middle frequently by the new spouse and the kids. And the step-parent should grow some thick skin; things will be bumpy. But regular family discussions, patience and hard work will prevent any serious resentment and animosity.

A related, but less common, tension can develop when a divorce occurs because one parent is gay. As homosexuality becomes more visible and accepted, fewer people remain in the closet, getting married and having kids, all the while knowing something is missing. But it still happens that people discover (or become willing to acknowledge) their homosexuality after living a straight life. This is both a delightful and a stressful realization for the parent, and it's often helpful to seek support in a coming-out group, or an organization for gay and lesbian parents.

Sometimes if kids are less than enthusiastic about their gay parent's new life (and perhaps his or her new lover), the parent may take that to mean that the kids are homophobic and that the main issue is sexuality. While homophobic attitudes still exist and kids may find their parent's coming out a little shocking, often sexuality is not the issue at all. They are likely more upset about the upheaval of divorce, or perhaps they feel a little abandoned by their gay parent's involvement in new activities. Or maybe they think that Mom's new girlfriend is a jerk because she really is a jerk (they probably think Dad's new girlfriend is a jerk, too). While coming out may be the best thing to ever happen to gay parents, they shouldn't pressure their kids to be equally as ecstatic. They very likely will come around after they have been allowed the time to mourn the divorce and adjust to their parent's new life and relationships.

Other issues may arise at the first birthday or holiday celebration after the divorce. Teenagers may feel like they are being pulled between two families. They may mourn the loss of family tradition. Or they may be suddenly shoved into an adult role; they become the one to serve a meal, or say the prayer, or make the family's arrangements. Special events in the teenager's life can also become a hassle after divorce. Who comes to the high-school graduation? Who teaches them how to drive? Who helps them pack and move away to university or college? If parents can find some friendly way to be together at these public events for their kids, it can take a lot of stress away from the teenager. I know one divorced family that has been able every year over the last ten to have a Passover *seder* together in their original family unit, adding the divorced parents' new spouses and families.

Economics is another big issue, particularly for women. Following divorce, women generally experience a decrease in their income, while men experience an increase. Custodial mothers, the vast majority of divorced women with children, take on most of the responsibility for the costs of raising kids. Though an increasing number of women continue to work full-time after they marry and have children, women still earn less than men, still perform the majority of child-rearing and homemaking tasks and are still more likely during marriage to get on "mommy tracks" at work that prevent them from moving ahead as quickly as their male counterparts.

By law, spousal support is based on the conditions, needs and means for each spouse and any child; the length of time the spouses cohabited;

the functions performed by the spouses during cohabitation; and any order, agreement or arrangement relating to support of the spouse or child. The objectives of support laws are to recognize any economic disadvantage arising from the marriage and the marriage breakdown; to support any children; and to encourage economic self-sufficiency, that is, the wife must get back on her feet quickly.

While these guidelines establish theoretical equality for the sexes, the courts have been slow to implement them in a feminist way. The duty to achieve economic self-sufficiency is still a priority in most Canadian courts. This is not difficult for women in well-paying full-time jobs with benefits. But few efforts are made to compensate a homemaking wife, or a woman who has accepted part-time work in order to take on most of the burden of parenting. One feminist legal scholar has argued that the goal of self-sufficiency taken to its "extreme interpretation in practice has meant that women who have been absent from the commercial job market are now being required to return to low-end employment to meet the legislated goal."[6]

Statistics Canada's first report on the payment of alimony and child support in 1992 showed that poverty was the fate of many divorced women. Relying on data from 1988 tax returns, the report found that fewer than 20 percent of single-parent families were getting some kind of support payment.[7] In 1996, the amount of arrears owed to Ontario children by deadbeat dads was almost one billion dollars.[8]

It's unlikely that any of these economic issues will be resolved any time soon. Financial hardship has a tremendous impact on single-parent families post-divorce. Incredible stress is added to the mother's already heavy burden; she may have to work longer hours, or move, or sell some of her possessions. It also adds to her resentment if her ex-husband is delinquent in his payments. She may feel guilty that she cannot support her kids as well as she used to. Many teenagers already work at part-time jobs for spending money or to save for the future; following a divorce they may have to chip in to the family's expenses or they may have to take on the full responsibility of their own support. Again, it's important that parents be upfront about their situation; it allows the teenager the opportunity to help out and to be realistic about the family's material conditions.

Dealing with the trauma of divorce is never easy for any of those involved. But sometimes, despite the best of intentions, despite counselling, despite help, marriages fall apart. It's important that parents listen to needs of their kids, even if occasionally it means rising above their animosity toward their ex-spouse. Sometimes, this may mean relying on the help of family, friends or a counsellor, to deal with their own pain and grief while at the same time trying to settle legal issues like support and custody, and performing the day-to-day business of raising kids. But if parents can offer their kids support and empathy, this will go a long way in rebuilding the family.

Notes

1. Statistics Canada, *Report on the Demographic Situation in Canada, 1990* (Ottawa: Statistics Canada, 1990).

2. Stephanie Koontz, *The Way We Really Are: Coming to Terms with America's Changing Families* (New York: Basic Books, 1997), p. 100-1.

3. Julien D. Payne and Marilyn Payne, *Dealing with Divorce* (Toronto: McGraw-Hill Ryerson, 1991), p. 9.

4. Katha Pollitt, *Reasonable Creatures* (New York: Vintage Books, 1995), p. 37.

5. Julien D. Payne and Marilyn Payne, pp. 8-9.

6. Patricia Wouters, "Promoting Sex Equality: A Charter Challenge to the Support Provisions of the Divorce Act, 1985," in *Equality Issues In Family Law*, Karen Busby et al. (eds.) (Winnipeg, MB: Legal Research Institute of the University of Manitoba, 1990), p. 191.

7. Diane Galarneau, *Perspectives on Labour and Income* (Ottawa: Statistics Canada, June 1992).

8. Jane Gadd, "Flaws found in deadbeat-dad plan," *The Globe and Mail*, July 19, 1996, p. A6.

Unexpected Losses: Grief in Adolescence

Sheri Findlay

Virtually no one gets through life untouched by grief. It is a universal experience affecting everybody at one time or another. As a phenomenon, grief has been studied for decades by physicians, psychologists and sociologists. As a theme, grief has permeated the art, music, plays and literature of all cultures through the ages. Clearly we don't yet entirely understand grief or we would have stopped studying it and writing and singing about it years ago.

This essay discusses grief, in particular, those aspects of grief that are likely to affect adolescents. No discussion of grief in teenagers would be useful without an understanding of some of the essential issues of adolescent development that were discussed by Miriam Kaufman in part one of this book. A knowledge of these developmental issues allows us to see in which ways teens can be expected to grieve differently from adults. In addition to a familiarity with adolescent development, a basic understanding of grief is needed. This is where we will start.

The death of someone we know is an external event which sets into motion an internal process known as "grief." Various definitions have been proposed, including "Grief: deep or violent sorrow, keen regret."[1] A more detailed medical definition is:

> **Grief Reaction:** The emotional reaction that follows the loss of a love-object. Somatic symptoms include easy fatigability,

hollow or empty feeling in the chest or abdomen, sighing hyperventilation, anorexia, insomnia, and the feeling of having a lump in the throat. Psychological symptoms begin with an initial stage of shock and disbelief accompanied by an inner awareness of mental discomfort, sorrow, and regret. These may be followed by tears, sobbing, and cries of pain. The duration of the reaction is variable but may last for over a year.[2]

The psychiatric literature uses the term "uncomplicated bereavement":

Immediately or within a few months after the loss of a loved one, a normal period of bereavement or grief begins. Feelings of sadness, preoccupation with thoughts about the deceased, tearfulness, irritability, insomnia, and difficulty in concentrating and carrying out one's daily activities are some of the signs and symptoms. A grief-reaction is limited to a varying period of time based on one's cultural group.[3]

The causes of grief are usually clear. Someone the person has known and had a relationship with has died. Generally speaking, the closer or more intense the relationship was, the more profound the grief reaction. However, the death of seemingly unimportant people in a teenager's life can also trigger a grief reaction. Whether the deceased was a classmate the teen wasn't known to be friends with, the sibling of a friend, or even a celebrity, such as a musician, the distress exhibited may go beyond what we think of as reasonable. In some cases, a close but private relationship may have existed. In others, there may have been an imagined relationship with the classmate, or a fantasy about the musician. Sometimes the emotional response of an adolescent confronted with the death of someone close may be labelled as grief, but might in reality represent an internal conflict related to the teen's developmental level and understanding of death at the time the loss occurred. These aspects are discussed later in this essay.

Why Are Teens Different?

We must begin by looking at what is unique about people at this phase of life. Adolescents are neither mature children nor immature adults. Nor are they "halfway" between the two. Adolescence is a stage of life that has many unique features. Physical changes of adolescence are encompassed by the word "puberty." Psychologically, adolescence is a time of striving for independence and autonomy. Many social changes occur during the teen years which culminate in the individual no longer being reliant on the family for support or guidance. Although eagerly anticipated by most teenagers, this increasing independence does come at a cost. In gaining a more adult identity, the teen loses self-identification as a child. Old relationships (i.e., family) are de-emphasized at the expense of new ones (i.e., peers). Loss is an unavoidable part of adolescence that no one is spared. New loss can not only add to pre-existing feelings, but amplify teens' feelings of loss of their former childhood self. Fortunately, most teenagers sail through adolescence and barely look back, the loss of the family being the last thing on their minds. Despite being frequently oblivious to the various changes going on around and within them, teenagers can be caught by an unexpected loss at a time when they are emotionally tenuous, and lacking a firm sense of self-identity.

One of the most important features that distinguishes adolescents from adults who are grieving is that the loss may be the teens' first experience with grief. And, as is the case for all first times, they don't know what to expect. The excruciating pain they feel, the restless nights, the feeling of nausea and all the other symptoms of grief are new to them, and they don't have the benefit of past experience to know that these feelings will subside slowly over time. How can they imagine ever feeling happy again, ever being enthusiastic, or even relaxed and free from worries? As much as we may like to simply say: "I know you feel terrible now, but one day you'll feel better," it is unrealistic to expect teens to incorporate this reality in their first experience with grieving a significant loss. As a parent, you may possess wisdom gained from experience in dealing with grief, but be forced nonetheless to watch your teenager struggle painfully through the same slow process for the first time. Frustrating though it may be, your words cannot hasten the healing.

When a mature adult hears about a death, anybody's death, the idea of one's own mortality is an inescapable mental exploration. A plane crash or random violence elicits the thought, "That could have been me." Friends and family are the next ones to be painted into the scenario, emphasizing the vulnerability of not only ourselves, but all our special relationships. Dwelling on one's own mortality or the possibility of losing the people we love and depend on can be painful. Most adults have learned to suppress these thoughts in order to carry on with everyday life. When did we learn to do this? The specific age is variable, but being able to deal with the constant threat of losing those we love is part of coming to terms with one's own mortality. By the time most of us reach adulthood, it is likely that we have spent some time reconciling ourselves to the fact that life is finite. In the transition from the magical thinking of childhood to the complex thinking of adulthood, we learn that all people must die, and that death is irreversible and often unpredictable. This knowledge is usually passively acquired in the teen years, typically in a process of slowly consolidating isolated ideas. When a death occurs in the midst of this transition period, before teens have had time to reach their own conclusions and come to terms with the implications, the notions of finite existence and fragility of loved ones can suddenly be brought painfully into focus. An intense emotional reaction may result, which may be interpreted as grief out of proportion to the relationship that existed with the deceased. What teens may actually be grieving is their own sense of invulnerability and immortality.

Adolescents commonly have a world-view similar to invulnerability, described as idealism, whereby bad things happen only to bad people. We may find this surprising, given the overwhelming evidence to the contrary in daily newspapers and the evening news. However, remember that children are deluged with books and movies with happy endings, where the good guys win and the bad guys get what they deserve. Happy endings are certainly the norm for all children's stories, and this continues to be true with most entertainment aimed at teenagers. It isn't necessarily the case that this situation needs radical change, but we need to be aware of the impact that such exposure has on young people. Those teens whose world-views have not evolved past idealism may develop an overwhelming sense of having been cheated when faced with a loss: "This wasn't supposed to happen to me"; "This isn't the way things are supposed to be"; or "What did I do wrong?" Incorporating this loss into a new coherent, more mature world-view is a difficult process that may go on for years.

Considering a teenager's evolving understanding of death, it becomes clear that a single loss can have different implications as the teen passes through the sequence of developmental stages. A death seen through the eyes of a child is viewed in a concrete manner, and is limited to the notion of never seeing the deceased again. Children and some early teens see no implication for their own mortality or for the mortality of others and, although the death may clash drastically with their sense of idealism, they are not yet ready to let go of this worldview. As the child matures, he or she may feel the need to re-evaluate this experience. Seen in retrospect through the more sophisticated eyes of the adolescent, the death has new implications. This process of regrieving can be more difficult for the adolescent than the initial loss he or she experienced as a child. Parents may not understand why their teen is suddenly talking about someone who died years before. It will be more difficult for teens undergoing this process if those around them feel that they are being inappropriate, or seeking attention. It needs to be understood that regrieving a loss that has apparently been resolved for years is a developmentally appropriate process. The grief is real and the process is normal.

The Symptoms of Grief

The physical and psychological manifestations of grief may be obvious in some teenagers, and more subtle in others. There is a wide variability in "normal grief," with some symptoms predominating in one individual, and different symptoms in another.

The most universal manifestation of grief is sadness. People describe this in many different ways, including a sense of emptiness, melancholy or sorrow. What we see on the outside typically is crying. However, crying is such a culturally determined expression of emotion that some young people, especially young men, may not give way to it. Instead, they may exhibit a paucity of emotion, irritability, loss of happiness or loss of a sense of humour. These are all normal reactions to grief, and no effort should be made to ameliorate them. There is no amount of crying that is too much or too little. Some people choose to grieve privately, and this needs to be respected. It is not necessary to draw out the quiet griever by forcing discussion about the deceased. It is enough to make it known that you are willing to talk about it at any time the griever wishes. Most teens eventually do want to talk about the experience, but may be wary of bringing up the topic when all the adults seem to have already resolved their sorrow and gotten on with life. Knowing that the subject is not taboo allows them to broach it without worry.

The lingering sadness can be the last to go, and, even decades later, feelings of loss and sadness can be sparked by a memory or anniversary.

In addition to sadness, difficulty with concentration and attention are extremely common during early grief. Teens can have great trouble doing homework or reading assignments, and long tests can be difficult for them to complete. The school needs to be aware of the adolescent's situation and may need to allow for extra time for assignments. Even in leisure time, teens may choose activities which are very distracting, such as television or video games, staying away from those activities that would allow their minds to wander, such as reading, listening to music, or arts and crafts. These are reasonable coping mechanisms in the short term and probably don't need to be addressed.

Irritability or moodiness, a part of everyday life with some teens, is seen quite frequently in teens who are grieving a loss. Small things can set them off, and they can seem grumpy for a good part of the day, especially with their families. The struggle to deal with their grief is overwhelming and can leave them with little emotional reserve for everyday frustrations, such as a pesky younger sibling or a parent who asks one too many times about a chore. Those in close contact with grieving teens should be understanding of the turmoil they face, and may need to develop a temporary thick skin. In general, the behaviour needs to be addressed only if it crosses the line into depression or violence.

Sleeplessness is a very common symptom of grief and is almost inevitable at some time during the grieving process. For some teens, the main problem is falling asleep; they are unable to avoid the flood of images or emotions that enter their minds as soon as their heads hit the pillow. They may try to distract themselves, but are unsuccessful. Some may even start to avoid going to bed until they are exhausted in the wee hours of the morning, thereby ensuring that they will quickly fall asleep. Some may try to facilitate sleep by using sedatives such as sleeping pills or alcohol. For others, the main problem is not with falling asleep, but with staying asleep. They wake up very early, often at three or four o'clock in the morning, and are unable to get back to sleep. During these quiet times, their minds are flooded with memories and thoughts of the person they have lost.

Regardless of the type of insomnia, the result is the same: exhaustion. During the day they will be tired from too few hours of sleep and poor-quality sleep, sometimes to the point of falling asleep in school. There is no perfect solution to this very troubling symptom. Sticking to a routine is probably the best approach. Going to bed at about the same time every night, and doing the same things before bed (watching the news, taking a shower, reading a book, or whatever) can be helpful. Sedatives are only temporary fixes and should be avoided. Although they can help with falling asleep, they often wear off halfway through the night and can lead to early-morning awakening. Some sedatives can leave teens groggy in the morning, and alcohol can leave them hung over. Many sleeping pills, including those available over the counter, are habit-forming and therefore have the potential for abuse. Other strategies that can be helpful include eliminating caffeine (coffee, tea, colas) and avoiding naps during the day. Teens should be encouraged to remain as active as they were before the death. Finally, it can be useful to limit the time teens spend in their room, particularly on the bed. The bed should be reserved for going to sleep at night. Despite these simple tactics, some may continue to have problems. Most teens in this situation can be reassured that eventually their sleep will return to its normal state.

When sleep finally does arrive, many find that their daytime grief has seeped into their subconscious and permeates their dreams. Wish-fulfilment dreams are common, in which the teen dreams that the death never occurred, or that the dead person has come back to life. Life in the dream is back to normal. Upon awakening some may even forget that anything has changed. Then, as the full impact of the death hits them again, they become sad, and may even feel guilty that they had been dreaming about being happy.

Alternatively, some dreams can be frightening or painful. If the death was accidental or violent, dreams can focus on the circumstances, real or imagined. True nightmares can wake the teen from sleep with a fright, and leave unshakable memories for the remainder of the day. These experiences can make the whole idea of going to bed very upsetting. As with insomnia, there is no simple solution for making upsetting dreams go away. Patience, reassurance and providing the opportunity to talk out their feelings can go a long way in helping teens cope. Having their feelings validated and knowing that what they are going through is "normal" can be comforting, even though the symptoms persist.

Physical complaints during grieving are common, and typically include a sense of nausea, a knot in the stomach or stomach butterflies. Poor appetite and lack of interest in food often result. Temporary weight loss is common and, unless dramatic, is probably not a cause for concern. Teens should be encouraged to attend all meals with their families and eat what they are able to. The complaint of feeling full after eating only a small amount of food is often voiced. This can be worked around by having many small meals during the day rather than three large ones. Some people tend to eat more when they are upset, and this can have the opposite effect — weight gain. Again, unless dramatic, this is not a major cause for concern. If the adolescent's main source of food is from the household, then an effort should be made to have mainly healthy food available from which to choose. Diarrhea and constipation are also frequently seen during the acute stages of grief, and are not causes for alarm. The problem is usually transient and improves without specific treatment.

A variety of other physical symptoms can accompany grief, often in the form of what are known as "somatic" symptoms. These symptoms are often pain-related, with headaches and stomachaches the most commonly experienced. These symptoms are likely the result of many factors, including decreased sleep, irregular eating patterns, increased psychological stress and increased anxiety associated with minor pain. The lack of a specific medical diagnosis doesn't make the pain less real to the person suffering the symptom. It is not imagined or fabricated discomfort. Understanding, support and reassurance are the first line of treatment. If the complaint is persistent or disabling, however, the teen probably needs to be seen by a physician. If no cause is found, the teen will probably be reassured that there is nothing seriously wrong and that the symptom is expected to improve gradually over time.

Specific Circumstances

Most of the discussion until now has been of a general nature, outlining the symptoms of grief and the interrelationship between adolescent maturity and the ability to grieve. We will now explore some specific circumstances that are common causes of grief in teens, and discuss unique issues in each scenario.

Death of a Parent

The death of a parent is, for most teens, the most disruptive possible loss. In addition to losing a person who has until that point played a pivotal role in their lives, they are losing their home life, their daily routine, their sense of stability, and often the surviving parent for a time. When such a major loss occurs, teens may feel cheated, almost to the point of feeling persecuted, or singled out for such a tragedy. They ask themselves what they did wrong and what they did to deserve this punishment. Not only is the parent gone for the present, but all the future roles that parent would play are now gone too — roles at graduations, at weddings and as grandparents. Each of these scenes must be rewritten, with the parent not there. Grieving the loss of the future, idealized parent can be the most painful aspect of all.

Adolescents are not immune to the many adult concerns that will need to be addressed in the upcoming months. Financial security in many families is at risk, and teens worry about their quality of life. The redistribution of household chores and having to take on more responsibility around the house can interfere with their pre-existing agenda. Teens can be put in situations that require degrees of responsibility not yet reasonable for their level of maturity, such as becoming the primary caretaker for younger siblings. The time needed for various new duties at home may interfere with normal teenage activities, such as seeing friends after school, participation in extracurricular activities at school, getting a part-time job and dating. Worrying about these day-to-day problems can leave an adolescent feeling guilty and selfish. Statements such as "Your mother died and all you can think about is yourself" may echo in their heads, even without them ever being said aloud. It is very important that teens be allowed to carry on with all those activities that they engaged in before the death; otherwise, the loss is being compounded by further loss. Some may choose to stay home more, at least initially, but this should be something they do out of choice, not obligation.

There may be teens who will need encouragement to carry on with their previous activities. The need to stay home to protect the surviving parent from being alone may be overwhelming to some teens. There will be anxiety for the teen who has to re-establish relationships with friends, teachers and acquaintances. They anticipate awkward silences, and know that other teens won't know what to say to them. They may worry about "breaking down" in public if someone offers condolences. Despite all the reasons to avoid returning to normal daily living, most teens understand the need and willingly face the challenge. Those who do not may need help from others. This help may come from a friend, someone who is able to stay close by for the first few days after returning to school. It is also essential that the teen sees that those around them, especially the surviving parent, is making strides of their own toward resumption of normal activities.

Understandably, surviving parents are often not as available to the adolescents as they would like to be. Obviously their own grief plays a large part in this, but there are many other factors, including financial worries, having to return to the workforce, finding new living accommodations and coping with increased family and household responsibilities. Many teens are put in the position of having to care for a grieving parent, placing a parent's needs above their own. They see that the parent is worse off than they are, and the teen can quickly become the stronger of the two. For parents, the loneliness of having lost a partner can be somewhat lessened by developing an unusually close relationship with their teenagers. This may be a therapeutic situation for both teen and parent, but, if prolonged, it can run the risk of jeopardizing adolescent development. Feelings of guilt can surface when the teen realizes the time has come to start making new relationships. Unless these feelings can be expressed openly and dealt with, the guilt can lead the teen to turn down opportunities to go out with friends in order to stay home with the parent, or delay going away to college. It is therefore essential to enlist the help of friends and family members for extra support. Someone who is outside the immediate family, and therefore not also grieving the loss, can be a valuable sounding board for teens. This allows them to discuss not only their grief, but also any feelings of guilt about separating from the surviving parent. The parent, in turn, must develop social supports from outside the immediate family. It is crucial that teens receive the message that they are free to recover from grief at their own pace, which will sometimes be faster than the parent's. To deliver this message, it may be necessary for parents to suppress their own desire for closeness with the teens, no matter how hard this may be.

Teens who live in single-parent homes obviously have a huge struggle ahead of them if they loose their parent. No doubt the grief process will be overshadowed to a certain extent by practical issues: "Where will I live?", "Who will support me?" and "How can I go on alone?" The feelings of isolation, desertion and hopelessness may be profound. If the other parent is available, he or she would be the obvious choice for guardianship, but this is often not practical if the parent was previously not involved in the teen's life. Other options might include grandparents, other relatives or close family friends. If possible, teens should have input into their own living arrangements, and every effort should be made to keep siblings together. The transition period may be very difficult for the teen, who is likely to feel unconnected and uprooted in any new environment, no matter how nurturing. Rejection of anyone who tries to "replace" a lost parent is likely; therefore, guardians should initially assume parenting roles with great caution. Basic "house rules" will have to be respected, but gaining trust or intimacy will take time, and the teen needs to be allowed to lead the way.

Death of a Grandparent

For many teens, the death of a grandparent is the first experience with grief. The degree of closeness the adolescent had with the grandparent determines the extent of the grief reaction. A grandparent who had the role of a surrogate parent may be grieved almost as a parent would be. The death of a grandparent that lived out of town and was only peripherally involved will have much less of an impact. A normal distance often develops between teens and extended family during adolescence. It is frequently the case that teens spend much less time with grandparents, aunts, uncles and cousins during this period of development compared with when they were younger. During the adolescent years, it is normal to feel more strongly connected to one's peer group than to one's family. When a death occurs during this time, teens can suddenly feel very guilty about their lack of involvement with the person they lost. They can feel that an opportunity for closeness or getting to know that person has been lost, and they may feel regret at not having been able to say goodbye. Teens should be relieved of this burden they place on themselves. It is likely that the involvement they had with their grandparent was age-appropriate. Hearing this from an adult can be very valuable and reassuring. Teens may appreciate the opportunity to say goodbye in their own way — by creating a memorial or speaking at the service.

Death of a Sibling

The death of a sibling can create great emotional conflict in a teenager. The circumstances around the death are extremely important in order to understand what a teen may be feeling. A sudden death, in addition to leaving teenage siblings stunned, may overwhelm them with feelings of guilt. They will question why their lives were spared, and it will be impossible to answer the question: "Why wasn't it me?" Guilt that they are still alive when their sibling is dead may lead them to challenge their own mortality and tempt fate by engaging in risky behaviour. Parents, who are experiencing their own severe grief, may misinterpret their teens' behaviour as not loving or remembering their dead sibling, or abandoning the family at a time of great need. It is essential to include all siblings in a family's grief. Teens need to know that the entire family, including their parents, have the same unanswerable questions they do.

If a sibling had been sick with a chronic disease or died from a terminal illness, then chances are the teen has had to put his or her life on hold as all the family's time, energy and emotion has been centred on the sick child. A well teen can easily be overlooked by parents who are having to cope with a dying child. When the sibling dies, in addition to feeling overwhelming sadness and grief, the teen may experience a feeling of relief that the teen is unable to share with his or her grieving parents. After the death, parents and other family members often idealize the dead sibling, talking about how wonderful the child was, how smart, and what a promising future the child had. The surviving teens are unable to avoid seeing comparisons being made between them and the sibling, and can come to resent the dead, "perfect" sibling. These feelings of relief at the death of a sibling and resentment toward the dead sibling may be very normal, but they leave an adolescent feeling guilty and wondering: "What kind of a person am I if I feel this way?" Even the most understanding of parents may be unable to see what the surviving teens may be going through. In these circumstances it is valuable to have a person outside the immediate family with whom the teens can talk through these feelings.

Death of a Peer

The death of a friend or classmate is unique for adolescents as it is likely the first time that they have had to experience grief publicly. In such circumstances, teens are not in the confines of the family, to whom they normally look for guidance and role models for appropriate "grieving behaviour." They will see how those around them, such as teachers and coaches, handle the situation. Although the deceased peer may not have been a close friend, and the deep feelings of loss and emptiness are not present, a sense of shock is often felt that is much stronger than that which would be felt by adults experiencing a similar, apparently peripheral loss. Again, this has to do with the sudden realization of mortality, the loss of invulnerability and the letting-go of idealism. It is important for schools and parents to provide a forum for discussion of the issues raised by the death of the peer. A memorial service organized by the school can be useful in providing closure and putting the death into context for the peer group.

Death as a Result of Suicide

Guilt is the emotion that often becomes overwhelming when someone we know has died as a result of suicide. Guilt that we didn't, or couldn't, stop the person, guilt that we didn't notice he or she was having a problem or didn't tell someone, and guilt that in some way we may have contributed to the person's suicide. These feelings can leave teens with a sense of helplessness and ineffectiveness. Endless "what if…" scenarios play out in our mind, as we wonder what we could have done differently to prevent the suicide. If the person who has died was someone close, such as a family member, a best friend, a boyfriend or girlfriend, we are left with a feeling of abandonment and desertion. It is nearly impossible not to take suicide personally, not to believe that suicide is a reflection on us as individuals. "If I were a more valuable person, he wouldn't have done that" and "Am I so worthless that I'm not worth living for?" There is also typically anger that the person "chose" to leave, and didn't care about the people who would be left behind. The suicide is seen as selfish and inconsiderate. This abundance of strong emotions such as guilt, anger and doubts of self-worth can be preoccupying, sometimes to the extent that normal grieving does not occur. An adolescent can be so overwhelmed with these emotions that the loss itself almost takes a back seat for a time, and the deceased is not mourned in the usual way until much later. This interference in the normal process of grieving can last years, decades, or even a lifetime. Often it is helpful to remove blame from the dead person by making it understood that most people who commit suicide have mental illness and are thus not "themselves" when they take their own lives.[4] The illness they had, whether it was depression, severe anxiety or schizophrenia, was responsible for the death in the same way that cancer or heart disease can be the cause of death. This knowledge may allow the teen to overcome the anger and guilt in order to realize the loss and move forward with mourning.

When to Get Help

The majority of individuals who are unlucky enough to lose someone during their adolescence manage to cope. With the help of family, friends and other members of their community, such as teachers and guidance counsellors, teens slowly return to their daily tasks and to those developmental tasks that society expects of them. There will be some teens, however, who need professional help through their time of grief. Warning signs can be confusing because they may be difficult to distinguish from normal grieving, and even from normal adolescence. Sadness during grief is normal but severe depression, thoughts of suicide or reckless behaviour (such as drinking and driving, drug use, or excessive fighting) are not. Depression may be seen as inability to get out of bed in the morning, to care for oneself, or a complete inability to eat. The depressed teen may be reluctant to leave the house, see friends or attend school. Withdrawal from all activities that the teen was once involved in is a worrisome sign. Many of these symptoms can be normal if they are not severe and are brief in duration. Persistence of severe symptoms for weeks, or mild symptoms for months, merits a trip to the doctor.

There are some circumstances in which we should probably anticipate the need for extra support for the teen. These include death as a result of suicide (especially if it was a parent or sibling) and death as a result of violent crime. Most teens in these situations should be given the opportunity to talk out their feelings with someone who is uninvolved. Accessing these kinds of services for teens can be difficult, but a good place to start may be with family physicians or paediatricians. If they are not comfortable counselling teens, they should be able to recommend an alternative. Services can also be accessed through the school, such as guidance counsellors or school psychologists. A single visit may be all that is necessary, but some teens may benefit from regular ongoing visits. Even those who aren't inclined to see someone regularly will at least have learned that help is available if they want it at some time in the future.

Conclusions

Mourning a loss is never easy, even for those lucky individuals who are secure in their self-identity, comfortable with their own mortality, and possessed of a world-view that has room for unexpected death happening to good people.

The typical adolescent, however, is asked to confront grief at a time when he or she is armed with none of these. One might reasonably wonder how it is that adolescents ever manage to survive the process. Part of the answer undoubtedly lies in the willingness of family and friends to provide a patient and non-judgmental forum for their teen to talk things out.

Notes

1. *The Concise Oxford Dictionary, 7th edition* (Oxford, UK: Oxford University Press, 1987), p. 438.

2. *Taber's Medical Dictionary, Edition 16* (Philadelphia, PA: F.A. Davis, 1989), p. 764.

3. Harold I. Kaplan and Benjamin J. Sadock, *Clinical Psychiatry* (Baltimore, MD:Williams & Wilkins, 1988), p. 301.

4. Harold I. Kaplan and Benjamin J. Sadock, *Comprehensive Textbook of Psychiatry, 5th Edition* (Baltimore, MD: Williams & Wilkins, 1989), pp. 1414.

part three

Parenting Different Kids

Behind the Scenes: Parenting Activist Teenagers

Tara Cullis

It was two in the morning in a strange hotel in Minneapolis, far from our Vancouver home. My thirteen-year-old daughter, Severn, and I had arrived at midnight for an environmental meeting called the "Ecommunity Conference," and nothing was going right. On reaching the hotel we'd learned that few of the promised luminaries such as Al Gore had actually come to the meeting. Our computer printer refused to spit out the speeches we had to make at 8:00 A.M. And worst of all, we had just realized that our speeches, advocating for the importance of neighbourhood, community control and livable cities, were to be presented in the colossus across the vast parking lot opposite the hotel — the Mall of America, the largest shrine to concrete and consumerism south of the forty-ninth parallel. (Yes, the West Edmonton Mall in Alberta, Canada, is bigger.) Our hotel room and our plane fares, we had just realized, were all being paid by the mall: The conference was a public-relations expense to counter its image of waste and excess. Our effort, coming so far and missing several days of school and work (as usual, we were unpaid) might well be counterproductive: The organizers had opposite goals to ours.

It was at that point that Sev — tired, hungry and anxious — looked around those four unfamiliar walls, and suddenly wailed. "Mum, what on earth are we doing here!"

My poor little girl! She should have been in bed! She shouldn't have been missing school! I shouldn't have been neglecting my other daughter! (Sarika, then nine, had stayed at home with Grandma.) And maybe I, too, had better things to do …

At moments like that (and there have been many), I've really wondered if we're doing the right thing, allowing our daughter to take on the fatigue and stress of international environmental work. Parenting an activist teenager is no picnic. It's a big investment of time and commitment, and a lot of hard work. One needs skills, and the will to teach them: Children aren't born knowing how to research, organize files, keep accounts, do public speaking. It involves dealing with a very idealistic person, which is challenging because you have to practise the ideals you preach. It costs a lot of money, if you have it, because a child will make you put your funds where your mouth is. It involves dealing with a young person who is exposed and sensitive to sad stories, depressing statistics, injustices, cynicism and wrongdoing. So it carries the threat of sadness, of depression at a vulnerable time of life. It involves a shelving of your ego, a transference of satisfaction from your own work to vicarious achievement; at times, it seems you have to put your own life on hold. It demands discipline to respect the delicate line between helping, which is necessary, and taking over, which is taboo (yet tempting: it would be so much easier!). It involves doubt: There aren't guidelines. It involves stress: It's all extra in an already busy life. It can throw off the balance in a family: Not only does it demand that parents devote a lot of time to the activist child's needs, it might also bring a public spotlight to that child. It requires a perspective wise beyond reason to accept the way some critics attack anyone — even a child — who tries to improve the world. It involves setting an example, a twenty-four-hour-a-day job since children see everything! And it requires providing inspiration. It involves, in short, tremendous parental support.

Back at the Mall of America the next day, after wrestling the printer into submission, the speeches had gone off well after all. We felt our messages may have reached some receptive ears, and we'd met some intriguing thinkers. During a short break in commitments we found ourselves lined up for the mall's roller-coaster. With us was another speaker, Roland Wiederkehr, the right-hand-man Mikhail Gorbachev had picked to head up the International Green Cross (his environmental organization) as the original executive director. A Swiss, he'd been serious, stiff and formal, though in his own way friendly, until Severn persuaded him to embrace the Mall's ironies, be a child with her and join us on the ride. After roaring down the long water-chute in a hollowed-out log, water ricocheting everywhere, formality was history. Tie drenched, three-piece suit sodden, hair madly dishevelled, a beaming Roland radiated delight. It was a thrill to share this hilarious moment of transformation with a man of his calibre. Having brought him to her level, Severn and Roland became fast friends.

That's the other side of the coin, the seductive aspect of parenting an environmental activist. Just as the effort starts to seem absurd, just as you begin to feel guilty, your child — and you, if you are the companion — are rewarded by tremendous fun. You might find yourself hiking to a mountain wilderness festival through a snowstorm in August, or listening to drums throbbing all night long on the wind outside your teepee. You might be meeting a foreign prime minister, travelling to Beijing or Rio, serving salmon pit-roasted under great old trees, voyaging in a flotilla with biologists and birders, dancing in a button-blanket around the fire on the dirt floor of a native Big House, or travelling to a new city where your child will meet other young people whose hearts beat to the same drummer. And you begin to see valuable things happen to your son or daughter. He or she develops skills and competence, often very quickly. Facing the causes of frustration and depression and striving to alter them give a young person a sense of personal control, of power, which is very healthy. Often, environmental or human rights battles are lost; yet even in failure, a pride develops in knowing one tried. Sometimes — I admit it's rare — the efforts result in success! And this is invaluable in building the character of a vulnerable young person. A youngster who has worked hard, with people she respects, to right a painful wrong and has been successful faces a difficult world with the beginnings of a priceless and patient confidence. Watching that blossom in a young person is wonderful. And there's another reward too. It's inspiration, which is a highly underrated joy. It is one of the ways a child can meet people who make her heart soar, and hear stories of respect, courage and achievement which make her burst with pride to be human. It counters the destructive cynicism so many youngsters embrace. A young person who draws the family into her activist efforts can give that family their most valued possessions: hard-won, suddenly overwhelming experiences that glow in the memory as treasured jewels.

When I balance the pros and cons, I realize these issues are like everything else: Both parent and child get out of it in proportion to what they put in. Hard work equals great, sometimes inexpressible satisfaction. But it's still hard work!

A question I've often been asked is, "Is it fair to saddle children with the problems of the world?" This is a sensitive and reasonable, and highly important, question, one which I pose to myself. It's worried me a lot.

In our house, bad news is a constant companion. Because both my husband and I work on environmental issues, phone calls and visitors introduce new disappointments daily, new losses, new frustrations and great sadness. Perhaps because he and I were both brought up in more optimistic times and in secure and happy families, we can with effort remain optimists; but it's so hard on our children. We have always included them in all our environmental efforts and adventures, partly because such campaigns often involve travel (usually to places which are both beautiful and culturally unique!). The girls have hiked and camped with us on wilderness campaigns and travelled with us to work with remote cultures since they were infants. But as they fell in love with nature, their sensitivity to its destruction or loss became ever more acute. In the 1980s we were working very hard supporting the Haida people of the Queen Charlotte Islands, or Haida Gwaii, in their struggle to protect the beautiful southern half of Moresby Island from logging. The children learned many Haida songs and ancient stories around distant campfires there, and loved to hunt and gather on the rich beaches near tilting totem poles and moss-covered old house posts. Back at home, many's the time I would go in to kiss Severn good night, only to find her weeping with furious frustration at the foot-dragging of the then-premier of our province, Bill Van der Zalm, to work with the then-prime minister of Canada, Brian Mulroney, on a national park reserve for South Moresby. At times like that I am careful to explain that he had his reasons, that our opinion is not the only one, that he could in fact be right! But, that seems to cut little ice. Perhaps by then it's too late. It's important that parents remember all along to teach children to look at both sides: they have to let kids know that parents do not just accept what they are told, but weigh the information; and that children must do the same. But my experience has been that children have terrific faith in their parents and tend to take their positions on issues. I assume this changes as the children mature! But at seventeen, Severn still tends to agree with us.

As far as dealing with the onslaught of truly bad news, however, which every child has to face now that the holes in the ozone, global warming (climate change), and species extinction are common knowledge, I have always told myself that teaching a child how to do something about the problems she hears of is an important route to mental health. Whether this is really true I can't tell you. Severn, my eldest child, who so far has had the most success in having an impact on decision makers, is today a well-adjusted and optimistic teenager. My youngest, Sarika, at fourteen, has commented that all the bad news means there is nothing to look forward to. I'm hoping that cutting back on pessimistic comments in our household, and helping her increase her experience in making a positive difference, will compensate. Whether it will I cannot yet tell.

Birth order in a family has its impact, but it's complex. In our case, our eldest daughter went into environmental work and was successful in making a difference. The resultant expectations sent our shy younger daughter into retreat; she let us know that she would not be going into public speaking. Yet she agreed to her elementary-school principal's request that she give the Arbour Day speech to Vancouver's mayor — and made a dynamite presentation. The principal was bowled over: He had not known she had that talent. And when Severn went to high school and grew out of the small local club she'd founded — ECHO, for the Environmental Children's Organization — Sarika, at ten, took over the club enthusiastically, enlisting a dozen friends and organising trips to the countryside. So one has to be careful. In the anxiety not to impose standards set by an older child, it's easy to forget or deny that a second child might have similar skills. Activist Craig Kielburger, the powerfully effective thirteen-year-old Canadian from Ontario who went to India in 1996 in the immensely successful effort to publicize the plight of child labourers in rug factories, is a second child. His elder brother, Mark, was an environmental activist as a teenager and the winner of many awards such as the Ontario Medal of Good Citizenship. Mrs. Kielburger recalls, "I used to worry about Craig, because Mark was a very good public speaker, and Craig used to say he'd do it too. I told him there are other things in life, that everybody's different. I felt he'd be in the shadow of his brother. I don't worry about that any more!"

Another issue that often comes up when people ask about kids and activism is: "How much of this is really her idea and her work, and how much is yours?" That question is an important and interesting one. Obviously the possibilities are vast. Politician, feminist and author Rosemary Brown, when asked if her children were activists, responded firmly: "They never had a choice!" Whereas Mrs. Kielburger comes from the opposite background: "I don't know where these kids came from! My husband and I were totally uninvolved, I swear to God. The two most dead-beat parents! Look what they did to us!" But Mrs. Kielburger is very supportive. Today, she works full-time, unpaid, for Craig's organization. In fact, she donates the use of her kitchen and computer equipment to the other volunteers who assist Craig. In my experience, an activist child means that at least one adult, usually a parent, has to give a lot of time to that child. The more productive the child, the more parental time is involved. Yet this observation does not mean that the child is a front for adult action, that the daddy or mummy is the real author of the speech or the concept or the ideas. Quite the reverse! It is the scut work, not the glory, that becomes the responsibility of the parent. As Mrs. Kielburger says, "We're the drones, the secretary, the drivers."

Even when a child's projects are quite limited and reasonable, a lot of adult time must be invested if these efforts are to succeed. Children simply aren't born knowing how to do everything: Someone has to teach them what they want to know. Further, someone has to look out for them and keep them safe. "Naturally, they [the parents of other children] are worried about security," Mrs. Kielburger adds. "People always ask, 'Let me speak with your mother.'"

Perhaps because they'd participated in demonstrations and celebrations all their lives, our children were activists from the cradle. Following my parents' example when they took me as a child in Vancouver on a walk in support of the human rights efforts in Selma, Alabama, I and my husband took our children on the annual Vancouver Peace March from the time they were in strollers. When Severn was in kindergarten, she organized her friends into a parade and marched round our neighbourhood on Bernard Street in Toronto's Annex district with signs to "Save the Wilderness." She made herself a beautiful sweatshirt with the same message, and wore it for years. Her travels with us in her early years had involved her in issues too adult for her full understanding: the long battle supporting the Haida's fight for South Moresby; the marches and the hikes to glorious alpine festivals in support of the Nlakapamux people's efforts to protect their ancestral Stein Valley (the largest unlogged watershed in southwestern British Columbia); the fight to help the Penan, the nomadic native people being displaced by logging in Sarawak on the island of Borneo; and especially our efforts to support the Kayapo people of the Xingu in their struggle to protect the Brazilian rainforest. It was Severn's concern for these naked, elaborately painted friends she'd made deep in the Amazon in a tiny native village threatened by dams, mining and burning that pushed her to start her own environmental group. Severn embraced our causes and our points of view fully, which concerned me somewhat, as I've mentioned. But it seemed healthy that, instead of becoming depressed about the problems, she wanted to find a way to contribute to solutions.

At this point she was nine years old, and in Grade Five. Her friends were enthusiastic about starting a club; they, too, wanted to make a difference to the animals and trees and Kayapo children. So they all came over to our house. Their talk went round in enthusiastic circles. They ate lots of pizza and drank quarts of juice, but little headway was made on their wish to start a group. Finally I mentioned that one way to start might be to make a list of things to talk about (called an "agenda"), such as choosing a name and writing down some goals. I also said that lots of people find it works even better when someone writes down the decisions made (in notes called "minutes"). Well, that's all it took for them to be off and running. I thought my contribution was done, and went back to the kitchen. But soon they were calling out for further input. First, they wanted a succinct but comprehensible synopsis of environmental issues — a request I found challenging. Then, they wanted equally succinct, and equally challenging, advice on various choices of action. But then they were flying on their own. They chose the name Environmental Children's Organization, or "ECO" — later changed to "ECHO." They elected to work on the Amazon and on the Penan in Sarawak.

They decided to put together slide shows and write speeches to teach high-school students about these and other environmental issues. Since I had a slide table and many useful slides, my collection was fair game; and since "cleaning up" seemed to mean merely picking up the fallen slides and getting them all onto the same table, it was up to me to restore order. I taught the children how to work the projector and the screen, how to organize a speech, and the basics of public speaking. And no eleven-year old can drive a car, so transport fell into parental laps by default. Soon the children decided they wanted to fundraise and at their next meeting came up with all sorts of ideas. They began making hundreds of pieces of attractive jewellery from Fimo and origami paper, which they sold to anyone who came near them — teachers, friends, parents, relatives. As the money came in bit by bit, I had to step in again to help them start a bank account and teach them to keep financial records — a task that needs careful supervision. Having heard of the muddy waters that logging caused in Sarawak, the club decided to buy a water filter for a Penan village. Older activist teenagers helped out enthusiastically and were great role models. Two volunteered to help the children learn the writing skills, editing and layout — and fundraising — necessary to publish newspapers for their organization. The children made four wonderful newspapers.

This took a lot of work. But it was great fun. And childcare is time-consuming in any event. Further, as an activist myself, with activist friends, and well aware of much of what the children needed to know, I felt unjustified in keeping all this useful experience to myself. I knew that the things they needed to know — running meetings, organizing, filing, bookkeeping — were very basic and useful life skills, worth the teaching. And third, I found I couldn't bear to tell a child: "You have a wonderful idea, but you can't fulfil it because you are too young and ignorant." I felt that a larger, priceless knowledge might result — the knowledge of how to turn dreams into reality, and the confidence that comes with it. I also thought that perhaps their actions, as youth, just might have an impact.

The office support, however, is serious business. Regardless of the area the child is working in, paperwork can become really formidable. Keeping a child current with her phone messages, helping her answer what tends to become mountains of mail, teaching her to set up and maintain accurate accounts and a filing system, to say nothing of tracking speaking schedules and accompanying her on travels, become ongoing maintenance chores. Even today, at seventeen, Severn dreads that ever-building pile of mail in her in-tray, despite its wonderful postmarks.

This whole dimension is arduous for a young person and can become overwhelming. Craig Kielburger now receives so many phone calls, letters, and requests to speak that his mother has four full-time volunteers working in her kitchen. Working to coordinate not just Craig but numerous other youngsters to fill the invitations, she feels she in essence runs a volunteer speakers' bureau. Besides the office and travel support, there are the actual issues with which the child is involved. Depending on the circumstances, a parent can find herself teaching her offspring how to research an issue, how to determine who to call for first-hand information, how to make notes and keep files. Then the child or the group will come up with a course of action. This is a difficult moment for parents! The more an effort is the child's idea, the harder the parenting role. If it were up to the parents, children would take our advice and choose doable, cheap, tested projects; our role would then be so much easier! Instead, children are capable of coming up with complicated schemes which seem doomed to failure, or grand schemes that can be quite terrifying for the parents. What would you say if your child, like Craig Kielburger, decided to journey to India to research child labour? It's a huge responsibility for a parent to agree to this. Severn and her ECHO group of Morgan Geisler, Michelle Quigg, Vanessa Suttie and Tove Fenger decided to travel to Rio de Janeiro to appear at the 1992 Earth Summit as a conscience to world leaders. What would you have said to this idea?

It is this daunting moment which is the most crucial in parenting (future) activists. Usually such grand ideas are simply impossible — the family does not have the leeway to adjust to the plan's demands and no one with the requisite talents leaps into the breach. But sometimes the glimmer of possibility shines through, tantalizing the family with the call of "What if ...!" Then you're really in trouble! Craig Kielburger's parents told him how concerned they were about his safety, his security. When Craig came up with volunteer, knowledgeable travel companions, and furthermore raised the funds for his projects by speeches to such groups as labour unions, his parents realized the trip was a possibility. When my eleven-year-old daughter announced her intent to travel to Rio with her friends, I told her that she didn't realize how much money it would cost, and that Rio was no place for twelve-year-old girls. But, deep inside, a flicker of excitement arose that these girls could dream so big, that they believed, in their youth and innocence, that their passion could have an impact on world leaders.

I realized it would break my heart to be the one to teach these youngsters at such an early age that there were limits to what they could achieve! I also knew that in a gathering of 30,000 world leaders and bureaucrats and business people and earnest environmentalists, the voices of children just might be the ones with a hope of being heard above the din. And another thought: I had already led two environmental expeditions into Brazil in support of the Kayapo natives and had learned Brazilian Portuguese. The coincidence that the Earth Summit would be held in Rio meant I happened to be uniquely suited to mentor the girls on such a project.

So we hesitated ...

A few weeks later a philanthropic donor flew up to visit environmental groups in B.C. He was curious to hear about the foundation we were launching and wondered if we had any projects he'd be interested in. Our organization was too young, then, to have developed such projects. But, as he left, the donor commented, "I've had a couple of chats with your daughter. I think her project to go to Rio is a good one, and I'm giving her a $1,000 grant to get her started." You could have knocked us down with a feather.

It was at that point I realized the trip might happen. Jeff Gibbs, a young family friend and the founder of the EYA (the Environmental Youth Alliance, which by the early 1990s spanned Canada and had crossed the Pacific to Australia), had already invited Severn to speak at a number of his national conferences. Since the children were only eleven, he knew their dream of going to Rio would need assistance, and offered to help the club put on an evening of speeches and slides at the local planetarium. The children leapt at the idea. He taught them what it takes: how to choose and rent the hall; how to design, print and distribute posters; how to determine how much to charge; how to develop the program; how to work the slide projector, the microphone, the lighting; how to promote and sell tickets; how to sell refreshments at half-time for extra income. Another friend, the fundraiser Harvey McKinnon, popped in to suggest the children type up blank cheques and insert them in the programs, and to put in a vigorous plea for funds before intermission. The evening was an enormous success. The earnestness and high spirits of the girls were profoundly moving. People jumped up and pledged $200 if others would match them. Which they did. I was astounded. At the end of the day the girls were staggered to realize they'd raised $4,700! Their Rio dream was coming closer.

Then the fundraising went into high gear. Now the girls took their Fimo and origami jewellery production line into full production and upped the arm-twisting of friends, relatives and kindly teachers. The Rio adventure was on.

I'd say the bulk of my work came then: researching the documents they'd need, the shots, a wonderful cheap apartment on the Copacabana, a brief trip to the Amazon *en route* home. I also had to unravel the extraordinary complexities not only of UNCED (the Earth Summit, or "United Nations Conference on Environment and Development"), but also of the Global Forum, which was the NGO's (non-governmental organizations') parallel convention to the Earth Summit. The girls decided that it was important to have a booth there, so they had to develop a display and lots of materials in several languages. One friend, Sharon Halfnight, stepped in to teach them how to design and make a colourful banner to identify themselves: It made all the difference.

Luckily, another parent, Patricia Hernandez, was also able to take the two weeks off work and accompany the children. A Colombian, she is at ease in South America and was ideally suited to keep everyone cheerful and comfortable. Despite the heat, humidity, pollution, fatigue, noise and sheer complexity of doing anything in Rio, she always gave the impression of having a wonderful time. My husband was a speaker at events in both forums, so he accompanied us too. I realized that I would have to give up my ideas of representing my own environmental organization at the meetings, other than in networking with the many environmentalists at the conference. It was impossible to do more! The children's hot and sweaty days began at seven o'clock in the morning and ended long after dark, doing endless homework to keep up with school. What with shopping for groceries in the fascinating Rio *mercados*, visiting the delicious *suco* (juice) bars, cooking breakfast and dinner, making bag lunches, and above all packing into the little taxis to put in the stifling ten-hour days at the outdoor booth, there was no opportunity to do anything else.

At the booth the children's first visitor, TV camera in tow, was Jean Charest, Canada's then-environment minister. The children soon gained their media legs. They were interviewed by television crews from a dozen countries, they explained their fears and hopes and passions to scores of interviewers, they debated their futures with hundreds of passers-by. At night they wrote wonderful speeches, and when they asked us for pointers my husband listened carefully to their talks and trained the girls in projection and delivery. Whenever they got a chance to take a stage, they delivered these talks, at first stiffly and with uniformly serious faces, then gradually allowing their energy and exuberance to give the words wings. Their audiences were respectful, encouraging and enthusiastic; and the girls' skills soared. There was no doubt they were having an impact; word was spreading.

I was convenor and M.C. of the "Day of the Children" at a third, parallel conference: the Earth Parliament. Many groups, including ECHO, were on the agenda. As the children spoke, the head of UNICEF, James Grant, began excitedly taking notes. Afterwards he came forward. It was essential, he said, that he take copies of the speeches to then-prime minister Mulroney, at his hotel that evening. But he also went to Maurice Strong, chair of UNCED, and request that Severn be given time to speak at a plenary session at the Earth Summit. As a result Sev got the chance to speak to the world's leaders, and she made the most of it, adding elements of all the girls' presentations into her compelling speech, which resulted in tears and a standing ovation.

It has been interesting to observe that, since then, she has had invitations to speak all over the world, opportunities to contribute articles to magazines, the chance to publish a book, many offers for television work, and, what is more, awards of all sorts. She has accepted many of these invitations and put in untold hours of hard work. She has developed persistence, and grace under pressure. Over time she has become a very accomplished writer and television host. Five years later, the invitations continue, and my involvement as a parent lessens annually: Sev's experience has outdone mine.

It makes me think. It's been astounding how much people, often total strangers, will help a person or a cause. They will go out of their way to teach, to make introductions, to clear the way to success. It's enough to confound your cynicism! Activists, especially young ones, could get nowhere without this remarkable generosity in society, this will to help them make the world a better place. If you think about it, I'm sure you will see it all around you. Teachers exhibit this altruism all the time, as do scout leaders, coaches and other volunteers of all sorts. In this context, a parent of an activist is merely one such citizen, and it is not surprising that we are happy to give the support we do. This also explains why some remarkable young people have been able to become effective activists even without their parents' help. Oher adults have been their mentors, teachers and cheerleaders, and have been proud to play the role.

These experiences have also made me think about the nature of celebrity. It was a great speech in Rio, but if you or I had given it, it would not have been heard of again. It was news because it came from a young girl. And once you get in the news, others hear of you; word spreads; invitations come in, which, if accepted, lead to other invitations and more renown until you wonder if people organizing events realize there are any other kids in the world! Celebrity seems to build on itself. This often feels unearned and baffling.

Yet experience does build up, does lead to reliability and professionalism. In my experience as a parent, at least, activism, when combined with large doses of luck and hard work, has not only been a terrific education for young people, but also a strict and challenging training ground for a number of highly useful skills. Although Severn went into her causes with only one goal, of helping to turn around our destructive ways, she is emerging with unexpected spin-offs: identified and developed talents which may well be useful to her in a career.

I asked my daughter what she feels is a parent's major role. Her analysis emphasizes the emotional support an activist child needs. First, the parent has to be a role model. She must live up to the standards she teaches. Then, she has to inspire. I have no idea how this is done, unless it's in those dreaming moments after lights out when you sit together in the dark, pushing the envelope of possibility. After that, the parent has to help the youngster keep perspective. She must teach balance, keep a firm eye on school grades, physical health, stress levels, common sense. Of course, that's daily stuff for any parent. And when successes arrive, says my daughter, you sure keep me from getting a swelled head!

My credo is that we are not here on earth to do harm, but to do good. My daughter seems to have absorbed this credo, and to have acted on it. To assist her in this endeavour has been one of my ways of living up to it. That doing so has provided us both with completely unexpected rewards has been an unlooked-for joy.

Coming Out: Parents of Lesbian and Gay Teens

Margaret Schneider

On the first Wednesday of every month, in the city where I live, a group of adults meets in a comfortable room in a church basement to talk about their experiences as parents of gay sons and lesbian daughters. They are part of an international organization called P-FLAG (Parents, Families, and Friends of Lesbians and Gays). Some of them have known about their children's sexual orientation for many years and have learned not only to tolerate, but to accept and appreciate it. Other parents are attending their first meeting because they have just found out that their children are lesbian or gay; they are upset, afraid and shocked. Yet others have known about their children's sexual orientation for a while, but have never talked to anyone about it. This is the first time they have ventured out of their own closet. These parents come from all walks of life and represent many ethnic groups. What they have in common is their recognition that, in spite of some extreme and usually very negative reactions to the news that their children are gay or lesbian, they are still parents, with all the attendant responsibilities. Ultimately all these parents will have to come to terms with what it means to them to have a gay or lesbian child.

In this essay I explore what parents need to know and understand about homosexuality in general, their children's experience in particular, and their own beliefs and feelings in order to continue to be effective parents. After presenting some general, factual information about homosexuality, I explore the foundation of attitudes and beliefs about homosexuality, describe the experience of growing up lesbian or gay, and finally, examine the parents' role in supporting their gay or lesbian children.

General Information

Most people have no reason to seek information about homosexuality until the issue touches them personally. When they do, what they find is frequently inaccurate, consisting of all the myths and stereotypes so ubiquitous in our society. Accurate information can often be reassuring to parents because it shows how erroneous the myths and stereotypes are, and because it helps parents to understand the realities of their gay or lesbian children's lives. This section provides answers to the questions that parents tend to ask most frequently and presents some information that will help parents think about their lesbian or gay children's sexual orientation in a more positive — or, at least, less negative — way. Even parents who describe themselves as liberal, and who know gay or lesbian people and count them among their friends, acquaintances or colleagues, find themselves upset when their gay or lesbian children come out to them. They express a variety of concerns and pose many questions, the most common of which are addressed here.

What is homosexuality?

Like heterosexuality, homosexuality is a physical, erotic and emotional attraction, with the capacity to fall in love; the difference is that it involves attraction to people of the same sex. Although homosexuals have persistently been accused of being child molesters, paedophilia (that is, a sexual interest in children) is in no way linked to homosexuality. Just as some heterosexual people, mostly males, are attracted to children, so, too, are some homosexual people — again, mostly males. However, most homosexuals, like most heterosexuals, have no sexual interest in children.

In Western cultures, at various times in recent history, homosexuality has been considered to be a sin, a crime or a mental illness. Each of these views needs to be examined critically.

Whether homosexuality is a sin is a question of personal belief as well as religious doctrine. Although it might be assumed that most religious faiths hold that homosexuality is a sin, there is, in fact, little consensus on this issue among theologians and other religious scholars. Although highly vocal religious leaders have vilified homosexuality, equating it with the downfall of the family and loss of general moral fibre, other religious leaders and scholars argue that homosexuality is an acceptable variation in the development of human sexuality.

There are two significant reasons for the re-evaluation of homosexuality. First, until recently, homosexual behaviour was equated with adultery, as was any sexual behaviour outside the bonds of heterosexual marriage. The concept of a loving, stable, monogamous relationship between persons of the same sex simply did not exist in society in general. As gay men and lesbians have become more visible in the past twenty-five years, it has become evident that many are indeed in long-term relationships, with many of the positive characteristics of heterosexual marriage.[1] Research investigating the quality of lesbian and gay relationships corroborates this.[2] These findings mean that homosexuality is no longer *ipso facto* adulterous behaviour. In other words, a focus on the integrity of the relationship rather than on the sexual orientation of the individuals has provided a new perspective on the issue of sin, and, in some cases, a new response from some religious groups.

The second issue which has led to the re-evaluation of homosexuality is the question of whether people choose to be gay or lesbian. Until recently, homosexuality was widely considered to be a "lifestyle choice." However, it appears that sexual orientation is established at a very early age, if not before birth, and, once established, cannot be changed. Many theologians argue that if it is not a choice, then it cannot be considered a sin, any more than can the colour of one's skin or the shape of one's nose.[3]

Parents who are concerned about sin and religious doctrine may be encouraged to know that many denominations are re-evaluating their position on homosexuality. Depending on their denomination, parents may be able to find support from their local faith community.

In some jurisdictions, same-sex sexual contact is a crime. In other jurisdictions, certain sexual acts between consenting adults, such as anal sex, which is most often associated with male homosexual behaviour (but practised by heterosexuals, too), are illegal. In more liberal parts of the world, such laws are slowly being repealed. Equally important, they are being offset by non-discrimination clauses that are being included in human-rights codes, civil-rights codes, public policy, and in the personnel policies of large and small corporations and institutions. In short, while a segment of the population believes that homosexuality ought to remain illegal, there is a significant trend toward removing it from criminal codes and protecting gay and lesbian people from harassment and discrimination.

While there are conspicuously varying views on the criminal and moral status of homosexuality, there is much more consensus on the question of whether homosexuality constitutes a mental illness. Until the mid-1960s, the research, such as it was, seemed to indicate that homosexuals were mentally unstable. However, this research was biased, did not conform to rigorous scientific standards and reflected the researchers' preconceived judgments. More recent research has clearly demonstrated that there is no difference between heterosexuals and homosexuals in their psychological and emotional well-being.[4] People who are gay or lesbian have the same range of strengths, vulnerabilities and personality characteristics that heterosexual people have. In fact, on the basis of personality-test results it is impossible to distinguish heterosexual people from homosexual people. Thus, regardless of anyone's opinion about homosexuality itself, being gay or lesbian, in and of itself, is not a barrier to establishing a career, getting an education, finding meaningful friendships and an intimate relationship, or being a productive member of society.

While there are some psychiatrists and psychologists who continue to maintain that homosexuality is a mental illness that can be "cured," these individuals represent a marginal group within their professional associations. Most professional associations, including the American and Canadian psychological associations and the American Psychiatric Association, have stated clearly that homosexuality is not a mental illness.

It is my belief that homosexuality is not immoral and ought not to be a criminal offence. It is my scientific conclusion that homosexuality is not a mental illness; rather, it is a different pathway in the development of one's sexuality. The real problem for gay and lesbian people is the discrimination they face as a result of the negative beliefs and attitudes held by others.

Why is my child gay/lesbian? Did I do something wrong?

Although there has been a lot of recent publicity about research into the origins of sexual orientation, no one really knows why people are heterosexual or homosexual. There seems to be at least some biological basis for a person's sexual orientation, but scientists are far from being able to identify a hormone, a gene or any other biological characteristic which is unequivocally associated with the development of one sexual orientation or another. We do know, however, that some theories, though persistent, are clearly incorrect. For example, whether either parent was particularly close to or distant from their child does not "make" a child homosexual. Sexual abuse does not make a child homosexual, and "being around" gay or lesbian adults will not make a child homosexual (any more than "being around" heterosexuals ensures that a child will grow up heterosexual). It isn't because parents let their daughter wear trousers too often or play sports too often. It isn't because they didn't make their son play football and hockey. In short, there is nothing that a parent has done to "make" their child homosexual, or could have done to prevent it. Parents have no control over their child's sexual orientation, are not responsible for it, and therefore have no cause to feel guilty.

Can my gay/lesbian child become heterosexual?

The short answer to this question is "no." People who are homosexual cannot be changed into heterosexuals no matter how motivated they are to change. From time to time, a variety of professionals claim they can effect change in homosexuals through processes such as religious conversion, psychotherapy or behaviour modification. In fact, these programs have a very low "success" rate and, in spite of the claims, they do not truly change people's sexual orientation. Instead, they can be damaging to the person's self-esteem, especially if the individual is coerced into treatment.

So, what is changing? To answer that question, it is important to understand that most people are not exclusively heterosexual or homosexual. A significant percentage of heterosexual men and women have had a same-sex experience resulting in orgasm, while a significant proportion of homosexuals have had opposite-sex experiences. Also, many homosexuals were married to opposite-sex partners before they finally were able to face the fact, or discovered that they were gay or lesbian and decided to come out. What this means is that homosexuals can behave heterosexually if they are highly motivated. And what stronger motivation can there be than avoiding the stigma and rejection that homosexuals face in our culture and from many of their own families? So, homosexuals who believe that their life will be ruined or that they are essentially bad people can be motivated to give up relationships with same-sex partners and perhaps begin having sexual relations with opposite-sex partners. This is not the same as changing their sexual orientation.

Frequently these individuals lead celibate lives, but they likely still desire same-sex partners, have same-sex fantasies, and still feel romantic and erotic emotional attachments to people of the same sex. But, no matter how hard they try, they do not have these feelings toward people of the opposite sex. They may be able to perform sexually in a heterosexual relationship, but on emotional, erotic and romantic levels the passion is simply not there. A sense of fulfilment is absent in these relationships, and in spite of outward appearances they are just "going through the motions." In addition, the inability to rid themselves of same-sex attractions can be damaging to their self-esteem.

Many gay and lesbian individuals feel a great deal of pressure to try to be "straight." Who wouldn't, if they believe that their life will be ruined, that they will go to hell and that everyone will reject them? Parents might feel that they want to encourage, or even push, their child to try to be heterosexual. The question to ask is whether a life of simply "going through the motions" is what parents would hope for their child in his or her future relationships.

The Future and Gay and Lesbian Children

Parents have many fears and concerns about what the future will be like for their gay son or lesbian daughter.

Masculine women/feminine boys — the image of an effeminate, limp-wristed, lisping, mincing gay male or a hyper-masculine, boot-stomping, leather-jacketed lesbian haunts the imaginations of the parents of lesbian and gay children. Is that my child? Is that who my child will become? Is that who my child socializes with? Is that who my child is going to bring home to dinner? There are a number of ways you can address these questions — by looking at the research, by looking at our culture and by looking at your child.

Recent research does indicate some connection between gender role (that is, the degree to which an individual adheres to typical masculine or feminine behaviour as prescribed by his or her culture) and sexual orientation. Boys who are "effeminate" in their mannerisms and choices of toys or favourite activities are more likely than gender-typical boys to become homosexual. The same is true for girls who are tomboys.[5] The key word, however, is "likely." Not all gender-atypical children grow up to be homosexual, and not all homosexuals were gender-atypical as children. Therefore, in practice, it is not possible to detect the sexual orientation of a particular person simply by looking at him or her. So, for every parent who says, "I thought he might be gay — he was always quiet and artistic," there is another parent who says, "But he doesn't look gay — he was captain of his football team."

Although there is some connection between gender roles and sexual orientation, it does not warrant the extreme characterizations of gays and lesbians which predominate in Western culture. These images persist, not because of research results, but because of historical and cultural factors. In the early 1900s, it was believed that same-sex desire in homosexuals was simply one manifestation of "sexual inversion," the desire to be the opposite sex. The cultural expectation was that homosexuals would act like the opposite sex. Homosexuals themselves held that belief and consequently adopted and exaggerated cross-gendered behaviour. Acting like the opposite sex was part of the social role of being homosexual. Later in the century, as gender roles for men and women in general became more fluid and flexible, so, too, did the social role of homosexuals.

Today, gay men and lesbians are much more likely to represent the full spectrum of masculinity and femininity, and are much less likely than in the past to be gender-atypical. Yet, the stereotypical images of homosexuals endure for a number of reasons. The most obvious is that these images are rarely challenged. In addition, believing that gay men want to be like women and that lesbians want to be like men makes same-sex attraction more understandable. In fact, some gay and lesbian adolescents initially believe that they need sex-change operations when same-sex attractions begin to emerge.

Another factor is that gender-atypical homosexuals are the most visible. With few exceptions, the media continue to portray homosexuals stereotypically. At events such as Pride Day marches, the television cameras focus on the more flamboyant participants; ordinary people don't make exciting news footage. Furthermore, the stereotype tends to be self-reinforcing. Whenever we see someone gay or lesbian who is stereotypical, it serves to support the stereotype. Whenever we meet someone who does not fit the stereotype, we dismiss that person as an exception to the rule.

What does this information mean for parents? Whether a child is going to be "appropriately" masculine or feminine from the parents' perspective can be a cause for concern. The degree to which they expect their children to adhere to traditionally masculine and feminine gender roles will be determined by the parents' cultural, ethnic and social background. Even parents who endorse more flexible gender roles probably find it hard if their children deviate conspicuously from whatever is normal for them. This is, in part, out of a sense of protection — no one wants their child to be the object of ridicule, harassment or violence. But there is also a deep-seated aversion in many cultures to gender-atypical behaviour. In fact, when people are asked why they don't like homosexuals, the most frequent replies are that gay men act like women and because lesbians want to be men. Yet people are hard-pressed to articulate exactly why cross-gendered behaviour is bad or undesirable beyond: "It just is. It's unnatural." Although our culture clings tenaciously to prescribed gender roles, it is important that parents think about where their ideas about gender roles come from and whether it serves anyone well to demand that their children, whether homosexual or heterosexual, adhere to rigid gender roles. This is particularly significant if their teenager has been gender-atypical throughout his or her development.

Gay and lesbian youth are just as susceptible to the stereotype as anyone else is. Typically, adolescents have limited exposure to gay and lesbian people. They may believe that the only way to be gay or lesbian is to act out the stereotype, but find the idea distressing if it's not their style. Alternatively, as adolescents often do when they're trying on different roles, they act out in a big way. For some gay and lesbian youth, stereotypical behaviour can be part of a phase which parents may simply have to live with for the time being.

The So-Called Gay Lifestyle

"Lifestyle" is a term that is frequently bandied about when homosexuality is the topic of conversation. There is often the assumption that there is one unified lifestyle pursued relentlessly by homosexuals, driven by an excessive interest in sex and characterized by flagrant promiscuity. The assumption is fuelled by media attention focused on bars, bathhouses, public parks, and other meeting-places used by some gay men to initiate casual sexual contact. This image is often vivid and alarming to the parents of gay and lesbian youth.

The fact is that there is no single lifestyle for lesbian and gay people. The lesbian and gay population represents the full range of socio-economic levels, occupations and religious denominations. It also encompasses a wide range of personal values. As discussed earlier, being homosexual often includes the possibility of having a long-term monogamous, loving relationship. At the same time, it is also the case that the visible gay male subculture still does contain a number of different venues for gay men to meet partners for casual sexual encounters, although gay activists have put a lot of effort into public education advocating the practice of safer sex. The primary reason for these casual encounters is quite straightforward. Either through socialization or because of a biological predisposition, men in general are more able to separate the emotional and physical aspects of sexuality. In this regard, gay men have more in common with their heterosexual counterparts than with lesbians.

It's also important to understand that, because it is sexuality that sets homosexuals apart, people who are gay or lesbian have had to examine their own sexuality more than have heterosexuals. One of the results has been the development of a subculture which supports and encourages discourse on sexuality in its art, newspapers, theatre and political commentary. Furthermore, because gay men and lesbians view themselves as oppressed by a parochial and narrow heterosexual view of sexuality, they are reluctant even to censor views which most people would find extreme or offensive. If one is to judge the subculture at all, it is important to consider the social context in which it emerged and continues to exist. Furthermore, it is as biased to judge the gay and lesbian subculture by the most visible, sexually focused components as it would be to judge heterosexual culture by highlighting Playboy clubs, strip joints and prostitution rings.

What this means for gay and lesbian youth is that, even if they live in urban centres where there is a visible lesbian and gay community, there are unlikely to be appropriate places for them to socialize. This may exacerbate the youths' sense of isolation, or, conversely, lead them into adult situations which they may not be equipped to cope with.

The Internet has provided one way for adolescents to track down a tremendous amount of information about gay and lesbian issues and to communicate for the first time with other gay and lesbian youth. Ironically, however, adolescents who surf the net around the world may know nothing about the supports for gay and lesbian adolescents in their own communities; the electronic connection may actually be a disincentive for youth to find out what's happening closer to home.

Isolation is one of the most critical challenges facing gay and lesbian youth. Therefore, it is important to assist adolescents to find gay and lesbian peers, gay and lesbian youth-oriented support groups and other age-relevant social venues. Organizations such as P-FLAG can provide parents and their teenagers with helpful information.

Part of all parents' responsibility is helping their teenager negotiate the tribulations of his or her developing adolescent sexuality. When the adolescent is gay or lesbian, the responsibility is the same, but the context is somewhat different. Parents will need to become familiar with a subculture that may feel entirely foreign to them. They will need to become comfortable with their child's sexual orientation in order to initiate a dialogue. Ultimately, though, parents must realize that the style of intimate relationships their children pursue as teenagers and into adulthood is a matter of choice and will depend on the values and the common sense that the parents have instilled in their children.

When Your Teen Comes Out

People realize that they are gay or lesbian in very different and individual ways, although there are some common patterns in the coming-out process. This is the process by which an individual comes to realize that he or she is gay or lesbian, and integrates that knowledge into an understanding of who they are.

Gay or lesbian people often grow up with a general feeling of being different, even before their overtly sexual feelings emerge. They may feel their emotional attraction to people of the same sex is stronger and has a different quality than it seems to for others. Some, but not all, boys feel different because they're not interested in rough-and-tumble sports. Some, but not all, girls feel different because they are tomboys.

As puberty approaches, all adolescents develop an awareness of their sexual feelings. Lesbian and gay adolescents become aware that their feelings are for people of the same sex. Boys tend to experience these feelings as a general sexual attraction to other males, while girls tend to experience these feelings when they develop a "crush" on a particular girl. In other words, the way that gay and lesbian adolescents become aware of their feelings is very typical of the way all adolescents develop this awareness.

Throughout this process, young people struggle to find meaning in their sense of being different. Even as early as age six or seven, these boys and girls find a label for their difference, even if they are not yet sure what it really means, and it's often a derogatory one — "fag, lezzie, homo." As their sense of difference becomes more overtly sexual, these adolescents begin to understand that the label "gay" or "lesbian" applies to them. One of the positive aspects of the increased public awareness of and dialogue about gay and lesbian issues is that adolescents have the vocabulary with which to label themselves. This provides a framework for them to begin to understand their sense of difference and what it means for them. Fifteen or twenty years ago, when that vocabulary was not as accessible, young people had no way to understand their feelings, which compounded their sense of isolation and confusion.

Although, in retrospect, some adults report that they were always very accepting of their sexuality, most gays and lesbians recall feeling isolated, deviant, bad and/or perverted. They believed all the things their culture had told them. These beliefs have a number of consequences for self-esteem and sense of identity. Most gay and lesbian youth find it very difficult to feel good about themselves in general because their culture is telling them they are essentially bad people. They also have difficulty coming to terms with what it means to their sense of identity to be gay or lesbian. Throughout adolescence most young gays and lesbians feel tremendously isolated. They have no opportunity to meet anyone else who is gay or lesbian and are afraid to talk about it with anyone who is heterosexual — particularly people in authority such as parents, guidance counsellors and teachers.

Adolescence is a stressful time at best. However, the combined isolation and feelings of being bad adds extra strain and places gay and lesbian youth at risk. They are more likely to suffer from anxiety and depression in comparison to their heterosexual peers; they have a higher rate of drug and alcohol abuse and a higher rate of suicide attempts. In fact, it is estimated that 30% of all teenage suicide can be attributed to conflicts about sexual orientation.[6]

Some teens may try to "make themselves heterosexual" by engaging in a lot of heterosexual sex. At the other extreme, some young men may seek homosexual contacts in the only way they know — by hanging around cruising areas where they might be picked up by homosexual men. Impulsive sexual acting-out poses a variety of risks whether an adolescent is heterosexual or homosexual — the risk of STD infection, of unwanted pregnancy, of being exposed to sexual violence, and of being exploited.

Many lesbian and gay adolescents become the targets of violence when their peers suspect or find out about their sexual orientation, and there is certainly anecdotal evidence that even some teachers harass students they know to be gay or lesbian. These circumstances place them in physical danger and exacerbate the negative feelings they have about themselves. It is not uncommon for school performance to be affected. Grades may drop and adolescents may be forced to switch schools if that is an option, or quit school to avoid violence and other forms of harassment.

In summary, gay and lesbian youth face a number of risks. Most do survive adolescence relatively unscathed; a minority do not. Imagine the difference it would make if gay and lesbian adolescents felt they could turn to their parents for guidance and support.

When children come out to their parents, the parents may not feel very rational but may, at the same time ask, "How can I continue to be an effective parent in spite of my feelings about my child's sexual orientation?" The desire to be a loving and effective parent may coexist with a highly charged, negative emotional response to the adolescent's disclosure. What are some strategies that parents can use to deal with their own feelings and maintain their role as effective parents?

First, it's important for parents to think about how they might feel a month, a year or ten years from now. Parents who initially thought that having a gay or lesbian child was the worst thing that could possibly happen find their attitudes changing in ways that are surprising to them and to their children. While some parents may never want to carry a placard in a Pride Day parade which says "I love my lesbian daughter," it's safe to predict parents will not always feel the way they do initially. Sometimes parents find themselves gradually becoming more tolerant, then accepting, of their child's sexual orientation. Other times parents are jolted into changing. As one parent said about her own reaction, "I knew I was going to lose her if I didn't smarten up." Another parent was moved when he heard about an adolescent who killed himself because he was gay. The parent was struck by the fear that this might happen to his own son if he continued to be rejecting. Parents need to become aware of the costs of rejection, to themselves and their child.

Many of the things parents can do are the same things which apply to good parenting in general. One strategy is to take sexual orientation out of the picture and see what is left. Consider, for example, a gay teenager who is staying out too late at night and will not tell his parents where he has been. The parent may be tempted to say something like, "I don't want you staying out all night with your gay friends who are taking you down to those bars where men pick up boys." This is not very helpful, since there are actually two issues to be addressed here. One has to do with the parent's fears — real or imagined — about the son's involvement in the gay subculture. The other is about staying out late — an issue which has nothing to do with sexual orientation. It might be tempting to focus on the gay-related issue, blaming any and all conflicts with the adolescent on his or her sexual orientation, but many of the difficulties of raising a gay or lesbian child are no different from the difficulties encountered with heterosexual youngsters. The parents' task is avoid to letting sexual orientation obscure the generic issues.

When teenagers come out to parents, they don't become different people. They are the same people they were before they came out — it's just that the parents now know something new about them. As youngsters work through the process of coming to terms with their sexual orientation, they will continue to use the judgment, problem-solving skills and values they were taught and raised with. The struggles that adolescents face as they deal with the difficulties of being gay or lesbian in a homophobic culture provide opportunities for parents to assist their child by imparting their own values and experience.

As parents come to terms with their child's sexual orientation, it is crucial to keep open the lines of communication. Children come out to parents in many different ways. Sometimes parents find out purely by accident — for example, by finding a suggestive letter or book. Sometimes they pick up on the hints their children are dropping, thereby forcing the parents to confront the child. Often adolescents plan their coming out and sit down with the parents and tell them directly. Regardless of the circumstances, children will look to parents for support, although the degree to which this is true will naturally depend on the relationship which existed between the parents and child before the disclosure. Especially when the child makes a point of coming out, it is a sign to the parents that their son or daughter has enough confidence in them to feel safe in telling them, that their child needs their support and cannot continue to lie to them about who he or she really is.

In most cases, the decision to come out to parents is made after a great deal of planning, anticipation and worry. No matter how well adolescents knows their parents, they may not be able to predict how the parents will react. Indeed, some parents never speak to their children again, throw their children out of their home, or even beat them up. Consequently, coming out to parents means taking a big risk. In most situations, coming out to parents is a tremendous compliment. It's a sign that the child trusts the parent and wants to share something. This requires that the lines of communication remain open.

What Parents Can Do

Parents usually have lots of questions, often focusing on their son's or daughter's sexual experiences. How do you know you're gay? Have you had sex with a person of the same sex? Have you ever tried sex with the opposite sex? If you haven't, how do you know you're gay? Even if the family has had a history of having open and frank discussions about sexuality in general, the child may not be accustomed to or comfortable with discussing his or her sexual experiences with his or her parents. Just because a child comes out does not give the parent permission to delve into parts of the child's life that ordinarily would be private. A good guideline might be that parents ask only questions they would ask of their heterosexual children. Another useful guide is to use "I statements" in communicating. For example, parents may be particularly worried about their gay son being at risk for HIV infection. Asking something like "Are you practising safer sex?" broaches the topic of the child's own sexual activity. A more comfortable way of asking the question might be a statement such as "I'm worried about you being at risk for HIV infection." That gives the child the opening to respond in a way that addresses the parent's concerns, but at the same time does not necessitate an explicit discussion of his sex life.

Parents experience a wide variety of feelings when their children come out to them. But as bereft, angry, afraid or bewildered as they feel, it's important for parents to focus on how their child must feel.

What do children want when they come out to parents? The short answer is that they want the parent to continue to be a parent even in light of this knowledge. They want to be able to share with their parents all aspects of who they are and, probably most of all, they want and need love, support and acceptance.

In order to focus on the teenager's needs, parents will have to get their own needs met elsewhere. While the child may be prepared with information in the form of books or articles for the parents to read, it is not fair to put the child in the position of being the sole support and educator of the parents.

Parents will need to seek out information on their own. This will be relatively easy in large urban areas, but may require more ingenuity in smaller towns and rural areas. The difficulty is that it will take time for parents themselves to "come out of the closet." Looking for relevant books at the public library or the local bookstore, or phoning a parents' support group or attending a meeting might seem out of the question. But, in the end, these are the things parents will have to do in order to get the information and support they need.

Studies of race and ethnic relations show that one of the most effective ways to become comfortable among people who are different from ourselves is to meet them and talk to them on an individual level. The same is true with regard to sexual orientation. Parents often say they found it initially difficult, but eventually helpful, to meet their child's gay or lesbian friends, if the adolescent has any. It is also helpful to seek out and talk to lesbian and gay adults. It is a way of taking something that seems extraordinary and making it feel ordinary.

Coming Out as a Parent

Parents who otherwise feel relatively comfortable with their child's sexual orientation often nonetheless are reluctant to tell friends, relatives or co-workers about their child. At first they may not feel it is necessary to talk about it at all. However, eventually it becomes increasingly awkward to avoid telling people, especially close friends or relatives who ask whether John has a girlfriend, or if Mary would like to be introduced to the nice boy next door. At this point, parents are embarking on a process of self-disclosure very similar to their child's own. They will have to make considered decisions about whom to disclose to and how to cope if there is a negative response.

In the end, through exposure to accurate information, through listening to the experiences of other parents, through talking to their child and the friends he or she makes, parents will begin to realize and really believe that there is nothing shameful about homosexuality. They will be proud to say that their teenagers had the strength of character to deal with their sexual orientation in an open and honest way. As parents begin to understand this, they become able to cope with negative reactions and delight in the positive reactions. As one parent commented, "Once I realized that my child's sexuality was not my problem, I began telling everyone. I was surprised at the number of people I had known for years, at work and at the health club, who told me that they had a gay son or lesbian daughter, or that some other member of their family is gay."

Parents who have learned to accept their gay or lesbian child have a role to play in educating a largely homophobic culture. They don't have to be activists to fulfil that role. By being open and accepting — by continuing to be parents — they can demonstrate that homophobia has no place in loving, supportive families.

Notes

1. It is important to acknowledge that gay and lesbian individuals do not uniformly endorse long-term, monogamous relationships. There is a segment of the gay and lesbian subculture that argues that the heterosexual model of relationships is the source of oppression for gay men and lesbians, and as such is an inappropriate model. This voice from the subculture — primarily that of the gay male subculture — advocates open (non-monogamous) relationships, serial monogamy, and the value and pleasure of casual sexual encounters. This

information may not be reassuring to parents, but it is important to keep in mind that there is a visible and vocal part of the "heterosexual subculture" which advocates (although not always as openly) similar types of non-monogamous sexual arrangements — witness the "*Playboy*" philosophy."

2. P. Blumstein and Schwartz, *American Couples* (New York: Marrow, 1983); and M. Mendola, *The Mendola Report: A New Look at Gay Couples* (New York: Crown, 1980).

3. The question of choice does arise, however, when some gay men and lesbians come out when they are well into adulthood. In these instances individuals may describe themselves as having made a choice to finally admit to themselves that they are gay or lesbian, and to come out. Sometimes these individuals are married, may have children and have tried everything in their power to live like heterosexuals. But there comes a point when living with this deception becomes intolerable, and they decide to come out. This is a choice about whether to continue living a lie, not a choice about what sexual orientation to espouse.

4. J.C. Gonsiorek, "Results of Psychological Testing on Homosexual Populations," in *Homosexuality: Social, psychological, and biological issues*, W. Paul et al. (ed.) (Beverly Hills, CA: Sage, 1982).

5. J.M. Bailey and K.J. Zucker, "Childhood Sex-Typed Behaviour and Sexual Orientation: A Conceptual Analysis and Quantitative Review," *Developmental Psychology* 31, 1 (1995), pp. 43-55.

6. J.B. Bradford, C. Ryan and E. Rothblum, "The National Lesbian Health Care Survey: Implications for Mental Health Care," *Journal of Consulting and Clinical Psychology* 62 (1994), pp. 242-82; and P. Gibson, "Gay Male and Lesbian Youth Suicide," in *Death by Denial: Studies of Suicide in Gay and Lesbian Teenagers*, G. Remafedi (ed.) (Boston: Alyson Publications, 1989).

Adolescents, Mothers and Adolescent Mothers

Judith S. Musick

The ideas discussed in this essay come from my experiences designing, running and evaluating programs for adolescents and adolescent mothers, and from studying their lives.[1] These experiences provide access to many different sources of information: interviews, diaries, drawings and letters that reveal myriad aspects of girls' lives; conversations and observations in homes, schools, teen centres, social-service programs, adolescent health clinics, and the streets of communities across the United States and several other countries. These data shed light on what works and what doesn't, and, most important, *why*. They offer insights for those who work with preadolescent and adolescent girls, and for parents seeking to divert their daughters from teenage motherhood, or help their daughters through it.

The focus here is on teenage *childbearing*. Although each year many adolescents get pregnant, a significant number choose to have an abortion. It is the decision to keep and raise the child one has conceived that has the most obvious and serious consequences — for adolescents and the children they bear, for their families and for society as a whole.[2]

Because the media (and, certainly, policy makers seeking easy answers) continually shift their focus from one oversimplified, unidimensional "cause" to another, the public fails to realize that teenage childbearing is not so much a problem as it is symptom of all that has gone wrong for these girls, both before and after they give birth. Consequently, the public also fails to realize the wisdom (indeed, the common sense) of approaches that emphasize promoting strengths rather than preventing problems. That is, one "prevents" teenage childbearing by nourishing the interests, abilities and skills of girls, before and during adolescence; by building on their capacities for commitment, caring and leadership; and by showing them what they *can* do rather than telling them what they cannot. It is wise for us to remember that none of us responds well to being viewed in terms of our worst potential.

The need to create a climate that promotes positive development is especially acute for disadvantaged girls — those growing up in resource-poor, risk-laden environments. However, this need is not exclusively that of the disadvantaged. Factors that increase risk for poor and minority girls are present to some degree even for girls in more-advantaged circumstances. Thus the lives of teenage mothers hold lessons for the parents of any preadolescent or adolescent girl, and can also be informative to parents of teenage boys. Although fathers — both absent and present — play important roles in raising or lowering their daughters' susceptibility to early childbearing, mothers play the leads in this particular drama.[3]

Paths to Teenage Motherhood: The Role of Mothers and Others

In addition to the more obvious negative forces impinging on the lives of girls who become mothers in their teens, a cluster of underlying, intertwined factors affects their development and lessen their ability to do right for themselves. These are the *hidden dimensions* of teenage childbearing — indirect but powerful determinants of motives and behaviours that lead girls toward early motherhood and away from other options. Given the influence of these forces, much of the current discussion of adolescent childbearing is simplistic and short-sighted — both that regarding the reasons adolescents have babies and that concerned with incentives for them to take more productive routes.

Even girls with a great deal of potential can be held back by psychological barriers that prevent them from seizing and making use of educational, vocational or social opportunities. These barriers are created by the experience of growing up and remaining strongly embedded in troubled families, *without meaningful, sustained exposure to other ways of being and other kinds of people.* One example of how this works concerns the developmental effects of sexual abuse. I have studied and written extensively about this issue and will not go into it in depth here, except as it relates to the need to create healthier pathways for girls. Researchers find a very high incidence of sexual victimization in the backgrounds of teenage mothers. This creates a vulnerability and patterns of behaviour whereby girls move from sexual abuse within the family and extended family environment during childhood and puberty, to sexually exploitive relationships (usually with older males) outside the home in early adolescence and middle adolescence.[4]

Although men are overwhelmingly the perpetrators of sexual abuse, mothers often create the climate for it to occur, and all too often fail to believe their daughters, or to intercede. Sexual exploitation means that adults are failing the children in their charge, and, frankly, it is not only the men who harm those whom they should be protecting, but also the women who turn their backs, betraying their daughters' trust. Such experiences send a powerful message to a still-developing young girl, that her well-being is less important to her mother than having a man, and that females are powerless when it comes to males. Here two young mothers describe their feelings about such betrayals:[5]

> *Mothers should be real careful about the people they date or plan to get married with … and don't ever choose a man over your own flesh and blood.*

> *I never met my father so I don't know what it is to have a father, but I do know about stepfathers because I have had them. Some of them take advantage of you. They resemble animals that don't even respect their own family.*

In the years before adolescence, controlling a girl's body is a form of controlling her mind. In this way, inappropriate sexual socialization acts as a kind of "brainwashing," shaping the girl's sense of who she is and what she can do. If her earliest lessons about her sexuality are taught through force, coercion or trickery, her capacity for self-efficacy is affected, and the sense that she controls her own body, and thus her own destiny, is diminished. Sexual exploitation, especially ongoing abuse without rescue, teaches the girl an ugly and often lasting lesson: that her needs count for nothing, and her actions make no difference.

Although boys also suffer sexual abuse, they tend to externalize their feelings, identifying with their abusers and becoming sexual predators themselves. Girls, on the other hand, are more likely to internalize negative messages about themselves and continue to seek and find themselves in the victim role. As one girl said,

> *Girls, I think they don't give a care because they get sexually abused and they will go around just jumping into any other guy's bed. After it happens they feel so cheap and sleezy and they don't care about life anymore. [They think] "they are hurting me, so why shouldn't I hurt myself? They don't care. Why should I care?" So they will go out and, you know, ruin their lives more.*

That is one way premature and exploitive sexual socialization affects later self-confidence, by creating a defeatist attitude. Another equally significant effect is diverting girls from the key developmental tasks of preadolescence (often referred to as the "school years"): acquiring the array of skills necessary for success in the world beyond home and neighbourhood — first the world of school, then that of society. If a girl's experiences rob her of the energy and motivation for this task — and make no mistake, premature sexualization is very diverting — the price will be high if measured by her sense of industry, efficacy and pride. It is a price she may well spend the rest of her life paying. Here is how another girl ties these issues together:

> *I feel so sick for the way I grew up. There are so many things I've been through that I never should have. I always feel like going back to the age of twelve and doing it all over again. I hate the fact of having sex so young. I would like to forget that part of my life. Too bad I can't. I should have stayed in school and went to college and went on to be somebody.*

Clearly, the experiences of the years before adolescence shape a girl's self-image and notions about who she is and what she can do. Without a solid base of skills in her psychological, social and intellectual portfolio to hold her on course, she is ill prepared for the many challenges of adolescence itself. This is particularly true in communities where there are many risks and few positive alternatives for young people; where there are many who exploit them, and few who shield and protect them;

and where there are few adults who actively guide them forward, and many who seek to subvert and hold them back.

When a girl is used by others in the years before her adolescence, the girl's identity is shaped to those others' desires. What happens, then, when she reaches adolescence itself, when the resolution of identity issues is the paramount developmental task? "Who am I?" asks the adolescent. "Someone who exists to meet others' needs" is the answer for girls who have been so used. "Where am I going, and what will I do with my life?" "Only what *others* think I should do," answer those whose experience teaches them little else.

Experiences of sexual abuse are harmful for any girl, yet those from more affluent families generally have greater access to hobbies and sports, and lessons and therapy. Living in communities with greater resources and supports, they also have better educational opportunities and other role models and domains for developing competencies. Such "external" factors help compensate for "internal" difficulties. Although their relationships with their mothers are still critically important, these girls have more opportunities to observe other ways of being and doing, and they are less likely to be isolated and locked into the troubles of home.

Whether risk is due to sexual victimization, parental substance abuse or family violence, those working with at-risk young women cannot break the hold of difficult or toxic life circumstances without serious, sustained efforts to expand girls' horizons and increase their repertoire of interests and skills. Counselling and social services are necessary, but they are far from sufficient for achieving such goals, even if the "only" risk factor is poverty.

The young women I know are repeatedly exposed to forces that prevent their choosing — and sticking to — positive routes to productive adulthood. Thus, what outsiders objectively view as opportunities and options — alternatives they could choose instead of early motherhood — are not subjectively, psychologically available to them, because (a) the emotional risks of setting themselves apart from the emotionally significant people in their lives is too threatening; (b) the rewards are too far off and nebulous; (c) the foundation of necessary experiences and skills is absent; and (d) absent also are the adults to guide and support consistently and give them psychological permission to follow other paths — to dare to live different and, yes, better lives than those around them.

These conclusions are based on my observations of a phenomenon I call *failure at the moment of potential growth*. In this situation the young woman drops out (of school, training or a program), or she becomes pregnant on the brink of a significant positive change or new direction in her life. Often this concerns something she seemed to have wanted for herself, or at least said she did. I began to wonder if this overtly self-sabotaging behaviour meant the young woman was not psychologically ready for change, if it represented being different from the significant others who confer and validate her sense of identity — her sisters, friends and, especially, her mother. Not wanting to jeopardize her connection to these important attachment figures, she fails on the brink of success. In this way, dropping out and becoming pregnant may serve as (unconscious) escape mechanisms for a young woman who is not emotionally ready to step into unfamiliar territory and risk "losing" those on whom she depends for emotional sustenance. Thus, adolescent childbearing has a special meaning in relation to being unprepared for such change, and mothers of adolescent girls have a special role in this regard. For a girl to choose (and stick to) a direction that will make her markedly different from her mother requires considerable resolve, especially if her mother fails to encourage and support her in taking this path.

For many girls, achievement means travelling to a new land, where they may have little in common with others. It therefore requires the will and ability to identify and become attached to new reference groups; to find and bond to new, emotionally significant others — those who are successful in wider worlds beyond home and community; to do as one girl says she does: "Look for respect and encouragement to better myself." Change calls for potentially risky transformations in her relationships with her mother and other family members, friends and partners. Even though success does not really estrange her from them, she may unconsciously fear that it will. At the same time, if she is determined to move ahead, she may deliberately distance herself from those whom she feels are holding her back, almost as if she believes that becoming a winner requires separating herself from losers — even if these are people she cares deeply about. Perhaps, in her struggle to succeed, she must also defend herself against similar weaknesses in herself. Distancing may thus be a marker of the young woman's sense that she must change partners to change herself — whether such partners are friends, family or mates. It also signals a need to see herself as different from others in order to do so.

> *Ray was immature as far as growing as a person. He didn't want me to grow and I refused to let anyone stop my growth. He didn't want me to go to school. He was real aggressive, he liked to fight. He fought me once and I refused to get into a relationship where I was afraid ... He was a fool. I'm glad I didn't marry him.*

> *I was to myself. The girls around me, I think all of them are silly. Those are the type that run after men ... they got baby after baby.*

> *We need to move cause nobody likes me. They would pull me down. They think I'm conceited 'cause I go to school ... I stay to myself ... I'm always on the go. I try to stay away from a bad environment ... trying to get in school and work. It's only to better myself. I don't want to live over here. I got in school and got a certificate to work computers. I won't have nothing if I just sit.*

Teenage motherhood can serve as a means of escape from any potential challenge or change that the girl finds too difficult or frightening. To turn back at a moment of potential growth is a way to avoid — at least temporarily — the risk that one's success may alienate significant others — perhaps forever. As one young woman observed: "I think when one person's not doing good, then you know it's really hard to see someone else doing good ... A lot of people just discourage me."

In spite of (possibly, because of) a depriving or troubled relationship, many a girl still longs for her mother's love and approval, and keeps searching for it, often fruitlessly. Interestingly, in a study of former teenage mothers in a model welfare-to-work program,[6] we observed that a number of the more successful young women had found and attached themselves to men with strong, loving mothers. Perhaps they did this in order to find a more enabling mother for themselves — someone to help them raise themselves up and furnish them with the example, guidance and encouragement they knew they needed to move up and out in the world. These young women seemed to know (intuitively, if not always consciously) that such relationships are essential ingredients in the construction of better lives for themselves and their children. Here two young mothers describe their perceptions of how their partners' family life differs from their own:

> He has someone to sit down and ask, "How do you feel today? How are things going with you?" I don't have too many people to ask me those questions. It's basically on me to sit down and say to myself, "Well are you okay today, Andrea? How do you feel?"

> Lou's mom, his sisters, they're all really nice to me. They work hard constantly. Always working. [Lou's mom], she's really nice. She's a church lady. I think [she] really raised them up good. She did a good job. I wish I had a mom like that.

These young women not only found new partners, but new and better mothers as well.[7]

Broadening Horizons: The Role of the World Beyond the Home

Just as a failure at the moment of potential growth signifies anxiety about the emotional consequences of change, having a baby (or having *another* baby) also signals the girl's awareness that she is unprepared to successfully make (and maintain) a transition to a different kind of life, whether in her education or in her social skills, experience or exposure. What can we expect intervention to accomplish? Were young women's experiences sufficiently transformative that they are now truly equipped to do something other than what they are already doing? Programs aim to help girls "feel better about themselves," but, realistically, they cannot feel better unless they can "do better" as well. Does the young woman have skills she didn't have before she was in the program? How well are these consolidated, and can they be flexibly used in a range of settings to help her set and realize new goals? How motivated is she to improve and use her new skills? Ambition based on ability can be fulfilled; such ambition is the rudder that keeps girls on course through the turbulent years of adolescence and young adulthood.

People keep saying that issues such as teenage pregnancy are complicated, but are they really so difficult to understand? *All* young people need real grown-ups to help them become decent human beings and contributing members of society. All young people need a web of caring adults as protectors, mentors, models, teachers, guides. All young people need adults who hold and reinforce high expectations for them, personally helping them acquire the skills to meet these expectations, or finding and linking them to others who can do so. Young people need even more support if their struggles to succeed make them different from the most emotionally significant people in their lives.

Although girls' mothers play key roles in preventing teenage motherhood, they are surely not the only players in this endeavour. If girls are to avoid the detours and derailments of too-early motherhood, the broader environment in which development occurs must be transformed. Much of what needs to be changed is at the societal level, from images in the media to opportunities in the worlds of education and work; however, personal change can be accomplished with the assistance of those who know and work with young people — teachers, counsellors, health and social-service providers, and so on. Nonetheless, a shift in their perspective and in approach will be necessary. The time has come for them to form new partnerships to help girls find new and more productive pathways to adulthood than motherhood. These must be partnerships beyond their own worlds of schools, health and social-service organizations, and community institutions — partnerships with a much broader universe of people and places as well.

I once met a young woman whose story started me thinking about and searching for these new pathways. Donna was twenty years old when I met her, and the mother of a four-year-old child. She had attended a model program for adolescent mothers that was part of a multisite demonstration. My co-researcher was looking at the young women who had done well in this program — that is, those who stayed to complete their high-school education[8] and job training, and I was studying participants who had dropped out. Donna had left after only eight months, before obtaining her high-school degree or beginning job training. Thus, according to the research criteria, she had "failed." After interviewing her, however, I came to believe that it was as much the program's failure as hers. Indeed, in a number of ways, Donna was a success. She was providing a stable and stimulating environment for her daughter, and had — on her own — permanently ended a long and self-destructive relationship with a violent man. She also had obtained her high-school-equivalency diploma at a nearby community college. Yet, she was still unsure about a career, and no one anywhere had provided guidance that fit her interests and talents. Tall, attractive and very distinctively dressed, Donna was an enterprising and artistic young woman. On very little money, she managed to create a warm, interesting home for herself and her child, and to design and make her own clothing and jewellery. The training opportunities offered by the program she abandoned were mainly for dental or medical assistants, cosmetologists or computer operators.

Now I ask you — where is the fashion industry in the lives of creative young people such as Donna? Where are the training opportunities for designers, managers or buyers-to-be in large retail chains (such as the GAP or The Limited) or in the large fashion stores of her state, such as Nordstrom's or Neiman Marcus? Where are the apprenticeships, or job-shadowing or mentorship programs to stimulate and nourish the aspirations of high-school-age youth and offer them a vision of what they could do? Where are youth-entrepreneurship initiatives? For that matter, where are the arts programs that used to be part of every junior-high-school and high-school curriculum? It is generally recognized that every time a school district drops art (or drama, music, sport, or any special-interest club, group, etc.) because of lack of funding — or because of a misguided notion that such activities are "frills" — it loses five or ten or twenty young people who could use the skills, knowledge and self-confidence gained there to move themselves several more steps up the ladder.

Consider for a moment how well-meaning programs for young mothers might inadvertently compound their social isolation and lock them into cycles of self-defeating behaviour. Here three adolescent mothers discuss, in positive terms, the fact that they and their fellow program participants have certain things in common and are all equal:

> *Everybody was in the same position; everybody had kids, everybody was on aid, nobody was better than anybody else.*

> *I really felt comfortable in my surroundings … We were all equal. Nobody was different.*

> *You were with a bunch of girls that were having the same problems as you. They were young and had babies.*

Yet what they were doing in their education, work goals, parenting and reproductive behaviour offered ample evidence that these programs (in which they had felt so comfortable) actually had little real impact on their lives and were unable to counteract the powerful forces holding them back in the past and continuing to do so in the present. If you do not have something else you want to do — and are now prepared to do as well — if nothing has really changed, why not have another baby?

It goes without saying that we want young people to feel good about themselves, but, as noted earlier, they must be able to do good as well. Although feeling comfortable may be a necessary first step, it does not necessarily provide a sufficient foundation for taking the next step. Meaningful growth requires taking the risk of moving beyond the familiar. If those who work with young people do not see their mission as expanding young people's world-view, who will do it?

A number of years ago, I directed a multiyear research and demonstration program for mentally ill mothers and their young children. My colleagues and I continued to follow these families for a number of years, and found that some of the children were doing quite well in spite of being raised by mothers with serious psychiatric problems. In trying to isolate factors underlying these children's relative success, we found that one maternal child-rearing variable stood out: the mother's capacity to seek and use outside resources on her child's behalf. Mothers of successful children had created an *extended environment* by introducing their children to what the wider world had to offer. Recognizing that a range of other adults — teachers, coaches, tutors, recreational counsellors, religious leaders, neighbours and so on — possessed a range of skills and interests that *they* did not have, mothers sought these people out and actively encouraged their children to learn from them. At the same time, these mothers also reduced their children's isolation by encouraging them to socialize with their peers outside the confines of school, inviting schoolmates over to play (even in preschool), and allowing their children to spend time at schoolmates' homes as well. At the other end of the spectrum were mothers who subtly, but steadily, thwarted their children's attempts to move beyond their orbit and develop themselves as separate individuals. As these children approached puberty, they were markedly less competent in school, and in their social relations with adults and other children.

This situation has, I think, a number of parallels to working with girls growing up in difficult circumstances. These young women need different types of assistance, and perhaps different kinds of people to provide them. Although parents can involve educators; medical, mental-health, and social-service providers; community youth workers; and counsellors, no single individual or discipline or institution has all the skills — and all the contacts in the various arenas of education, occupation and avocation — to help girls (and boys) discover and develop a range of interests and talents.

Youth-serving institutions willingly provide case management for problems that call for psychological or medical or educational intervention. Why not other kinds of "case management" linking girls to theatre groups, photography classes, summer internships, special-interest clubs and camps, entrepreneurship opportunities? What about finding other people beyond our own sphere to create and sustain young people's commitment to such initiatives? Parents, too, can work at making these links to strengthen their daughters' options and widen their horizons. Creating environments that genuinely promote potential, rather than simply trying to prevent problems and repair damage, calls for new sets of players and possibilities, and it calls for these on more than a sporadic, drop-in-the-bucket basis. Having spent much of my career with adolescent mothers, and girls judged to be "at risk" of becoming so, I know that prevention is not the best approach. Promoting positive development, that is, steering girls toward competence and confidence, is the only way to divert them away from teenage motherhood.

Teenage mothers are everyone's children, even if "everyone" does not yet realize it. I do not know about people in other countries, but Americans are very strongly wedded to the ethic of "every family for itself," "every person for his or her *self*." This means that those not directly involved with youth who need resources and assistance see them as other people's problems, and other people's failures, when in reality they are not. Parents focus only on their own children and family rather than making links with the wider community of children and families. Those of us working with young people must engage new partners in our efforts to open their eyes to new ideas, people, settings and experiences beyond the boundaries of their current world. Organizations, industries, groups and individuals from "outside" have indispensable roles to play in directing the energy, idealism and talent of youth in positive ways, and forging partnerships with parents to join them in this enterprise. It is the responsibility of adults to (gradually) introduce and socialize youth into their future roles, and not to allow that to happen by default. We want to make sure that all our young people — boys as well as girls — have as their dominant role models grown-ups who lead constructive and principled lives. Such adults can be found in rural areas and small towns as well as large cities. They can be found in developing countries as well as highly industrialized nations. I have met extraordinary people working with disadvantaged girls in Africa and South America. Often these leaders are educated women, from the privileged upper classes in these countries. For example, one of the founders of a very innovative program[9] for street girls in Kenya is a lawyer and former high-ranking member of the government who left her post to do this work. Her partners in setting up the program were women from the fields of social work and health/family planning. The point here is that these adults are *there* psychologically, and the girls they work with know and appreciate it. They also have power and access to people and resources that open doors for these girls. Although it is critical that adults from the community — especially parents — be involved (and employed) in programs for youth, young people's sources of inspiration and assistance need not always be similar to themselves. It is the relationship that counts.

Conclusions: Helping Our Daughters Find and Follow Positive Paths

It seems to me that the lives of adolescent mothers offer many lessons for mothers raising daughters today, no matter what their circumstances. This essay therefore concludes with suggestions based on these lessons, with the caution that these are not prescriptions for parenting, but rather ideas informed by research and practice with preadolescent and adolescent girls. In some instances, the suggestions overlap and interconnect, and many apply equally to the mother whose daughter becomes pregnant and decides to keep her child.[10]

Many of these suggestions also apply to the raising of sons. Factors such as a mother's relationship with her child and her relationships with others, her interest and involvement in her child's life, and the example she sets by her own — all impart valuable and lasting lessons for sons as well as daughters.

Mother-daughter relations are important throughout life, but have heightened salience in the pre- and early adolescent years. Even as girls resist it, they long for maternal wisdom and standard-setting. Many of the young mothers I study attribute their early parenthood (and the troubles leading up to it) directly to their mothers' lack of involvement and guidance. Be involved in your daughter's life. Don't be afraid to stand up for what you believe is right. Don't be intimidated by your daughter's anger or accusations of being "old-fashioned." Don't be afraid to say that teenage motherhood holds girls back and keeps them down: It does. Don't be afraid to tell your daughter, "You need different friends" if you feel her friends are leading her down destructive paths. Monitor the men she goes out with: The majority of teen mothers' babies are fathered by adult men, not by peers.[11] In general, the younger the girl, the wider the age span. Girls are more vulnerable to being exploited in relationships with older men. Further, going with an older man she believes will "take care" of her is just another way of believing she'll be rescued by Prince Charming, rather than making her own way in the world. Don't be afraid to say: "That guy is too old for you." Stay involved in your daughter's life. There are too many dangers today to leave her development to chance.

A daughter's identity is tied to the models of womanhood and work you provide. She forms her identity not simply by what you say, but by observing how you live your life. For example, if you were a teen mother, it will not be enough to simply say: "Don't do as I did." Rather, you must consistently encourage her to follow other routes to adulthood and to see what they are. What skills does she have? What skills might she be acquiring? Is she exposed to a range of activities and people? Does she have the opportunity to develop interests and skills in domains such as sports, hobbies, arts, as well as school-related skills? Feeling competent is based on *being* competent. Share your skills and interests, and find others with other skills and interests to impart. That is, create an extended environment. Make sure she doesn't have too much empty time on her hands. The old notions about "idle hands" and "idle minds" are all too true in regard to preadolescent and adolescent girls.

Reflect on how you really feel about issues such as relationships with men, sexuality and responsible sexual behaviour, and about the messages you may (inadvertently) send. Everyone has "domains of silence" — unresolved psychological issues that cause us to fail to say (sometimes, even to see) certain things if they threaten to create emotional conflict or pain. If we have not dealt with our own experience or our own pain, our own inner struggles may keep us silent when we need to speak. For example, counsellors may fail recognize sexual abuse (or any type of family violence) if they have denied or repressed their own experiences of or feelings about similar victimization. Similarly, how can we teach our daughters about healthy, respectful relationships if we ourselves remain in disrespectful relationships — relationships that harm our daughters indirectly, if not directly? How can we consistently and steadily teach our daughters about responsible sexual behaviour and family planning if we are conflicted in these domains ourselves?

What about the issue of change itself — of our capacity to move beyond our own borders? Do we create barriers for our daughters because we fear "losing" them if they choose to take different roads? Might our own timidity and self-imposed limits constrain our daughters' desire and ability to grow or to make positive, self-affirming changes? What things do we fear to change in ourselves? Whatever holds us back will hold our daughters back as well. We, too, need to take positive risks: It is never too late. Remember, our daughters are watching.

Finally, being supportive of a teen mother is a delicate balancing act. It calls for the capacity to help without taking over, and the willingness to be there while also encouraging personal responsibility.

Notes

1. Some of the quotes presented in this essay have been excerpted from these publications: Judith Musick, *Young, Poor and Pregnant: The Psychology of Teenage Motherhood* (New Haven, CT: Yale University Press, 1993); Janet Quint and Judith Musick, with Joyce Ladner, *Lives of Promise, Lives of Pain: Young Mothers after New Chance* (New York: Manpower Demonstration Research Corporation, 1994); and Judith Musick, "They're Our Kids, They're Everyone's Kids: New Pathways and Partnerships for Youth," 18th Annual Konopka Lectureship, University of Minnesota, Minneapolis, May 1996.

2. Current estimates indicate that, in the United States, which has very high rate of teen childbearing for an industrial nation, only a very small number of teen mothers choose to give up their babies for adoption, probably in the range of 3 to 5 percent as of 1988. However, many young mothers do rely on other family members to raise their children, especially if they were very young when they gave birth. Because the collection of data on teens and adoption is a difficult and time-consuming process, there are not yet accurate numbers from more recent years for U.S. teens (information from a personal communication with Christine Bachrach, National Institute of Child Health and Human Development, U.S. Department of Health and Human Services,

1997). In developing countries with high rates of teen childbearing, one seldom finds girls relinquishing their babies for formal adoption.

3. To give just one example, in a recent study of unlawful sexual activity between adult males and adolescent girls, most teenage mothers saw their own fathers' lack of involvement, abandonment or abuse as leading to their being attracted (or vulnerable) to the adult men who had fathered their children. However, these girls were equally likely to blame their mothers' lack of caring, or personal behaviour, such as substance abuse, for their early sexual involvement with older men who exploited them, got them pregnant and eventually abandoned them (data from a collaborative study of the American Bar Association Center on Children and the Law, and the Progressive Foundation, Washington, D.C.; final report by Sharon Elstein, Kathleen Sylvester and Howard Davidson to appear in Fall 1997).

4. I have covered this topic in various publications, but perhaps in greatest depth in the book *Young, Poor and Pregnant: The Psychology of Teenage Motherhood* (see note 1).

5. These young women were participants in teen-parent programs run by the Ounce of Prevention Fund, an innovative initiative for children, youth and families in forty low-income communities across the state of Illinois.

6. Janet Quint and Judith Musick, with Joyce Ladner.

7. It is worth noting that young women's relationships with their partners' mothers often outlast their relationship with the men. Clearly, the phenomenon is not unique to teenage mothers. A divorced woman may also remain close to her former mother-in-law, especially if she has a positive influence on her life.

8. In this program, completion of education meant obtaining either a high-school diploma or a graduate-equivalent degree.

9. One of its components is a camp, away from the city and its distractions, that helps girls step back and begin the process of disengaging from self-destructive behaviours. The camp is based on an Outward Bound type of leadership development.

10. Being the mother of a teenage mother is a complex and highly emotional situation for many women. Some new grandmothers are still quite young and are raising young children themselves, while others are just entering or re-entering the worlds of education or work after raising their children. Now there is a dependent baby with a still-developing adolescent for a mother — an adolescent who needs her mother, but who may also resist her. Clearly grandmothers need help coping with and managing this complicated and stressful new role.

11. This helps explain why there is relatively little information available on teenage fathers, and why programs for adolescent mothers have so much difficulty engaging these men.

What is Independence?: Teens with Physical Disability or Chronic Illness

Miriam Kaufman

It's hard to imagine the reality of having a child with an activity-limiting problem. Most people think they would not be able to cope, but almost everyone faced with this situation adapts to parenting a child who is "different," in a society that is intolerant of difference.

Many of these problems are diagnosed at birth or in early childhood. In the years after diagnosis, a process of enormous change takes place, as parents learn about the condition; accommodate to the changes in their lives necessitated by frequent doctors' appointments and treatments; advocate on behalf of their child in the health and educational systems; and, like every parent, get to know their child as a unique human being. By the onset of adolescence, these parents have learned to "expect the unexpected." At the same time, the bedrock of the relationship is a clear, stable vision of who the child is. During adolescence, this vision can be shaken, leaving the whole family feeling unanchored.

Finding a balance is the hardest part of this process. How to be supportive without being overprotective; how to offer your child a vision of unlimited potential while acknowledging barriers to achievement; how to role-model assertiveness and politeness simultaneously — the list goes on and on. Whenever parents feel that balance tipping, they blame themselves for not being the perfect parent — wise, patient, an effective advocate, a tireless fighter. But balance is hard to maintain when circumstances are constantly changing.

Unplanned change may be especially upsetting for a family with a child with special needs. Change that is a result of hard work, such as physical therapy or education, or outside intervention, such as medication, is often positive; but change that just happens is often negative, with a worsening of the condition, increasing limitation of activity or the diagnosis of another disorder. It is not surprising, then, that the changes of puberty may be greeted with trepidation.

Indeed, chronic conditions can have an impact on the process of puberty. Conditions that are associated with a difficulty in taking in or absorbing adequate calories (such as cystic fibrosis or inflammatory bowel disease) may slow the process of puberty. It is difficult to look like a child while feeling like a teen. Some conditions (such as spina bifida) are associated with early puberty, which means that the adolescent has to deal with puberty before her peers, maybe even before puberty is discussed at school. She may feel singled out by having these changes happen while her friends' bodies are still those of children. Treatments from earlier in life (such as radiation or high-dose steroids) may slow growth generally or prevent the development of a specific part of the body. Puberty also has an effect on the disease process. Insulin needs may change at this time. Some illnesses may actually improve. New drug side-effects may become evident as levels of various hormones increase.

Some of the changes are small, some are major, all take time to get used to. Although some of these transitions happen only to people with illnesses, many are more universal, like going to a new school, moving to a different city or getting a new job. These transitions may be more significant, or harder to deal with, if the adolescent is also coping with a chronic condition. While major changes can be hard, they can often be positive, a sign of growth and learning.

Teens with long-term conditions have a lot in common. They also have a lot in common with other teens who are not affected by any medical problem.

I have asked teenagers what they would like to say to a teen who has just found out that he or she has a serious condition. I got answers like:

"Just look around when you are in the hospital, you'll realize it could have been worse"; "Show your parents and doctors you're capable, then tell them, not the other way around"; "You are going to gain respect for other people, like you never had before"; "If doctors and nurses are getting on your nerves, let them know"; "Don't be scared, just go with it"; and "You are still the same person." Attitude has a big impact on how disabling any condition is. It can be very difficult to be singled out when you are an adolescent. But standing out from a crowd isn't always bad, and teens may even be able to turn it to their advantage.

Family Life

Parents get used to being in control of their kids' lives and health care. At adolescence, children are ready to take more control, and it may be hard for parents to adjust. Teens who have been recently diagnosed with a serious illness are likely to have difficulties coping for a while. They might feel that they are healthy and strong and they can't accept that this isn't true any more. They are essentially the same person they always have been, and need to figure out what parts of their lives won't change. They will explore their capabilities. They need time. It takes most teens a year to adjust to moving to a new home and school. Teens who develop a serious illness or disability face a much bigger adjustment.

The idea that "bad blood" in families causes many chronic conditions is common to many cultures. Some parents have been raised to feel embarrassed by chronic illness or disability, and may not tell their relatives about the teen's condition. Close family members who are aware may be able to help with decision making around disclosure, as can religious leaders, teachers and social workers. Parents often feel their children's problems are their fault, and this is especially true of parents who have children with disabilities or illnesses. They might feel personally responsible for passing on the gene, or for not taking care of themselves well enough when pregnant. Some parents believe that problems their child has been born with are there for a purpose — as punishment, or to make the family stronger. It is helpful when parents make an effort to remove guilt or blame from themselves and their children. Every teen faces many challenges, and illness or disability can be hard even with the most positive of attitudes.

Many adolescents with disabilities complain about being overprotected. Detecting potential risks is an important part of the job of a parent of a younger child; however, parents of teens have to step back and let their teen experiment and take some risks. Parents can also set limits when it is clear that the level of risk is unacceptable. If a teen does not yet take responsibility for medication and other treatments, parents can help him plan how to take over his own basic care. It is important to recognize that it is his disease, and part of taking charge of his condition is for the teen to decide who will learn about his condition and when.

We tend to use war metaphors when talking about illness. We use words like "battle" and "enemy." It can be helpful for parents and young people to see an incurable condition more as a (not very likable) companion in life. Your teen and her condition can cooperate with each other, rather than fighting.

It is often faster to "do for" a child with a disability. With the pressures of other children and busy schedules, it can happen that someone is not given the opportunity to dress or feed himself. You may have tried to teach him at an earlier age. Self-care may even have become a battleground. However, teens often become uncomfortable with others attending to their intimate needs. The development of day-to-day life skills is crucial to self-esteem and autonomy. Less hectic times may afford opportunities to learn skills. Teens may not need any real teaching. It may be that you need to ask them what the steps in a particular task are, and then give them time to practise alone, offering yourself as a resource to help solve difficulties.

Most teenagers buy their own clothes, either with their mothers or with friends. You may have bought large, loose clothing to save time in the past. But clothes are pretty important for teens, and it is helpful if you give them at least part of their clothing budget to spend on things they really want. You could suggest that they consider clothes that are fashionably baggy and look for things that might make them easier to put on, such as a large neck opening or deep armholes. Assume that they will make a few mistakes in their selections and don't get too upset about them.

Teens can move into taking responsibility for their medication. This might be hard for them because they may not like the reminder that they are sick; they can be so busy that they forget; and they may not have a convenient schedule for the medications. They can look at modifying the medication schedule (within limits) so that they can take their pills at the same time as other parts of their routine, and they can find pill containers (weekly ones, or a small piece of jewellery that can hold a few pills) to take with them each day. When they go on a trip, it is a good idea to carry two sets of pills, and pack them in separate bags in case one gets lost.

Most parents can't believe that there are adolescents who wish they could take part in jobs around the house. But chores play an important role as we grow up. Teens who are not required to do household chores because of a disability can feel they are not contributing members of the family. Their desire to take part in these day-to-day jobs is a wish to "pay their dues" to the family. It is a way to foster independence by developing creativity in tasks of daily living, and enhances practical household skills that will be useful when they are out on their own. A teen who is feeling like a burden may enjoy having the rest of the family dependent on him for a meal, a clean living room or a table that is set for supper every night.

Family discussions about a teen's illness or disability can show that, while parents think that the siblings know "what's wrong," they may have a distorted view of the situation. The diagnosis may have been made long ago, a very basic explanation may have been given initially, or the disease or treatment may have progressed or changed over time. Siblings may feel resentful of the extra attention they see their brother or sister getting; they may feel embarrassed and try to keep their sibling or the diagnosis a secret from their friends.

When we have children, we assume they will outlive us, and it can be terrifying for parents to live with the knowledge that their child is likely to die young. Some parents avoid talking about death, hoping to prevent it from happening. One child may already have died of the same illness. Siblings may be worried that their sister or brother will get sicker, or even die, and may keep their distance to protect themselves emotionally. It is important for family members to acknowledge their feelings, and to get professional counselling if needed.

The decision of when to tell a child that she is dying is complex, and very difficult for parents to face. They do not want the teen to give up hope while there is any, but if they try to hide it, the teen will sense that there is something wrong that can't be talked about. Discussing it gives both sides a chance to grieve. A teen may want to be involved with planning her funeral. The process might help her deal with some of the overwhelming feelings she is having. Dying is a process, not something that happens in an instant. If she can be actively involved, she may feel more in control.

For Teens, Life *is* Friends

Young children usually have families as their primary resource. Although they have activities and friends, the family is the focus. At the beginning of adolescence, parents provide most guidance and opinions. This changes during adolescence, when teens function much more in the realm of peers. Unfortunately, several studies have shown that disabled youth tend to have a drop off in the number of friends they have as junior high and high school progress. Often children are in the same school for several years and the other kids learn about their condition and can see beyond it. In grades seven, eight or nine, many students go to much larger schools where most of their classmates are strangers. Often these other teens are feeling insecure and self-conscious, and aren't willing to take the risk of making friends with someone who is visibly different. If the teen is having difficulty making friends, it may be easy for the parent to encourage him to find what he needs within the family. In the long run, this benefits no one.

Sometimes new opportunities to see friends can be created. A teen can be picked up from school an hour after classes have ended. If nothing is happening, she can always study in the library. She might join an after-school club so that she can meet people with the same interests. It may then be an easier step to invite other students to her house to see a relevant computer program that she has, or something else relating to their mutual interest. Or she can arrange something more casual, like going with a bunch of kids to the mall after school. A friend might be willing to invite her and several other friends over, which may break the ice when the new people can see that it isn't a big deal. She also may have been excluding other people with illness or disability as potential friends because of worries that other teens will think she wants only friends with a similar disability. Parents can help teens find groups through their local hospital or disease-disability-specific foundation.

Having a close friend is the best practice teens can get for growing up. They learn how to be intimate with a non-family member. They can talk about things that worry them that would be embarrassing to reveal to you. They try out different ways of behaving and communicating (not to mention different hairstyles and clothes). Friendships help them feel more comfortable being with people their own age. Teens who have not had much experience with friendship may think that, if they have a fight, the relationship is over. Parents can be reassuring by sharing their own experiences of friendship. If they have difficulty making or keeping friends, the clinic they go to may have a social worker who can offer some practical help.

Teens who haven't had as much chance to be around other people the same age (because of being in the hospital or spending more time at home) often have a hard time knowing how to act. Friends may be able to help with this, telling them if there are things they are doing (like joking around too much or talking too loudly) that are turning people off. They can even ask their friend to signal them if they are behaving in a way that might bother other people. They can watch other people together and see what they do. They may notice that people are often included when they show that they are interested in a conversation by looking at the speaker (without staring), nodding their head every once in a while, and smiling when something is funny. They may be spending so much of their energy worrying about how they are doing that they forget about the other people.

Teens with chronic conditions often struggle with the question of disclosure. Some decide to tell everyone they meet, so there are no surprises. Others do everything they can to hide the truth. There is no obligation to tell potential romantic partners, or anyone else, about a diagnosis. In a long-term relationship, a big secret can be destructive, but that doesn't mean that disclosure must happen at the beginning of a relationship. If an illness or medication affects activities, then some level of disclosure may be important, such as saying something like "I can't drink because of the medication I'm on."

A teen who realizes that he is attracted to members of the same sex may feel that this will be an additional burden for the family and be reluctant to talk about it. He doesn't want to be the one who is always causing "problems." The process will be easier if there has been exposure to gay relatives or friends while growing up. "Coming out" is not easy for teens, and it is important that parents try to respond in a loving manner, and not give a message that this kid is bringing yet more trouble into the family.

Every adolescent has questions about sex. Sometimes teens and parents have a hard time finding the answers when they relate to the specifics of their illness. The rarer the condition, the more difficult it may be to find someone who knows. Many teens (and their parents) will wonder if they can even have sex at all. They need to know that sexuality encompasses a wide variety of feelings and behaviours, and is not just limited to intercourse. When viewed this way, it becomes clear that everyone can have sex, although not everyone can have intercourse. Worries about reproductive potential will also have an impact on how a teen feels about his sexuality.

At School, Work and Play

Teens who miss a lot of school may find that they have trouble understanding assignments and getting organized, even when they work hard to catch up. They might have missed very important, basic information when they were sick. Long-term difficulties with learning and organization may result from radiation or other treatment. School counsellors and psychologists may not be aware of this and need to be educated. When they understand the issues, they can sometimes access special programs. There are often specific strategies that can help when the nature of the problem has been identified. Teens also appreciate knowing that there is a reason for any difficulties.

Going into junior high or high school or moving to a smaller town may mean leaving a special school and entering the regular stream. It is easier for the teen to adjust if she understands the nature of the system she is entering. The most difficult situation is going to a school where everyone is a stranger. Just one friend can make a huge difference, and can be a role model to other students.

Schools are full of physical and organizational barriers that can make participation difficult. Access difficulties may include those found in many public places, as well as high water fountains, narrow rows between the stacks in the library, and classes that are far apart geographically but close together temporally. Teens can fight to have barriers removed where possible, and develop strategies to get around the others (such as bringing a water bottle or plastic cup for the fountain). It may be more embarrassing for a student to speak up about something like lack of doors on washroom cubicles, and parents or health-care professionals can be enlisted in the battle. Other, less visible, barriers may also hamper the student. For example, a teacher may mark students' notes (including neatness), discriminating against students with learning problems, those who tire easily and anyone who doesn't think like a teacher.

Teens with a chronic condition can benefit greatly from starting to think about career plans even earlier than other adolescents. Teachers, and even parents, may have expectations that are too low, or may not want to project into a future that they think will be dismal or nonexistent. But because more planning may be needed to work around physical limitations such as fatigue and institutional limitations ("We've never taken anyone who has ..."), negotiations need to be started well in advance. Occupational therapists are often helpful with this, and supportive guidance counsellors are worth their weight in gold.

Getting a summer job or part-time job after school is a common part of life for teens. It provides experience, a social network, and the freedom that the extra money brings. Teens may have to deal with employers' concerns about their ability to work. If their condition isn't obvious and they have no special needs at work, then they do not have to mention it. If there are special needs, then teens may need to show that the condition will not interfere with their ability to do a good job. They may have to deal with an employer who is worried that the condition is contagious. Potential employers may not know that research has shown that "handicapped" employees have better-than-average safety records and do not affect an employer's insurance costs.

The sad reality is that employers have been known to fire teens who have something as common as diabetes. The teen who gives up learns nothing, but the one who goes back or writes a letter discussing her job performance and lack of sick days is learning how to fight for herself. She may even learn how to make a complaint to a government agency, like Canada's Human Rights Commission.

For children and teens, recreation is not just leisure activity, but an important venue for acquiring physical, emotional and relationship skills. But these activities that involve exercise, enjoyment, social activities and expressing a creative self are often the first to be dispensed with when "more important" things come up. Thus, in attempts to make sure that kids don't miss school, appointments may be booked during rehearsals for plays, sports practices or when friends are hanging out at the mall. Even when the teen is in the hospital, time can be made for recreation, even if it is just talking to a friend on the phone. Although it can be hard to fit into a schedule that includes numerous appointments and treatments, regular exercise provides socialization time with other teens. People who exercise regularly have more energy and more muscle strength, and feel better about themselves. Making time for exercise can help provide control over a schedule that is otherwise centred on illness.

Parents struggle with finding a balance between supporting their teen to believe she can do whatever she wants, and being realistic about limitations. Teens may be frustrated if their parents don't seem to recognize that some things are harder for them than for their friends, but will be unnecessarily held back if their parents assume they cannot do any sports or physical activities. Some teens may have a hard time imagining what physical activity might interest them and provide enjoyment. They could think carefully about what they might want to do, give it a fair trial, and replace it with something else if they don't like that particular activity. It might help if they make a rule that they can't quit one thing until they have decided on a replacement activity and have a definite start date. Teens may want to go on an Outward Bound-type trip, where their body becomes a tool used to surmount difficulties, rather than an enemy. Teens discover they have much in common with other teens and are less different than they thought. After the program, they are more willing to take physical risks, and parents are more likely to see them as being capable of these things.

Some kids may have particular health considerations that make participation in certain sports difficult. They could discuss the sports they want to play with their doctor, and get advice on how to minimize the risks. There are some interactions between exercise and medications, with increased drug side-effects during or after activity. On the other hand, exercise may help the condition, increasing mobility, decreasing pain, lowering medication needs. Changes in medication or meal times may be necessary.

Coaches sometimes have unfounded concerns about teens who are on medication playing school sports. A letter from a doctor can be useful, but parents often end up signing a release stating that the school is not responsible for any complications that may result from the sport. Even if the coach does not insist on one, a proper warm-up is essential (for all athletes) to avoid injury. Many sports injuries can be prevented with careful training, good warm-up and cool-down exercises, and protective clothing. Teens may want to get in touch with a national organization for sports for the disabled to see if there is an organization for the sport they are interested in, and whether there is an athlete in their area that they could talk with. These extra efforts are worthwhile for the pay-off for teens — getting to participate in activities, seeing themselves as a participants whose activities aren't limited by their illness or disability, and better overall health.

Teens with chronic conditions are as vulnerable as others to societal pressure about weight and appearance and may diet either in an attempt to look like everyone else or just to participate in it because it is a normal teen activity. They may wish for an unrealistically low (and unhealthy) weight. A higher-than-average weight may result from medications or the condition itself. Before going on a diet, teens need to examine their activity levels and talk with their doctor or nutritionist about healthy eating.

Some teens who get treatment (such as dialysis) at night lose the opportunity to sleep over at friends' homes. Doctors can often work out a treatment schedule that allows a teen occasional nights out. If the treatment is short, she may be able to go home for a half an hour or so late in the evening and then go back. If her friends know about her condition and the treatment, it may be possible for her to have them over and leave them alone for a bit (with a video and popcorn) while she gets hooked up. Some teens avoid activities with friends because they need to be able get to a bathroom quickly. They can prepare for outings by locating, in advance, public washrooms at the mall or in large restaurants and fast food chains, local hotels and bus or subway stations. If they are concerned that they might not make it in time, teens of both sexes can wear "light days" type menstrual pads, carry extras and always have toilet paper or tissue with them.

Driving can be an important skill for teens because it opens up possibilities and establishes the teen as "normal," even if he doesn't have access to a car. Some people do need to have major modifications made to a car, but many require only minor changes, and many people with wheelchairs drive regular cars. People who are deaf or hearing-impaired should know that they can get a licence. People who have "visual-spatial" problems may be able to do eye exercises to improve their possibility of driving. All teens will need support to learn to drive.

They can prepare by working on their ability to make independent decisions, improving coordination, reading the driver's handbook for their area and practising "commentary passengering" (talking to whoever is driving about what they are noticing). To be able to drive well, they must be mature and assertive (not aggressive). There is no specific way to learn maturity. It comes from having a variety of life experiences, from dealing with difficult issues, and from developing a world-view that extends beyond how things affect them.

Mixing Medications and Drugs

Teens with chronic conditions face conflicting messages about drugs. They are encouraged to take their medications, yet ads on television tell them that drugs are bad. They may have got a message that, if there is something wrong, there is a pill to try to fix it. It is critical that they realize the most of life's problems cannot be solved through drugs.

Because any one drug they take has more than one effect on their body, interactions between drugs can be quite complex. Risk occurs if teens' doctors and pharmacists are not up-to-date on all the medications that they are taking; for example, they shouldn't take any over-the-counter drugs (medications obtainable without a prescription) without first checking with their family doctor or pharmacist. Alcohol and marijuana and other street drugs can also interact with their medication.

We all have the right to know about possible side-effects and complications of any treatment. Physicians are sometimes reluctant to share information about side-effects, as they worry that it will scare kids off. However, with encouragement, they will usually discuss side-effects. Looking up side-effects at the library can be frightening, as every drug has a long list of possible nightmares, many of them rare. It is very important that a medication not be avoided because of what is perceived as a side-effect; the problem may not be caused by the drug, and, even if it is, it may be of short duration, or easily cleared up with a different dose. Side-effects such as acne, increased facial hair, or problems that result in restrictions in driving can be very distressing, and alternative treatments can be explored. Teens can help a doctor understand the impact of these effects. Many teens get oral contraceptives from clinics, as they worry that their regular doctor will tell their parents. Since these drugs can interact with a variety of medications, it is important that their regular doctor knows they are taking them. Doctors have an obligation to maintain confidentiality, but often don't think to discuss that obligation with teens.

Recreational drugs, including tobacco, can affect the performance of prescription drugs. Smoking can change the level of other medications in the body, a problem that can continue for several months after quitting. Alcohol is also notorious for drug interactions, and in addition may cause a temporary or permanent change in a medical condition. A decreased level of inhibition and poor judgment while drinking could have a more harmful effect on those with a chronic condition (such as causing them to forget to take their medication or diminishing theor ability to escape an unsafe situation or fight off an attacker). Interactions between marijuana and some medications have been documented: Teens are taking a chance if they smoke up while on another medication. The combination of alcohol and cocaine has been associated with headaches, irritability, memory loss, possible liver damage, increased heart rate and sudden death. Teens with chronic conditions may use drugs to feel like part of a group, to temporarily forget their problems or as self-medication for depression. It is wiser to find a counsellor who will work confidentially to find some real solutions to problems. Parents can facilitate this kind of treatment when they suspect an alcohol or drug problem.

Teens can go to parties prepared with a response to an offer of a joint or a beer. Easiest are answers like, "Not tonight, thanks" or "I'm the designated driver." If someone is pushy, they can always say, "I'm on more drugs than anyone in this room. I don't need to smoke, too." If they have friends who don't want to do drugs, they could try to go to parties and events with them. If they have learned to trust their feelings, they will leave if the situation becomes uncomfortable, especially when parents have made it clear that they will pick them up with no questions asked.

Doctors and Hospitals: Friend or Foe?

Doctors are a large part of life for many people with chronic illness or disability. Every teen should have a doctor who is willing to recognize her as a person with a right to privacy and dignity. Yet many teens have ongoing concerns about their health care. Teens complain that they know very little about their condition because their doctors won't tell them anything. They may never get to see the doctor one-to-one. Some doctors seem to have no awareness of cultural differences and how to make appropriate cultural references. Others try to scare patients into "complying." While in hospital, teens may not be warned or consulted about upcoming tests. They may be treated by different medical people whenever they go to the hospital or clinic, and feel that no one is really in charge of their care. They may have to repeat details of the illness and treatment over and over to new medical caregivers, or not be believed if they go for emergency treatment at a different hospital. Their appointments may be scheduled for the convenience of specialists, with no regard to their own quality of life.

There are ways for parents to support teens' efforts to have some control over and responsibility for their own health care. Parents can advocate for complete information being provided to the teen, and for some of the appointments to focus on the positive and on other issues that matter to adolescents, such as puberty changes or sex. Opportunities can be created for teens to see the doctor alone, so they can ask questions that might be embarrassing to air in front of parents, or discuss sensitive issues. Use of culturally appropriate examples by nurses, parents and others is helpful. Teens can develop strategies to ensure that they are told about upcoming tests when in hospital, and how to get information when the doctors are on "rounds." They can advocate for a "case manager" at the hospital, who would follow their treatment through all the different specialists, diagnostics and so on. They can carry basic information about their medical condition and treatments, to be given to any new specialists or attached to their hospital chart. If they require narcotics or other strong medications in a crisis, they might ask their doctor to sign a small card that indicates their usual dosage and that they are not addicted, with the doctor's telephone number on it in case they are refused appropriate treatment at an emergency facility. They could also work on getting appointments scheduled long in advance, clustering them together to miss less school and avoid important social times such as sports competitions or Friday-afternoon weekend planning.

Teens (like adults) may find it hard to cope with hospitalization, no matter how many times they go in. Having with them their own pillow and pillowcase, a washable comforter from home, good-luck charms, or even a stuffed animal can make their hospital room feel more homey. They can have more control of their routine if they figure out the daily schedule, determining when they *have* to be accessible to caregivers. They can make plans for the rest of the time, such as taking over a corner of the patients' lounge and getting other hospitalized teens to meet them there, bringing their own projects into the hospital with them, inviting friends over to do homework together or watch a video, having family and friends bring "real" food (if their diet isn't restricted). Nighttime can be the worst to get through, especially if they are woken up in the middle of the night. As they get better, they may not need the nightly check, but they will probably have to ask the doctor to take that instruction off their chart.

Anyone who relies on the medical system a great deal has to cope with changing doctors, often because the doctor moves or completes a course of study, or because the family or patient moves. It can be hard to find a new doctor, and the idea of educating the new doctor about one's medical history can be daunting. If options for a new doctor are available, teens can consider what is important to them. Do they want a doctor who has a comfortable manner, one who gives them the information they ask for and explains things well, one who treats them like an adult, one who is up on the latest research, or one who sees them as a partner in their care? Do the clinic hours or payment methods meet their needs? Having the previous doctor prepare a summary of all operations, procedures and important lab work they've had done can make the transition to a new caregiver much easier. The teen should get a copy of the summary. If the doctor won't supply a copy or won't prepare the summary, a trip to the medical records department at the hospital can sometimes be useful for obtaining some of the information. Sometimes it is possible to get a short summary of operations and procedures, although there might be a charge for this.

Although the vast majority of people who work in hospitals are not abusers, people do get abused (physically, verbally and sexually) in hospitals and institutions. This is especially true for children with chronic illness or disability. Abusers often pick out children whom they see as being vulnerable, so it stands to reason that kids who are different in any way, including having a chronic condition, are at increased risk for abuse. Abusers try to leave their victims with the feeling that what happened is the victims' fault, so children need to believe that no one has the right to treat them that way, and if anyone — a porter, a nurse, a doctor, a neighbour, a relative — does, they can tell someone about it, even if they've been warned not to talk. Teens who can't talk can be taught to scream, point or make gestures that will communicate what has happened. This problem can be hard on parents; we want our children to cooperate with appropriate care and behave politely, but it is essential that they have tools for protecting themselves.

No matter how well-intentioned and necessary treatments have been, teens may feel abused by doctors and nurses. They may have many memories of being held down for procedures, of having painful things done to them. Parents may feel guilty about subjecting their children to this, and then deny the effects to mitigate that feeling. Teens need a chance to be able to discuss how the system has affected them.

Transitions

Many parents have a hard time accepting the movement of their children away from the family sphere. Parents of a child with a chronic condition may have an even harder time with this: their role as nurse/physiotherapist/dietitian/advocate may have become a major part of their self-definition. The transition, first to peers, and eventually to moving out of the home, is accompanied by the development of an adult relationship between parents and their children. Letting go of responsibility for care and accepting that teens are old enough to form their own opinions and make their own choices are difficult contributions parents make to independence.

Conditions that result in physical dependency may lead teens to think that they cannot be independent. But independence is a state of mind. None of us is totally independent. We all need our families, friends and others to survive. Every teen and parent must invent a personal definition of autonomy. An important first step is increasing responsibility for decision making.

All of us should advocate for fairness in our communities and in society. Role-modelling, fighting for change, and encouragement to take responsibility for making change can be powerful lessons for adolescents. Effecting change may involve writing letters, making phone calls, being an activist. Sharing these skills may not make every teen a committed activist, but teens will learn that fighting for what they need often works and helps them feel in control and powerful.

As teens with a chronic illness or physical disability finish adolescence, they may find it hard to see friends leaving home before they do. They can be encouraged to work toward independence by moving into space that is a bit separate (such as a renovated basement). Families need to let go of teen-type curfews and some other rules. Sometimes teens will want to spare their parents the expense of college or university as they figure they won't live long, or perhaps won't fully utilize an education. But they can continue their education for enjoyment or fulfilment even if they don't have a large chance of a long life. Besides, what if they live for twenty years?

Growing up, moving out and creating families of their own can be scary for teens who have faced extra challenges, as well as for parents. No particular model must be followed, and it is important that teens move at their own pace.

In the end, the teen with a disability is more a teen than a disabled or ill person. Some mature more quickly than others, some find their condition to be an almost unbearable burden, while others take it in their stride. Parents, friends and health-care workers who have a positive attitude (while still respecting the negative feelings that living with difference can engender) will help teens with chronic conditions develop and thrive.

Notes

1. This article is based on a book I wrote for teenagers with disabilities: *Easy for You to Say: Q&As for Teens Living with Chronic Illness or Disability* (Toronto: Key Porter Books, 1995).

2. Ability OnLine is a computer network for young people with chronic illness and disability. Their motto is "Putting children and adolescents with disabilities in touch with the world." Ability OnLine is a great way to get to know people. Everyone is on an equal footing. If a teen has a condition that is rare, this may provide a first chance to "meet" someone with the same thing. The service is free. The modem number is 416-650-5411, and their helpline number is 416-650-6207. Outside the 416 area code, they can be reached through Telnet, with any Internet service provider, at bbs.ablelink.org. More information is available on their Website at www.ablelink.org.

Welcoming Our Differences: Daughters with Developmental Delays

Bridget Lynch

Marika was born with Down syndrome in March 1979. Her birth parents were encouraged to give her up for adoption. Her young mother, who was a recent immigrant to Canada and spoke no English, hoped to foster her out without relinquishing her. However, under Canadian law, her parents were faced with either giving her up for adoption or keeping her. Her birth father insisted on adoption, and, when Marika was put into foster care, her birth mother could only cry. This story was told to us by the wonderful older couple who fostered Marika until she was ten months old, when we adopted her into our rambunctious family.

I grieve with her birth mother at this separation, forced on her by a husband and culture who said, "She's not perfect, give her up." I also feel deep in my heart that Marika is my daughter, with all the emotional bonds that relationship claims. Her birth parents have long since moved back to their homeland. But each year, on Marika's birthday, I feel special waves of mother love coming her way and count her doubly lucky.

When we adopted Marika, John and I already had three children under six years of age, two daughters and a son. We had always wanted to adopt a child with Down syndrome to bring up as one of our own. In the early 1970s, we had lived in France at L'Arche, a community which welcomes adults who have developmental delays. We learned from that experience the intrinsic value their lives have in our world. We wanted our children to grow up knowing there are values in being human, beyond intellectual or physical capabilities; that everyone has worth; and that at one level or another we all have development delays. We had another son, Kell, when Marika was eight years old. She was there at his birth and welcomed him with joy. His coming nestled Marika into the heart of the family, where she belongs.

It is important for me that I write of Marika's adoption. For years I felt that I didn't have the right as a mother to speak up on behalf of kids with developmental disabilities because I had never lived the experience of giving birth to a child with a disability. I feared I would be accused of not knowing what it was really like, of appropriating a voice. I felt that somehow my feelings wouldn't count because I have never been disappointed or devastated by her disability. I have certainly been frustrated and anxious and fearful, but I have never been disappointed. It has taken me years to get past this, to simply say, "I am Marika's mother."

Through writing about my experiences with Marika, I hope to touch on universal aspects of mothering a teenage daughter who is different, not only by her intellectual capacity, but by cultural standards as well. Her abilities are limited by her intellectual capacity, but her acceptance within our culture is limited by bias. This difference has a direct impact on the type of relationship a mother develops with her daughter, for it is less a relationship of "in my own image" than may occur with other daughters. I don't expect Marika to achieve high grades at school. I don't expect her to excel at sports. I don't expect her to get a good job. I don't expect that the life she leads will somehow reflect on me, as I'm afraid I do with my other children. I have different areas of expectation for Marika, and they have more to do with her being happy, having a good sense of herself and being given opportunities to explore her fullest potential. All these are hopes most mothers have for their children, but they lack the overlay of competition that tends to accompany those hopes.

This different set of hopes highlights one of the most difficult aspects of mothering children with developmental delays. Generally their achievements are so far behind the norm that they are ignored. When Marika learned to roll over and sit, I was thrilled. It was beside the point that it was months later than the ages at which my other children accomplished this feat. When she learned to walk at the age of three, I wanted to run into the street and celebrate with the world! But I didn't. Few people would have understood our sense of victory.

At the age of four, Marika underwent an assessment to classify her learning abilities in order to identify her needs within the educational system. Following the testing, I sat in a room with ten professionals who had participated in the assessment. They were there to tell me, the young mother, about my daughter's learning potential. No one looked directly at me. In serious tones I was informed that Marika was "educably retarded." She was officially classified and given a label by which she would henceforth be known. I asked what her IQ was and they replied that it wasn't the main focus of the testing (even though they had used the test to determine her label). I insisted. They demurred; it was as though I had no right to know. When they finally told me, I smiled and exalted inside. It was very low. Yet, what I saw was a fantastic little girl who was beating her odds even as we all sat there, a little girl who had a personality that negated IQ as a measurement of worth. She could walk. She was toilet-trained. She was an earnest little kid who loved to please and interact with others. Why couldn't these people see her worth instead of her disability? Didn't these solemn "experts" see how happy she was? When I left the interview, I felt a new burden had been placed on Marika. Not only did she have Down syndrome, but she had a new label as well, and I wondered how such a little girl was going to carry such a weight.

Soon thereafter her five-year-old sister, Caeli, was entering senior kindergarten, and Marika came along to the first day of school. The other children didn't know Marika and they gathered around her, noticing she couldn't talk properly and didn't look quite like other four-year-olds. I watched this from across the room and thought to myself, "Here we go." I was mentally putting together an explanation about Down syndrome, when I heard some of the children ask Caeli, "What's wrong with her? Why doesn't she talk right? Why does she walk funny?" Nothing malicious, just curious. But I held my breath as I watched Caeli put her hands on her hips and declare with a ferocity that left no room for questions, "That's just the way she is!!" With that, the children looked at Marika and understood. There was nothing wrong. That's just the way she is. Forget the labels, which are someone else's convenience. That has been my guiding principle ever since.

Although Marika was born with Down syndrome (a combination of physical symptoms and not a disease), she is not like every other person with Down syndrome. To generalize about people with Down syndrome is the same as generalizing about people from the same race or culture; there are similarities, but they never override the unique aspects of the individuals. Often people with developmental delays are perceived in a universal way, and the individual gets lost in the generality. It may be easier as a culture to deal with them this way. When we recognize their individuality, then we are forced to recognize their essential humanity and their individual needs. This is the challenge that mothers of children with developmental delays face. Our kids are as unique as anyone's kids. They are individuals whose needs must be acknowledged in order for them to live with dignity and respect.

The school system is all too often the crucible of this dilemma. Here in Ontario, children with developmental needs were recognized only in the late 1960s as deserving of public-education funds. Prior to that, parents privately set up "schools" in church basements and community halls to provide their children with any semblance of an education. When the province mandated the right of these children to an education, most school boards chose to create segregated special education classes. During the last fifteen years, there has been a heightened public and political awareness of segregated versus integrated educational opportunities, with the ensuing debate about which form of education is most appropriate for students with developmental delays. Parents and educators have learned over the years that both settings are important and should be available, based on the needs of each child. However, in a historic decision, the Supreme Court recently ruled that the final selection of appropriate placement belongs to the individual school board and not the parents. Current cutbacks in educational funding, combined with the political and philosophical attitudes of local school board trustees, not necessarily the needs of the individual child, will determine where and in what type of setting these kids attend school. Students with developmental delays may be bussed a great distance to be educated away from friends and siblings in a setting that may not be appropriate, and their parents will have no recourse.

The issue of where a child is educated is not simply a question of having an appropriate setting for educational opportunities; it is also a question of providing a setting where that student will be able to grow emotionally and socially. This is at the heart of the dilemma about educational settings for children with special needs. Where are each child's social, emotional and educational needs best met?

When Marika started school, she was bussed to a segregated classroom in a school several kilometres from our neighbourhood in downtown Toronto. I was told that she had an integrated lunch program and gym program, as children from regular classrooms shared the gym and lunchroom at the same time. Marika was decidedly unhappy. She never talked about her school or named friends. She was terribly isolated and lonely. She loved going to Cherrywood, the alternative program at the neighbourhood school, to visit her sister's class and see neighbourhood friends. She very much wanted to be there.

Three years later, after many meetings with teachers, principals, parents, trustees and school board superintendents, a special arrangement was made, and Marika was integrated at the age of ten into a Grade Three classroom at Cherrywood. She was assigned a male teacher's aide who had never worked with a child with special needs. This integration was on a part-time basis of two days a week and was for a trial period of three months. Before further integration was possible, Marika had to prove to the teacher, principal and administrators that she could do it, that she could adjust to being educated in a normal classroom setting. It was a very tense time for us, and a confusing one for Marika. She didn't understand why she had to keep going to her old school, and she fussed every time the bus came for her. She couldn't understand what "part-time" and "trial basis" meant.

Meanwhile I would get calls if she pushed someone at recess or if she refused to settle down and work. The calls were appropriate; it was the underlying message that jarred. Marika was being watched and assessed rather than embraced as a member of the school community. I had similar phone calls about her siblings, but there was never a concern about whether or not they belonged at the school. Their antics were seen as normal.

Despite her frustration and acting out, Marika's personality was blooming within this neighbourhood school setting. I watched her self-esteem improve in a way that left me stunned. She was happy and talkative, and fairly burst with feeling part of the gang. Yet how does a mother let her daughter know she has to watch her every step, that there are many people who don't believe she belongs at her local school, that she isn't worth the trouble that inevitably comes during adjustments to a new setting? Marika was incapable of understanding any of this. I prayed and bargained with the principal and waited. The school board had put my daughter on the line in order to appease her "demanding" mother, and as a mother I had to participate in having my daughter prove herself. This was a horrific bind. If I hadn't had the support of other families at Cherrywood who wanted Marika in the school with their children, I might have given up.

Then, one day, her teacher's aide unexpectedly quit. A school secretary, Esther, volunteered to assist Marika in the classroom until a proper replacement could be found. Overnight, everything changed. Esther had never worked in a classroom, or with a child with special needs. Yet, one of those little miracles happened without which we'd all be dust. Esther loved Marika, loved working in the classroom, and she kept the position permanently. Marika's behavioral problems virtually ended. She settled in and moved full-time to our local school.

Unfortunately, within the field of special education there is very little material available for teachers in special education classrooms, or for teachers who have integrated students with special needs into their classrooms. Nor do most school boards provide special training for aides who work with these kids. All too often it is through the innate abilities of the aide, along with creative input on the part of the classroom teacher, that adequate educational opportunities are provided. Luckily for Marika, Esther was enthusiastic and resourceful in this area.

In one interesting exercise when Marika was in grades five and six, she dictated a story each morning to Esther. Marika's speech was very impaired and she required patience to be understood. Esther was able, through encouragement and persistence, to access Marika's incredibly active imagination. Each story was about a page long, and after the dictation she would draw a picture to accompany it. The stories were quite engaging and became known as the "Mary and the Toys" stories.

We have several notebooks of them, which in fact resemble a journal, as they often reflected life in our household, both the good and the bad. "Mary" represents the parent figure in the stories, and "the Toys," Marika. One scene told of the Toys getting up in the morning and making breakfast. Mary came into the kitchen and got angry and said, "What a BIG MESS!!" Aside from the fact that John and I saw ourselves more than once in these stories and were quite chagrined, we had never realized the extent of Marika's imaginative world. This was a revelation to us. These stories reflected the way she perceived the world and how she felt about her life. They enabled her for the first time to express herself. It was especially interesting that she used metaphor to fictionalize her reality. Most importantly, this story writing gave her a strong sense of self. Someone cared about what she thought. It was a brilliant exercise, but it left me with nagging questions.

There has been very little research done into the ways children with developmental delays learn. How do children with Down syndrome learn to read? Do they have particular ways of perceiving letters and numbers? Why does Marika tend to write from left to right? Are there special ways to teach speech therapy to children with Down syndrome? These same questions can be asked of students with other special needs. The outcome of this lack of research-based curriculum is that these students are not getting the opportunities to learn that they deserve. This unfortunate reality means that Marika and other students with developmental delays have not been given enough opportunity to develop their potential. Our children may be in the educational system, but there is a long way to go, whether they are in special-education classrooms or integrated into regular classrooms, before their learning needs are optimally met.

Marika graduated from Grade Six at the age of thirteen. She had become a valued member of the Cherrywood school community, and with glowing recommendations from both teachers and the principal, she continued to be integrated at the local middle school through Grades Seven and Eight. She was welcomed into her new environment by the school principal, who informed me during an interview, "Some educators don't believe in integration, and some do. I just want you to know that I do." Once again, I was one grateful parent. Marika changed teacher's aides through this time, and she adjusted to the changes well. She was following a modified academic course, and assuming some clerical responsibilities in the school office. Her enthusiastic approach to school helped her to become well known to staff and students alike as she collected daily attendance and specialized in celebrating birthdays. She was an active member of the school choir, and the enterprising music teacher encouraged her to play trumpet in the school band!

Towards the end of Grade Eight, she had a crush on one of the boys in her classroom. She got dressed up for the end-of-the-year school dance with much enthusiasm. Her teacher's aide, wonderful Rosemary, reported that this boy, who was respected and well liked by his peers, asked her to dance a slow dance — in front of his friends and teachers. Marika was thrilled beyond telling. When I heard this, I silently thanked him and the school community that was sensitive enough to provide an emotionally safe environment for that dance to happen.

During the graduation ceremony from Grade Eight, as she proudly walked across the stage in her funky dress, she received a resounding ovation from her 250 fellow graduates. They were as proud of her as she was of herself. Many parents of other students made a point of seeking us out to tell us touching anecdotes about interactions between their children and Marika. I began to see that integrating Marika had been a positive experience not only for Marika, but for many of her classmates as well. At the age of fifteen, Marika was happy and developing with confidence both emotionally and socially. She was a contributing member of her community and she knew it. But, as her mother, I couldn't help wonder: what next?

We had been successful in integrating her until this point, but high school was a different question. What were her needs going to be over these next years? The differences between her and her peers were widening. This was especially evident in her changing relationships and in her outgrowing some recreational activities. She was no longer being invited to birthday parties or having friends over. It was evident that her previous friends who were now teenagers had grown past wanting to involve Marika in their lives. I understood that. She also had to stop her ballet classes, which she loved, because she was too old for the group she had been dancing with. She had spent a couple of years as part of an integrated theatre group and loved acting, but the group broke up. She had to give up swimming, another passion, due to ongoing ear infections. It had been relatively easy to find appropriate schools and activities for Marika while she was young. It is a time of easier integration because the differences between kids with special needs and their peer group are not beyond bridging. The later teen years are proving more difficult.

During our search for an appropriate high-school placement, I visited the segregated classes available in our local board of education. These classrooms were often engaging, with dedicated teachers, but I couldn't imagine Marika's social and emotional needs being appropriately met within them. I wondered about the students I did see in these classrooms who had higher academic potential than Marika. Why were they still in these segregated settings? Our board of education had accommodated our request for Marika to be integrated and had subsequently developed a policy for the integration of students with special needs. Were these students not integrated because their parents didn't want them integrated, or because their parents didn't know what their options were? I was struck once again by the fact that, as a parent, I have to remain vigilant while looking after my daughter's needs, and have to continue to champion her possibilities.

After visiting many schools and talking with principals and teachers, I found a placement in a small high school for students with special adjustment needs. The school had not had success with a previous student who had Down syndrome, and there was a reluctance to take Marika. Once again she had to prove herself, this time against a negative perception about people with Down syndrome. But this time it didn't take long. By the end of the second month, she came home beaming her urchin smile and proudly wearing a sweatshirt with "Student of the Month" written across it.

At the first meeting I had with the faculty, I was welcomed into a cheerful group who not only appreciated Marika but recognized her possibilities. Prior to her being placed in the school, there had been tentative talk about, one day, her being able to join the co-operative education program, where she would be placed in a job in the community several mornings a week. The teacher responsible for the program felt there was no need to wait, that Marika had the social skills required for such placements. He felt she was more than capable to start immediately. I walked out of the meeting and drove away with tears streaming down my face. I hadn't realized the weight I had been carrying all these years until someone else lightened my load.

This illustrates another aspect of mothering a child whose needs are not generally recognized within the school system. We are always asking for attention for our child, asking that needs be met while trying not to feel that we are begging or being overly demanding. This can wear at anyone's sense of dignity. Sometimes I am tired of having to fight this fight, to insist over and over again that my daughter is worthy of the education and acceptance that is considered the natural right of other children.

The educators and trustees and superintendents who helped Marika to be integrated have often told me how wonderfully well she has done; that she proved herself, she earned her way; that she was somehow worth it. I want to scream as I stand there and smile in appreciation. All these children are worth it. I don't want my daughter to be on the receiving end of a Good Samaritan deed. She should have had the opportunities in the first place. As it stands, Marika has quite simply been lucky. Lucky that she has an engaging personality, lucky that she could be integrated at a time when there was a local political will to do so, lucky with her wonderful teacher's aides, and lucky that this school she is in hasn't been phased out, which is the current plan for it. Why do our children have to count on so much luck?

Marika was placed in a local high-school cafeteria to help make lunches. The women with whom she was placed had never worked with a student with special needs before. At the end of the year, Marika was one of the few students at her school to receive a co-op education award. The night of the award ceremony, the women she worked with and who had nominated her for the award were there to watch her receive it, obviously proud of her. I sat in amazement, realizing Marika was forging relationships and ties without me. She was not only winning awards for her work, but touching the hearts of strangers.

Outside the relatively safe realm of school, where Marika is known, is the less comfortable public world. As a mother of a daughter whose different appearance attracts attention, I am painfully aware of the looks and comments of strangers. Where I might not care what her siblings are wearing when we go out, I always make sure Marika is clean and well dressed. It is a habit born of years of strangers staring at her. I feel Marika has to look twice as good or she won't be acceptable. I don't want anyone feeling sorry for her or me. And I want her to feel good about herself.

During all her growing-up years, I cut Marika's hair at home. I realize that I did it not only for convenience, but to avoid the strangers in a beauty salon. One day when she was thirteen or so and I was feeling game, I booked an appointment at a local salon for her hair to be cut. She was a teenager. It was time for this initiation. The salon was full of patrons and chatter, and Marika's stylist, a young man, was gracious. She accepted the drape of the apron, the brushing of her hair. It was when he asked her to lean back in the chair and hang her head into the sink that she objected with a shriek. All eyes turned and watched her panic, her disturbance, her ungodly scream. That focus was almost unbearable. Yet, I talked both her and the shaken stylist through the shampoo, and she finally relaxed into her hair being cut. She was so proud of herself when it was over, unaware of the effect of her fuss. Another time, she needed her blood drawn at a medical lab, and her understandable fear resulted in her bloodcurdling screams of objection. Once again we worked through it, and she wore her Band-Aid for days as evidence of her triumph. More Marika victories. But I must admit I dread these moments, with her cries, the need for forbearance, and the prayer always in my heart that the strangers around us do not object to her presence or feel pity, but see her success.

During her years growing up, John and I have never treated Marika differently as a child within the family. At home she doesn't have special needs; she has the same needs for love, discipline, food, clothing, housing and attention as our other children. They are all unique and deserve individualized response. In fact there is an assumption among people I meet that she somehow takes more time and attention and worry. This has not been the case.

Her siblings have loved having her in their midst. When her older brother, Brendan, at the age of fifteen declared in a fit that he hated everyone in the family, he stopped himself short as if he had blasphemed (which he had, but that's beside the point) and said he didn't mean Marika. Her younger brother, Kell, who at the age of ten has recently grown to her height, recognizes her as his older sister (largely because she won't let him forget it), even as they play happily together. I tease them both and call them my twins, which they think is hilarious.

Marika has responsibilities in the household; she has to clear the table and clean her room, which she despises as much as her older sisters have. She can be ornery, and has taken to yelling at us in the best imitation of her sisters, the difference being that she doesn't tend to hold a grudge. If we get upset with her, she tells us in no uncertain terms to leave her alone, declaring with a sense of superiority, "I'm a student now." She has a devastating put-down look. Her sisters have been very important role models for her. She shares a room with her sister Caeli, with all the love and tangle that go along with that arrangement in most households. She spends hours in front of the mirror and tells us all to get lost when she has "homework to do." When her oldest sister, Erinn, was still in high school, she made a habit of taking Marika, then thirteen, out to Sunday movie matinees. They would both get dressed up and go out to the latest teen flick, Erinn aware of the curious looks that would come their way as she proudly flaunted their sisterhood.

Marika has developed physically and has now reached her full-grown height of four feet ten inches. She is fastidious about her personal hygiene; my worries about her being able to look after herself were quickly allayed. After her first period and fear around what was happening, she has become used to her monthly bleeding and looks after herself well. She has a natural flair for dressing and appreciates stylish clothing. She is fanatic about her long hair, and she loves polishing her long fingernails. She is a poised and self-confident young woman.

She has a passion for music and her interests range from Sharon, Lois and Bram to Whitney Houston, Barry White, and a current obsession with the music of *Joseph and the Amazing Technicolor Dreamcoat*. As a surprise Caeli took her to see the show with Donny Osmond for her recent eighteenth birthday. When she bought the tickets, Caeli wrote a note about Marika to Donny, asking if he would be willing to meet Marika after the show. He most graciously invited them backstage and treated Marika to the thrill of a serenade.

Marika misses her ballet and acting, although she was not exemplary at either. For her the achievement and satisfaction were in having participated, not excelling. When Marika danced in her recitals, making mistakes for sure, but dancing on and contributing to the whole, she radiated delight. Her enthusiasm belied the notion of competition and leading roles as being the goal of the dance. Unaware of those ambitions, she was her own star. Marika loves going to the theatre and movies. We know she has liked something when she comes home and goes to her room, shuts the door and re-enacts the drama. Her speech is still difficult to understand, although it is improving since the recent acquisition of a hearing aid. Sometimes she finds it easiest to entertain herself in her own world where she is in charge and she doesn't have to make herself understood to anyone else.

The highlight of Marika's year has been the two or three weeks spent each summer in an integrated program at a residential camp. While at camp, she rode ponies, swam like a dolphin and slept in the girls' cabin where gossip went on until midnight. Last summer, I asked if she could have some responsibilities at camp now that she was seventeen and her peers were counsellors-in-training. The director responded most positively, and Marika worked each afternoon in the kitchen, helping with the evening meal. She was so proud of her job, and knew that this was expected of her now that she is older. It is important to Marika that she be a contributing member of her community.

The process of maturation is slower in someone with a developmental delay, but it is there nonetheless. Marika is not a four-year-old in an eighteen-year-old's body. She has in fact matured and developed at many levels appropriate to her actual age group, despite her learning delays, with the experience that living for eighteen years brings to anyone. And she is still learning. She continues to surprise us with new words, more sophisticated thoughts, and an improved ability to express herself. I had not anticipated this ongoing learning, expecting instead that she would somehow reach a limit to her intellectual capacity. Now I expect this learning to go on for the rest of her life.

To that end we are sending her up to canoe-tripping camp this summer, where both her sisters are on staff and the average age of the camper is fifteen to sixteen. Marika will be the first camper like herself that the camp has welcomed. She will be canoeing, portaging and sleeping in a tent for three weeks with seven other teenagers from across North America. Her sister, Erinn, will be one of the guides on the trip, and is looking forward to this adventure with her sister. I am grateful for the opportunity they have to share it. The camp emphasizes community among the campers, as well as challenging each and every individual to reach their fullest potential. This is the biggest risk and challenge we have undertaken with Marika and I must admit I approach it with trepidation. How will the other campers treat her? Will she hold them back? Will she be able to paddle day in and day out, and carry her pack on long portage trails?

These are real concerns and I don't have the answers. I just know we have to take the chance and give her the opportunity. She is very excited about the trip and wants me to buy her a paddle, but I can tell that she also knows this is a big event. Once again, people are holding their breath to see if Marika can do it, but this time the risk is outside school, in the larger world. I am emotional about it. It is a true test of her abilities, of everything she has learned to date. She will find out what she is made of, as much as those travelling with her will discover their own weaknesses and strengths; she will be on par. This is a big separation and growing-up time for her. I only hope that I will be able to respect her new-found abilities and inevitable maturation when she returns.

This trip, its outcome unknown, is symbolic of Marika's future. She is in a protected environment now and I am worried about what lies ahead for her. Her life is becoming ineffably more isolated. We must continue to find appropriate recreation for her and to begin to think about Marika as an adult. I am concerned about her safety, her vulnerability, when the day comes that she leaves the school system. I wonder about the possibilities of Marika being able to enjoy a sexual relationship. I wonder how she will be able to connect with someone with whom she could share that type of relationship. I am realizing that she has permanent limitations. She will never be able to live on her own or travel alone on public transport. I am realizing that her environments, both working and recreational, are going to become more and more segregated in nature. That is inevitable and happens, to a certain extent, with everyone.

The integrated schooling and activities that she has participated in have prepared Marika for a future filled with possibilities she might otherwise not have been ready for. I want her to live as independent a life as she is capable of living within a supportive community. I have always felt that way about Marika. She doesn't just belong to this family; she belongs to the larger community as well. We are responsible as a society to look after not only Marika, but everyone who may need special consideration, whatever their need, at whatever point in their lives.

When we, as a society, narrow our definition of normal, pushing those who don't "fit in" to the edges, we are fooling ourselves. Marika has not only been my child, she has also been my teacher. For all I have done and provided for her, she has given me back ten-fold. The term "developmental delay" is such a misnomer. A label serves to separate the labelled one from the one who is doing the naming and labelling. It is an artificial and dangerous way to distinguish one human being from another. It leads to hierarchies and presumptions of worth.

Her older sister, Caeli, who once defended her as a five-year-old, is now nineteen and has just finished a Science in Society course. Several months ago, a genetic scientist visited the class to discuss genetic research. The issue of Down syndrome came up. As Caeli was telling me about the visit, my instinctive response was similar to the one I had had fourteen years earlier, when the kids in kindergarten were asking her about Marika. As a mother, I wanted to somehow be able to reach out and protect her from taking the emotional brunt of that debate. She said the discussion centred around finding a cure for Down syndrome and whether it was an appropriate scientific pursuit. The geneticist and many other students felt that it was. Caeli spoke up on behalf of people born with Down syndrome. She said that, while some people with Down syndrome may benefit from some types of surgery or medical treatment, she didn't think it was a condition that needed curing. Cures are for people who live in pain, for people who are diseased and sick. This was not an issue of science and medical advancement, but an issue of cultural bias. In whose image should we be made?

Contributors

Merryl Bear is the program coordinator for the National Eating Disorder Information Centre in Toronto. She has authored and co-authored articles and a book and overseen numerous public-awareness campaigns on food and weight issues. She has been included in *Who's Who of Canadian Women, 1996/7* (Toronto: University of Toronto Press, 1996/7) and *The World Who's Who of Women, 14th Edition* (Cambridge, U.K.: International Biographical Centre, 1997) and was named a "Woman on the Move" in 1995 by *The Toronto Sun*.

Pier Bryden is a recent graduate of the Child Psychiatry residency programme at the University of Toronto. She is currently working as a child and adolescent psychiatrist at York County Hospital in Newmarket, Ontario, and in the Women's Therapy Centre at the Clarke Institute of Psychiatry, in Toronto. She is a regular participant at the Sunday morning discussion group with Karin Jasper, Michelle Marshall and Leora Pinhas.

Tara Cullis is the president of The David Suzuki Foundation, an environmental think tank based in Vancouver with 17,000 supporters in Canada, the U.S. and Australia. Her Ph.D. from Wisconsin is in Comparative Literature and she taught non-fiction writing for five years at Harvard. She left in 1988 for full-time environmental work in British Columbia and the Amazon. She has worked extensively with native peoples around the world, has founded or co-founded eight organizations, and has won international awards for television documentary writing. She has been married to David Suzuki for twenty-five years, and they have two teenaged daughters.

Sheri Findlay is a paediatrician working in the Division of Adolescent Medicine at the Hospital for Sick Children. Her areas of professional interests include high-risk youth and street-involved kids. She lives in Toronto with her husband, Brandon, and their two-year-old son, Cameron.

Martha (Mardi) Fleming is on the youthful edge of forty, and lives with her husband and two teenagers in Ottawa, Canada. She works as an elementary school teacher and spends her spare time growing vegetables and flowers.

Rachel Giese works in Toronto as a writer, editor and broadcaster. She covers gay issues and popular culture, and has an interest in the social history of women and the family.

Jacqueline Haessly offers Peacemaking for Family workshops and intergenerational education programs through Peacemaking Associates, a training and consulting company. She is the author of numerous books, articles and curriculum materials on peace, and has contributed chapters to six business anthologies on the topic of business and social responsibility. Jacqueline has taught at Cardinal Stritch College in Milwaukee, Edgewood College in Madison and the University of Wisconsin-Milwaukee, and is on the faculty at The Union Institute College for Undergraduate Studies. She is currently pursuing a doctoral degree in Peace Studies with an emphasis in spirituality, family life education for peace and transformational leadership. She has been nominated to more than twenty Who's Who international biographies for her work in the field of peace and global awareness education. She and her husband, Dr. Daniel Di Domizio, have parented five children and share in the nurturing and homemaking tasks associated with the fun, love, tears and laughter of busy family life.

Debra W. Haffner is the president of the Sexuality Information and Education Council of the United States. She has been a sexuality educator for more than twenty years. She has a Masters of Public Health from the Yale University of Medicine and a B.A. from Wesleyan University, and is a Fellow of the Society for Adolescent Medicine. Debra Haffner has been married for fifteen years and is the mother of two children.

Kaca Henley is founder/director of YOU*NIQUE, a company that promotes self-acceptance and diversity, and uses interactive techniques, seminars and audiotapes to help people develop their own strategies to maintain self-esteem. Writer, editor, speaker and advocate for size acceptance, she is a former fat teenager, a mother and grandmother, and a volunteer with the children's rights movement and Ability OnLine (a computer bulletin board for children with disabilities). In her spare time, she translates fiction and poetry from Czech to English. She was named "Woman on the Move" by *The Toronto Sun* in 1994.

Karin Jasper is a psychotherapist in private practice at the College Street Women's Centre, specializing in the area of weight preoccupation and eating disorders. She is the co-editor, with Catrina Brown, of *Consuming Passions: Feminist Approaches to Weight Preoccupation and Eating Disorders* (Second

Story, 1993), and author of the children's book *Are You Too Fat, Ginny?* (Is Five Press, 1988). She is on the staff of the Toronto Hospital and is an adjunct professor in the Department of Adult Education, Community Development and Counselling Psychology at the Ontario Institute for Studies in Education at the University of Toronto. Karin lives in Toronto with her partner and daughter.

Cheryl Littleton counsels teenagers experiencing problems with drugs, alcohol and life at a substance abuse clinic in downtown Toronto. She has two teenage daughters. She feels that patience, a sense of humour and being absolutely unshockable are necessary for parenting, or counselling, teenagers.

Bridget Lynch supports alternative forms of education, champions community and the disenfranchised, acts as a midwife for women in childbirth and promotes postpartum culture. Bridget loves and admires her five children and appreciates the patience of her husband, John.

Michelle Marshall is a psychiatry resident at the University of Toronto, specializing in child psychology.

Kathleen McDonnell has been writing for both young people and adults for over twenty years. Her book,*Kid Culture: Children & Adults & Popular Culture*, was published by Second Story in 1994 and she is a regular contributor to CBC Radio. Her young audience play, *Loon Boy*, won a Chalmers Theatre for Young Audiences award in 1994 and is being re-mounted in 1997 by Carousel Players. She's also the author of *Ezzie's Emerald* (Second Story, 1990), a children's novel, and the forthcoming fantasy novel *The Nordlings*. She lives in Toronto with her mate and two daughters.

Judith Smith Musick was the founding director of the Ounce of Prevention Fund, a statewide initiative for teenage mothers in Illinois, and currently serves as the vice chair of its board. She is also a research faculty member at Loyola University's Erikson Institute for Advanced Study in Child Development in Chicago. She has spent the past twenty years developing and studying prevention and intervention programs for children, youth and parents, and conducts research and writes about the development of girls growing up in various high-risk environments in the United States and abroad. Judith Musick received her Ph.D. in child development and educational psychology from Northwestern University, and completed a post-doctoral traineeship in clinical developmental psychology at Northwestern's School of Medicine and Prentice Women's Hospital. She is currently conducting research on leadership and economic development with girls and women living in poverty. She lives outside of Chicago.

Leora Pinhas is a child psychiatrist specializing in eating disorders and feminist psychotherapy. She is currently completing a fellowship at the University of Toronto in the Department of Women's Mental Health and Child Psychiatry. She lives in Toronto and has recently become a mother of a little boy.

Carol Ricker-Wilson hated high school and did as little work as she could in order to pass. Blessed with a Humanities course in university — in which she learned, for the first time, that all knowledge was connected and integrated — she began to enjoy studying. She has taught for many years in alternative secondary schools, is presently seconded to York University's Faculty of Education in Toronto and is working on her Ph.D. in Women's Studies.

Margaret Schneider is a psychologist and an associate professor at the Ontario Institute for Studies in Education at the University of Toronto. She has published many articles on lesbian and gay adolescents and is the author of a book, *Often Invisible: Counselling Gay and Lesbian Youth* (Central Toronto Youth Services, 1988), and the editor of an upcoming book entitled *Pride and Prejudice: Working with Lesbian, Gay and Bisexual Youth.* She co-authored and narrated an audiotaped series for Open College, entitled *Contemporary Issues in Human Sexuality,* which is periodically broadcasted on CJRT-FM in Toronto. Margaret is on the board of directors of the Sex Information and Education Council of Canada (SIECCAN).

Alison van Nie completed undergraduate degrees at McMaster University, Hamilton, Ontario, and a graduate degree in education at Acadia University, Wolfville, Nova Scotia. Alison has previously lived in Nova Scotia, Canada, and Kenya, East Africa, while working in the fields of education and social services. She is presently living in Hamilton, Ontario, where she is a research coordinator in the Faculty of Health Sciences at McMaster University. She specializes in studies with a focus on quality-of-life issues and is interested in the incorporation of psychosocial elements of well-being into the concept of health. Alison is married to Johannes van Nie and they have four children.

Pat Watson writes children's fiction, as well as non-fiction on social welfare and social-justice issues. She is the mother of a pre-teen.

Gail Winter is a member of the Kingfisher Lake First Nation in the Nishnawbe-Aski Nation in Northwestern Ontario. She recently earned her Doctor of Education degree from the Ontario Institute for Studies in Education/University of Toronto. She and her daughter now live in Thunder Bay. Her academic interests include First Nations education, First Nations economic development, and research methodology.

About the Editor

Miriam Kaufman, **MD,** is a paediatrician at the Hospital for Sick Children in Toronto, and associate professor in the Department of Paediatrics at the University of Toronto. In addition to her involvement with teens with chronic conditions, she works with teen mothers and young women who have been sexually abused. She is the author of *Easy For You To Say: Q & As for Teens Living With Chronic Illness or Disability* (Key Porter Books, 1995) and a co-author of *All Shapes and Sizes: Promoting Fitness and Self-Esteem in Your Overweight Child* (HarperCollins, 1994). She is a consultant to the Canadian Paediatric Society's Adolescent Medicine Committee. Miriam lives with her partner, Roberta, and their two children, Jacob, twelve, and Aviva, nine. Two years ago, in a landmark legal decision, they and three other lesbian couples won the right to adopt their non-biological children.

Best of gynergy books

Lesbian Parenting: Living with Pride & Prejudice, *Katherine Arnup (ed.).* Here's the perfect primer for lesbian parents, and a helpful resource for their families and friends. "A book of such depth, strength and courage, that the unexpectedly great sense of pride in the face of rather obvious prejudice is magnificently inspiring." *The Family Next Door*
ISBN 0-921881-33-9 $19.95

Patient No More: The Politics of Breast Cancer, *Sharon Batt.* "This book is a must for all women and should be compulsory reading for all health care professionals." *The Journal of Contemporary Health*
ISBN 0-921881-30-4 $19.95/$16.95 U.S.

Beyond Don't: Dreaming Past the Dark, *Elly Danica.* With honesty and insight, Elly Danica continues her inspiring story of surviving and dealing with child sexual abuse. "A fluent, probing book, reflective work on [Danica's] painful transition from victim to fighter." **Michelle Landsberg,** *Toronto Star.*
ISBN 0-921881-40-1 $14.95

Imprinting Our Image: An International Anthology by Women with Disabilities, *Diane Driedger, Susan Gray (eds.).* "In this global tour de force, 30 writers from 17 countries provided dramatic insight into a wide range of issues germane to both the women's and disability rights movement." *Disabled Peoples' International.*
ISBN 0-921881-22-3 $12.95

Hot Licks: Lesbian Musicians of Note, *Lee Fleming (ed.).* Proud and eloquent, 23 lesbian musicians reveal their passions and politics, their musical influences and career highlights. "With cool photos and magazine-style page design, Hot Licks is a quick, informative, and colorful read, and brings together an impressive collection of lesbian voices." *Philadelphia Gay News.*
ISBN 0-921881-42-8 $24.95

gynergy books titles are available at quality bookstores. Ask for our titles at your favourite local bookstore. Individual prepaid orders may be sent to: **gynergy books,** P.O. Box 2023, Charlottetown, Prince Edward Island, Canada, C1A 7N7. Please add postage and handling ($3.00 for the first book and $1.00 for each additional book) to your order. Payment may be made in U.S. or Canadian dollars. Canadian residents add 7% GST to the total amount. GST registration number R104383120. Prices are subject to change without notice.